Environment, Agriculture and Cross-border Migrations

This book is a product of the CODESRIA 13th General Assembly, 2011

Africa and the Challenges of the Twenty-first Century

Environment, Agriculture and Cross-border Migrations

Edited by

Emmanuel Yenshu Vubo

CODESRIA

Council for the Development of Social Science Research in Africa
DAKAR

© CODESRIA 2015

Council for the Development of Social Science Research in Africa

Avenue Cheikh Anta Diop, Angle Canal IV

PO. Box: 3304 Dakar, 18524, Senegal

Website: www.codesria.org

ISBN: 978-2-86978-604-2

Typesetting: Alpha Ousmane Dia

Cover Design: Ibrahima Fofana

Distributed in Africa by CODESRIA

Distributed elsewhere by African Books Collective, Oxford, UK

Website: www.africanbookscollective.com

The Council for the Development of Social Science Research in Africa (CODESRIA) is an independent organisation whose principal objectives are to facilitate research, promote research-based publishing and create multiple forums geared towards the exchange of views and information among African researchers. All these are aimed at reducing the fragmentation of research in the continent through the creation of thematic research networks that cut across linguistic and regional boundaries.

CODESRIA publishes *Africa Development*, the longest standing Africa based social science journal; *Afrika Zamani*, a journal of history; the *African Sociological Review*; the *African Journal of International Affairs*; *Africa Review of Books* and the *Journal of Higher Education in Africa*. The Council also co-publishes the *Africa Media Review*; *Identity, Culture and Politics: An Afro-Asian Dialogue*; *The African Anthropologist, Journal of African Tranformation, Méthod(e)s: African Review of Social Sciences Methodology*, and the *Afro-Arab Selections for Social Sciences*. The results of its research and other activities are also disseminated through its Working Paper Series, Green Book Series, Monograph Series, Book Series, Policy Briefs and the CODESRIA Bulletin. Select CODESRIA publications are also accessible online at www.codesria.org

CODESRIA would like to express its gratitude to the Swedish International Development Cooperation Agency (SIDA), the International Development Research Centre (IDRC), the Ford Foundation, the Carnegie Corporation of New York (CCNY), the Norwegian Agency for Development Cooperation (NORAD), the Danish Agency for International Development (DANIDA), the Netherlands Ministry of Foreign Affairs, the Rockefeller Foundation, the Open Society Foundations (OSFs), TrustAfrica, UNESCO, UN Women, the African Capacity Building Foundation (ACBF) and the Government of Senegal for supporting its research, training and publication programmes.

Contents

List of Contributors

Henry de-Graft Acquah is at the Department of Agricultural Economics and Extension, University of Cape Coast, Ghana. He has a PhD from the University of Göttingen.His research interests include asymmetric price transmission, microfinance and rural finance, and Bayesian econometrics and statistics.

Maurice Nyamanga Amutabi is the Deputy Vice Chancellor for Academic and Student Affairs (ASA) Kisii University, Kenya. He was formerly a lecturer at the Catholic University of Eastern Africa (CUEA) where he taught courses in Research Methods, Political Science, Development, Peace and Conflict Studies. He is the author of *The NGO Factor in Africa: The Case of Arrested Development in Kenya* (New York: Routledge, 2006). He is co-author of *Nationalism and Democracy for People-Centered Development in Africa* (Moi University Press, 2000) and *Foundations of Adult Education in Africa* (Cape Town/Hamburg: Pearson/ UNESCO, 2005). He co-edited *Regime Change and Transition Politics in Africa* (New York: Routledge, 2012).

Victor Ngu Cheo is a senior lecturer in the Department of Journalism and Mass Communication at the University of Buea, Cameroon. His areas of interest include environmental and sustainable communication. He holds a PhD in policy and environmental communication from the Brandenburg University of Technology, (BTU) Cottbus, Germany.

Kwabena Nkansah Darfor, Department of Economics, University of Cape Coast, Ghana. His areas of specialisation include environmental economics, labour economics, and resource economics.

Sunday Shende Kometa, Lecturer in Geography at University of Buea, Cameroon.

Humphrey Ngoda Ndi is Associate Professor in the Department of Geography at University of Yaounde I, Cameroon. He specialises in human geography with specific emphasis on medical/health geography in particular. He has a special interest in remote sensing.

Justitia O. Nnabuko, Senior Lecturer and Acting Head, Department of Marketing, University of Nigeria, Enugu Campus.

Max Memfi Ntangsi, Department of Economics and Management, Faculty of Social and Management Sciences, University of Buea, Cameroon. He specializes in Education Management. He is the author of several scholarly articles and book chapters.

Jacob Nunoo, Department of Economics, University of Cape Coast, Ghana. His areas of specialisation include Labor Economics, Health Economics, and Development Economics.

Samwel Ongwen Okuro is a senior lecturer and head of the Institute of Cultural Heritage and Material Sciences at Jaramogi Oginga Odinga University of Science and Technology, Kenya. He has been a lecturer at Maseno University, Kenya, where he taught in the department of history and archaeology. His research interests and publications are on gender, human rights, and agrarian reforms in Africa. He has co-authored a book *Strategies Against Poverty Designs from the North and Alternatives from the South*.

Anta Sané holds a PhD in Political Science from Howard University, Washington, DC. Her areas of interest include Public Policy, Public Administration, and International Relations. She currently teaches an introductory course in Political Science and International Relations at Howard University. She is also an Adjunct Professor at the University of the District of Columbia Community College.

Chibuike U. Uche is researcher at the African Studies Centre, Leiden. Prior to joining the ASC, he was Professor of Banking and Financial Institutions at the University of Nigeria and a member of the Monetary Policy Committee of the Central Bank of Nigeria. *He* has extensive research experience in Nigeria, Ghana and Sierra Leone in the fields of political economy, business and financial history, financial institutions regulation and regional integration. His current research interest is foreign business operations in Africa. He has a PhD in Accounting and Finance from the London School of Economics.

Emmanuel Yenshu Vubo is a professor of Sociology at the University of Buea, Cameroon. He has been Chair of the Department of Sociology and Anthropology, and currently Associate Dean, Research and Cooperation. His research interests and publications are on the sociology of development, political sociology and the sociology/anthropology of intercommunity relations. He is currently a member of CODESRIA's Executive Committee and member of several learned societies including *Réseau International Afrique-Monde*.

Introduction

The book is a collection of selected chapters, all, except one, of which were presented during the 2011 General Assembly of CODESRIA held in Rabat, Morocco, on the theme 'Africa and the challenges of the twenty-first century'. The chapters have been brought together under three sub-headings: (environment, agriculture and cross-border migrations). The nine chapters cover the environmental question itself, environmental communication and governance, farmers' perceptions of and adaptation to climate change, the effects of hydroelectric dams on surrounding communities within the context of climate change, challenges for agricultural development especially in the context of land grabbing which has become a central issue in Africa's development, social protection for farmers and cross-border migrations. The challenge of bringing several contributors together to is making sense of the interconnectedness of the issues, the background of which is the continent's development.

The working hypothesis we have adopted is that Africa's development challenges can be attributed to its context or its human and natural ecology. One of Africa's leading social scientists, Peter Ekeh (1986) argued that one way of looking at Africa's development was to connect it to its environment and its historical moment which constituted its cybernetic component or the relationship between developing units and its environment. This conception is one of the parameters through which a pragmatic understanding of development can be understood. The environment and historical moment of development is the world time of development or the global imperatives that control or constrain development. Even before proclamations of globalisation as a recognition of the interconnectedness of the world system, Ekeh had seen the increasing internationalisation of the world as an essential characteristic or environment of Africa's development. The Cold War days in which his analysis was proposed had presented an ideologically bipolarised planet in which development was hemmed in between the competing models. Its social, cultural and political environment had been shaped by the dynamics of the polarisation. The natural environment seemed to portend and provide abundance of climatic stability in global relations of inequality and exploitation between rich and poor nations (whether capitalist or really existing socialist). The natural ecology of development was marked by three contrasting developments: the progressive depletion of resources within a competitive economy which did not envisage an end to the earth's limited natural base, increasing pollution that commenced with the Industrial Revolution but which had seemingly been ignored, and the fluctuation of the climate in some parts of the south between apparent stability/ abundance and natural disasters. It was during this period that Africa's agriculture entered the global scene as a supplier of cash crops for the western countries (in the main) alongside a predominantly residual peasant survival economy. It was then that one could witness what was presented as development models based on this type of agriculture existing side by side with food disasters consequent on natural calamities (droughts, floods, insect pests, and desertification). This was happening at a time when the global division of labour had assigned Africa to that unfortunate situation. Several attempts by African countries to think about their agricultures differently, as Ntangsi points out in his contribution, did not lead to much transformation. On the contrary, over time there was real regression such that after the end of the so-called Third Development Decade (the 1980s) Africa was largely dependent on food imports and, unfortunately, on food aid .

Global development has, however, changed with the end of that epoch, which itself was substituted ideologically by the proclaimed globalisation, the political and hegemonic dream of achieving a final phase of liberal economic orthodoxy captioned as neo-liberalism by its critics (Bourdieu 1998). That dream, less linear in its fortunes than conceived, has ushered in several transitions, some expected and organised or planned, while others have surfaced as offshoots of the longer term developments or as the chaotic outcomes of the dominant western development paradigm. This world time or epoch can be termed as a long and uncertain transition. Although initially witnessing the final emergence of the United States (US) as the lone superpower and the installation of a new *pax Americana*, others dreamt of a multi-polar world where the influence of the western powers would be mitigated. These two romantic dreams have not come to pass. Instead a new phenomenon is replacing the old cleavage between a developing/underdeveloped third world finding its uneasy way between East and West. This is a phenomenon of the emerging countries/economies cum nations which have forged a development clear of the dominant position of the US and the declining position of Western Europe. While it is the dream of some African countries, and provides fertile ground for new forms of cooperation, as is expressed in the current interest of Brazil, China and India in Africa, there is a new form of external intervention in the agriculture of the continent, namely land grabbing. Other newly rich countries are involved as Okuro (in this volume) has demonstrated for Kenya, as are white Zimbabwean farmers in Nigeria (Nnabuko and Uche, also in this volume). The intervention of this mode of farming promises higher productivity, high incomes, and new technologies but also implies marginalisation of poor farmers and other negative outcomes. The question is what this type of agriculture truly holds for Africa.

African countries are not just passive recipients of the fallouts of these new international developments through a new mode of agriculture, which is dependent on capital from the new financial giants. African countries seem to be dazzled by the prospects of the model but also wish to be part of the process either by taking part in an alternative to the G8 (as with South Africa's position within the BRICS), engaging in differing cooperation links (witness the regular China-Africa or India-Africa summits) or embarking on copying the model (better still, road) taken by the emerging countries. Ambitions range from specific targets such as attaining two-digit growth rates to broad or rather vague ones, such as being emerging nations by 2020 (Côte d'Ivoire), 2030 (Kenya) or 2035 (Cameroon). Is this mere mimicry or realistic aspiration? Whatever the case may be, the critical issue now is: how will it affect agriculture and social services? It is within such a perspective that the contributions of Ntangsi and Amutabi should be read.

The turn of the century also witnessed a major twist in the environmental question which has now become a social and political concern in the West (Latour 2004), but which had been largely framed as an exclusively natural process. Climatic change with enduring global effects was here to stay. The challenge of climate change has made itself felt through science and policy analysis to the extent that it has become a global concern since we share one interconnected world. As a major disruption in trends, climate change is a challenge at all levels, but more specifically to farmers. It confronts the practices of farmers and their farming systems which either adapt to or are simply dependent on the environment. Climate change issues have also departed from the domain of nature proper and become part of history, not only of natural history (of the fundamental sciences) but as part of human history or an offshoot of such a history (Maalouf 2009:277–89).

Climate change exacerbates existing risks to farmers, such as water stress, diseases and food security' (Paul et al. 2009:36). Climate change is characterised by 'increased temperatures, changes in rainfall patterns, more droughts, floods and recurrent extreme weather conditions' (ibid.:37). The El Niño effect, tsunamis and yearly tropical tornadoes are some of the visible indicators of what these changes are likely to produce. Natural catastrophes that defy prediction are likely to result from this situation. That may be why the call is to limit the effects of anthropogenic activities. Climate change is part of several disorders that have coincided with the transition from the twentieth to the twenty-first century (Maalouf 2009). Its very anthropogenic nature makes it a historic event, that is, an event which is within time and space, and is situated within the human realm. A number of chapters in this book tackle a wide range of issues related to these natural processes with the human interface: the environmental question itself (Sane), communication and governance (Cheo), farmers' perceptions (Acquah, Nunoo and Darfor) and dam projects in their social and natural environments (Vubo and Kometa), and from different approaches – reflections, empirical analysis, policy analysis.

The present world time of development is marked by increasing migration (consequent on globalisation) and the emergence of new areas of strategic interest. One such region that is attracting attention and gaining in importance is the Gulf of Guinea where the two developments can be observed. This area is strategic for its mineral resources (especially big oil reserves) but unfolding questions of security are occasioned by all kinds of sources of conflicts and manifestations of violence. It is an area of intense migrations that will change the face of the region that stands astride a vast portion of West and Central Africa and that brings two or even three regional cooperation groupings into contact (ECCAS, CEMAC, ECOWAS). The 2013 meeting on maritime security was an opportunity to examine the common ground that brings the states of the Gulf of Guinea together to start thinking in a single direction and explore ways of working together. One could also envisage a rapprochement towards the creation of a greater cooperation community bringing the states and people together. Migration will constitute an essential component in local issues of conviviality well beyond the diplomacy and regional bureaucratic structures of such a scheme. That will constitute a challenge to the dogma of sub-regional integration and the belief in its potentials for development, as well as to the survival of the scheme itself. The crucial issue is whether one can envisage a regional integration scheme without citizens. That is what the contribution by Vubo and Ndi attempts to examine.

This environment of development, which may be also the object of development, is a changing one; it is in transformation and transforming other realities. It is difficult to say what the future holds. The following chapters chart a way forward on how to come to terms with the predicament of a new era for Africa and the whole planet.

References

Bourdieu, P., 1998, 'Utopia of Endless Exploitation: The Essence of Neo-liberalism', *Le Monde Diplomatique*, December, <mondediplo.com/1998/12/08 bourdieu>, accessed 28 February 2013.

Ekeh, P., 1986, 'Development Theory and the African Predicament', *Africa Development* 13(2), 1-40.

Latour, B., 2004 [1999], *Politique de la Nature: Comment faire entrer les sciences en politique*, Paris: La Découverte.

Maalouf, A., 2009, *Le Dérèglement du Monde*, Paris: Grasset.

Paul, H., A. Ernsting, S. Semino, S. Gur and A. Lorch, 2009, *Agriculture and Climate Change: Real Problems, False Solutions*, Copenhagen: EcoNexus.

1

The Environmental Question in Africa: A General Statement

Anta Sané

Introduction

All works dealing with climate change in Africa agree that the continent stands to suffer the most from global warming. They also show that past history provides us with poignant lessons on the likely effects of future climate change, the greatest concern being the large infrequent disturbances to the climate as these will have the most devastating effects. In a sobering study from the Kenyan Tsavo National Park, Lindsey Gillson (2006) reveals evidence for a drought that coincided with the harrowing period of Maasai history at the end of the nineteenth century termed *Emutai*, meaning 'wipe out'. Ecological shocks such as that experienced by the Maasai are predicted to be a feature of global warming. Gillson explains that her work involved analysing sediments from the famous Tsavo National Park. The age of the sediments was obtained by using radiocarbon dating. Ananalysis of the pollen and charcoal fragments provided a picture of accumulated environmental change. John Lovett, who has been researching the impacts of climate change on Africa, says that we must learn from history and be prepared (Lovett 2006).

Prepared or not, the perils of climate change are already being felt across Africa. Andrew Simms of the New Economics Foundation has reported that although climates across Africa have always been erratic, scientific research and the experience of groups monitoring the situation indicate new and dangerous extremes. Arid and semi-arid areas in eastern, western, northern and parts of southern Africa are becoming drier, while equatorial Africa and other parts of southern Africa are getting wetter. The continent is, on average, 0.5 degrees centigrade warmer than it was 100 years ago; in some areas, the temperatures have risen by much more. In a part of Kenya, for instance, the temperature has become 3.5 degrees hotter in the past twenty years. As a result, in the past few years alone, 25 million people in sub-Saharan Africa have faced a food crisis because subsistence farming has become very difficult. The great tragedy is that Africa had played virtually no role in global warming, a problem that was caused by the economic activity of the rich, industrial countries. The rest of this chapter provides a comprehensive picture of the problem and offers feasible suggestions on how to deal with it. The chapter begins with a discussion of the 'law of change', the theoretical postulate upon which the analysis in this paper is grounded.

Issues of Change

Humans, like all other animals, and all plants, influence their environment, and are, in turn influenced by it. Mutual influence is part of life itself; a fundamental force behind the development, for centuries, of the many living things on our planet. We can envision this force as a law of nature: the law of change.

The concept *ecological balance* is often employed to simplify matters. The term implies a situation where the law of change works in various directions in a system of animals and plants, and that the various forces countervail in order to stabilise the system as a whole. But in a broader perspective, and in the long run, it makes no sense to speak about equilibrium, as the law of change is omnipresent. It works sometimes incrementally, with course corrections, sometimes by leaps and bounds, as ancient species and ways of life give way to the new.

Industrialisation, so far incomparably the greatest intervention by the law of change in our existence and environment, is due to accumulated knowledge, inventiveness and organisational talent. But we now see the limits of what this new make-up provides: pollution of air and water, noise, acidity of lake water, maltreatment of nature, the health hazards of many products and production processes, overcrowding, and the breakdown of traditional groups and values. All these are consequences of industrialisation or, at least, of a too rapid and, in part, obviously unpremeditated process of industrial growth. These consequences are the price we have paid for our un-paralleled per capita supply of goods and services and our un-paralleled population growth. Most of us only became genuinely aware of these consequences very late on.

It is imperative to keep in mind the link between material well-being and interest in environmental improvement when we consider the problems which African countries face with regard to soil, vegetation and water. The existence and increasingly critical nature of these problems are generally recognised and eloquently described. That the rich world's donors of development assistance should try to help towards their mitigation is undisputable. Indeed, it is not industrialisation which constitutes the main environmental dilemma for African countries. Industrialisation has not developed very far in Africa. Agriculture and animal husbandry, generally at a subsistent level, constitute the dominant pattern of the African economy. In their pursuit of survival, peasants exploit ever more marginal soil, ever poorer grazing grounds.

The problem of Africa, when it comes to the natural environment, as well as in most other respects, is not an over-hasty development, but a too sluggish one, or none at all.

Environmental Crises in Africa and the Developed Countries: A Brief Comparison

The environmental crises in Africa and the developed nations are Janus-faced: i.e. whereas the environmental crisis in Africa is one of under-consumption and inadequate technology, the environmental crisis in the developed countries is one of mass consumption and advanced technology. That patterns of production and consumption in the developed nations have had a severe impact on those nations' environments is now becoming apparent to citizens in those countries.

Today, about 20 per cent of Americans, for example, refuse to drink water from their taps, at least partly because they doubt its safety; there are dangers of floods (increased by the clearing of forests for farms and timber), the leaching of rubbish buried in landfills, and pesticide runoff in irrigation waters from agriculture. Many Americans are worried about the ways society generates energy and the resulting global warming, air pollution (as much of the 2,500 gallons of air inhaled in the US each day contains exhaust fumes, lead and asbestos), and ozone depletion and its relationship to skin cancer (Blatt 2004).

The relationship between poverty and environmental abuse is not as widely understood. Even so, on closer examination, it, too, seems inevitable. This relationship is painfully apparent in Africa. Affluent societies' appetites for exotic hardwoods do, of course, contribute to rampant devastation. American, European and Japanese corporations, constrained by severe restrictions at home, have been able to operate quite uninhibited in Africa. The royalties developed countries have paid for laying waste to African lands have been welcomed by African governments as much-needed nest-eggs for their countries' 'development'. Now, albeit late in the day, a few African leaders are beginning to take appropriate action.

Nonetheless, native slash-and-burn farmers are also contributing to the problem, as they cover ever wider territories to eke out food for the day from temporary croplands. In addition to the farmers, there are hosts of landless peasants who wage a desperate struggle to ward off hunger and malnutrition. Yet more still – millions – are in desperate need of firewood, especially for cooking. The scarcity of firewood is the real energy crisis for a majority of Africa's people. Anything and everything that can be burned is being torn out of the soil; barren circles around villages are widening. Gathering food for cooking is beginning to take all day for many.

Where the forest is gone, wells dry up, rivers alternate between flooding and running dry, topsoil is leached and washed away, and dams clog with silt. In this way, the poorest people are literally destroying their own future, as the very basis of future generations' existence goes up in smoke.

Poverty

Are problems of pollution and environmental degradation really the sole headache of the industrialised countries? Problems of conservation are mounting in African and other developing countries as well, but they are generally of a different kind compared to those in the industrialised countries: desertification (i.e. the process whereby vegetation and soil are debased to the extent that more or less permanent areas of desert-like barrenness materialise in arid tracts outside actual deserts), the wholesale razing of tropical rain forests, the pollution of highly productive coastal waters, etc.

In the last three decades, increasing attention has been paid to environmental questions in the debate on foreign aid and development. The reason is obvious. In many African and other developing countries, there is now ruthless exploitation of scarce natural resources and a dramatic degradation of the environment, which is threatening the basis of human existence. Thus, the customary view that environmental degradation is only a problem for the industrialised countries, and that environmental protection is a luxury which the developing countries cannot afford, appears increasingly obsolete. There should be no conflict between environmental protection and development in African nations. In many places, environmental degradation constitutes a direct threat to development. This is especially true of the efforts to improve the living conditions of the numerous poor in the rural areas. Active environmental protection is in many cases a prerequisite for development.

Environmental degradation in African countries is principally a result of over-exploitation of natural resources. This is, for instance, true of arable land, pasture, groundwater and forests. There is in addition profit-motivated devastation, especially in the case of the felling of forests. To subsist, people are forced to use natural resources in a way that drastically reduces the capacity of those resources to provide yield in the long term. The energy and food crises have created a vicious circle of poverty which has led to ecological disaster in many areas.

The decisive importance of environmental aspects has been better documented at the international level, and it has also been recognised more widely in recent years. A World Conservation Strategy was initiated in 1980 by a number of international organisations both within and outside the United Nations system. This strategy emphasises the connection between social and economic development and the natural environment, and suggests alternative approaches to development that take this connection into consideration. Environmental development is a major component of the work of the United Nations Environmental Program (UNEP). The aim is to achieve an integration of environmental and resource aspects in all of the United Nations' development efforts and to work out methods of integrating them into the development work of individual countries.

All development and development assistance cooperation must hinge upon the wishes of the recipient countries. Consequently, the frequently discussed question of choosing a suitable technology for a development project should be, first of all, a matter for the recipient country. The task for development assistance should be to help the recipient country to develop its own capacity to assess, receive and adapt the technology that is exported.

African countries and the developed countries must markedly increase their commitments in the sphere of land management, principally in village forestry, and the combating of desertification. The problems of soil erosion and desertification are especially acute in the Sahel area, where the advance of the desert constitutes an ecological disaster of enormous proportions. The very basis of human existence is being rapidly eroded over large areas by the desperate search by the poor for shrinking grazing land for their livestock and for fuel and water. Bilateral projects, which must be brought to the fore, should include planting of trees and village forestry, providing more efficient stoves which use less wood, and the restoration of areas around water-holes, which have been over-grazed in countries like Burkina Faso.

A corollary to poverty, inevitably, is hunger. The reasons for hunger in Africa are many; environmental degradation is one. Another is that African countries today produce raw materials for which the industrialised countries pay very little. In order to feed their own peoples, African countries are then forced to increase their production of raw materials at the expense of the environment. Signs of stress on the world's bio-productive resources are already apparent. If the production of major commodities of biological origin is viewed in per capita terms, it is evident that many of them have already exceeded their peaks. And as population and per capita consumption continue to increase, it is likely that more commodities will reach their peaks in the near future.

The earth's physical resources and expanding technology can sustain an average growth rate in food production of about 5 per cent. Even a humble population growth of 2.1 per cent per year, however, would lead to increased pressure on resources, higher real costs and environmental deterioration, factors which would further undermine global food prospects. Humankind has entered an era of scarcity as far as arable land is concerned. The declining availability of arable land suggests that expanding food production will depend on a wide range of resource-augmenting inputs like fertilisers, pesticides and high-yielding varieties.

But this leads to another problem. Not only is the production of fertilisers and pesticides energy-intensive, it is also expensive and dependent on global petroleum prospects. Producing one ton of nitrogen requires about 1.8 tons of oil-equivalent. Much of the fertiliser applied to farms is not utilised by crops and leaches into water systems where it poses environmental health risks through nitrate contamination. The presence of nitrates in drinking water may induce a disease called methaemoglobinaemia, through which the capacity of the blood to carry oxygen from the lungs to the rest of the body is reduced. Infants are most vulnerable to this disease. Moreover, the leaching of nitrogen fertiliser may lead to the problem of eutrophication. It has been estimated that more than 70 per cent of the nitrogen entering surface water comes from agricultural activities. If eutrophication is modest, it may be a source of food for numerous herbivorous animals, which in turn are fed upon by fish. But if the bloom becomes excessive, it may choke waterways and hinder navigation. And when the bloom decomposes, it depletes oxygen and may affect the fish population.

Most of the pesticides used in Africa and other developing countries include persistent organochlorines like DDT, aldrin, dieldrin, and heptachlor – all of which have already been banned or are heavily restricted in developed countries. Pesticides poison at least one person every five minutes in the third world, making a total of 250,000 people a year, of whom about 10 per cent die. This estimate, however, does not include the thousands who suffer from cancer, miscarriages and still-births, bear deformed children or suffer from the effects of pesticide contamination. The world produces about 1.8 tons of pesticides each year, an equivalent of 14 ounces per person on earth. Approximately 360,000 tons are exported to the developing countries. Despite this massive production of pesticides, the problem of pests is far from being solved; the bugs are fighting back by developing resistance against pesticides.

Future growth in agricultural resources will depend on the provision of more water and better water management in the arid and semi-arid areas. It will also depend on the drainage and management of surplus water in the humid and wet areas that account for well over 50 per cent of the world's remaining reserves of arable or potentially arable land. Water will continue to be a major limiting factor to food production. Producing one kilogramme of dry wheat grains needs at least 0.75 tons of water, and irrigating a hectare of rice requires up to 787,400 cubic inches of water in a season.

Food production faces the challenges of soil deterioration, despite the fact that some previously unutilised land is being brought under the plough. Soil deterioration is mainly a result of desertification, waterlogging, salinisation, alkanisation, deforestation, loss of farmland to other uses and general soil erosion. The problem is compounded by the lack of effective technology for reclaiming salinised and waterlogged farmland. And irrigating more land may reduce the availability of pastureland and intensify pressure on the remaining pastures.

Forests and Trees

The threat to tropical forests is a threat to many people's chances to survive on agriculture. The devastation of tropical forests in Africa has created an energy crisis that is of concern to most people. The ravaging of rainforests is radically changing our climate and life conditions, in spite of denial by some policy makers and observers. The threat comes from transnational forest companies pursuing maximum profit and slash-and-burn farmers struggling to eke out a living; though signs of resistance are beginning to emerge.

The rainforest is a 60 million year-old ecological system that is unique in its stability but, currently, about a quarter of a million square kilometres of rainforest disappear each year. At this rate, this would mean that within a span of a generation, there would be no such forests left on this earth. What happens when a rainforest disappears? One outcome is certain: the rainforest will never reappear. It is even questionable whether an ordinary forest would ever grow out of this devastation. In addition, modern climatic research points out that the clear-cutting of rainforests can heavily add to the increase of carbon dioxide content in the atmosphere created by the burning of fossil fuels.

The future of Africa is intimately bound up with the future of its trees. Wood and charcoal are African households' most important fuels. Furthermore, trees provide shade and protect crops from the scorching sun. They help retain moisture in the soil, thereby combating erosion. But more trees are felled than are being planted. Turning the tide to avert catastrophe requires planting millions of trees each year. Fuel, too, must be used more efficiently. With an average population growth of about 3.2 per cent per year, Africa's problem is acute, requiring mass mobilisation and firm political will to solve the deforestation problem.

Despite the abundant oil reserves in Africa, most of which has not even been tapped, the continent is facing two energy crises at once: an oil crisis in the modern sector and a wood fuel crisis in the traditional sector. The crisis in the traditional sector has to do with the fact that more trees are felled than are planted. Moreover, waste (plant mortality) is substantial: roughly three out of every five seedling trees are destroyed, with only two surviving ten years after planting.

Desertification

In 1973, two words became prominent in newspapers and television news around the world: Sahel and desertification. Sahel is an Arabic word denoting the belt of steppe and arid savannah south of the Sahara – from Senegal on the Atlantic Ocean to the west, to Sudan and Ethiopia on the Red Sea to the east. This roughly 310–496 mile-wide belt normally receives 2.5-15 inches of precipitation per year; but several years between 1968 and 1973 brought far below normal amounts of rain. Grass and other fodder disappeared, and millions of head of livestock perished. Deaths due to starvation among the nomadic herdsmen and small farmers of the Sahel were estimated at 200,000. The disastrous cycle of crop failure, famine, devastated pasturelands and cultivated fields has gone down in history as 'the Sahel catastrophe'. It also resulted in a considerable degree of desertification – defined earlier in this chapter as the process whereby vegetation and soil are debased to the extent that more or less permanent areas of desert-like barrenness materialise in arid tracts outside actual deserts.

Several types of land abuse can result in desertification. Two cases of the devastation of arable land in the arid regions of Africa are considered here: (1) Tunisia, an example of the situation on the northern fringes of the Sahara; and (2) Sudan, an example of sub-Saharan Sahel conditions.

The Mediterranean climate is characterised by long, dry summers and intensive periods of rain during the winter – a pattern that can lead to significant soil erosion if natural ground cover is weakened through farming, over-grazing, or the clearing of bushes and trees. The same practices denuded the mountains bordering the Mediterranean to the north and east some 2,000 years ago. Greece, Italy, Lebanon, Spain, Turkey, among other countries, offer numerous examples. As the population of Tunisia has grown rapidly (about eightfold) over the past 100 years, the pressure on land, water and wood resources in that country has intensified. Consequently, the following five ecological effects have been noted:

- Over-grazing occurs because too many animals are allowed to graze freely on steppe land for long periods. Grazing and the trampling of hooves of goats, sheep and, to some extent, camels weaken natural ground cover. As a result, topsoil is pulverised and is easily blown away by the wind or rinsed away by heavy rains.

- Wood derived from the cutting of trees and brush for household fuel, fencing or building material bares the soil, paving the way for ensuing erosion. Each family of farmers cuts approximately one hectare of marquis each year to meet fuel needs. The areas are cleared and then planted, making them extremely vulnerable to erosion.

- Salinisation of irrigated land results because the bedrock of southern Tunisia contains salt that in many places contaminates groundwater as well as soil water. Deposits of gypsum have caused the formation of alkaline crusts in the soil and salinisation with gypsum in irrigated fields. Salinisation due to insufficient drainage is believed to have ruined vast irrigated tracts in ancient Babylon, contributing to the fall of the empire more than 2,000 years ago.

- Water erosion and siltation in reservoirs are the outcome of the many fluvial reservoirs that have been built in Tunisia. Most of them lie in the mountainous and less arid northern reaches of the country. Dams have been constructed to supply the cities with drinking water, to irrigate various agricultural districts, and to control flooding. All of the reservoirs, however, are filling rather quickly with sediment.

- Wind erosion is symptomatic of the effects of the tremendous dust storms that carry soil particles from North Africa across the Mediterranean to southern Europe. Soil leaves Tunisia in other directions as well – e.g., eastward and southward. Clouds of red dust from Africa have descended from time to time on the Alpine glaciers – where the snow is coloured red – and on European coasts and cities. Precipitation occurs in the form of dry dust or as clumps of mud in rainstorm. Each of these storms represents the loss of millions of tons of African soil. The loss of wind-borne sand and soil particles from the Sahara and the Sahel over the Atlantic is even greater.

Sudan, the largest country in Africa, with an area of 967,247 square miles, contains a variety of climatic zones, ranging from Saharan desert along its northern borders to mountainous rain forests along the Uganda-Congo frontier to the south. Sudan probably has more territory affected by desertification than any other country in Africa.

A 1944 report by a Sudanese government commission on soil conservation revealed that the problem was known even at that time. The commission's conclusion was that soil degradation and erosion were more a consequence of human beings and their domesticated animals than of a change in climate. Its recommendation mainly concerned the region's surrounding towns, where it advised planting green windbreaks of trees and bushes around some centres. As we know today, the commission was only partly correct in both its diagnosis and suggested medicine.

Between 1968 and 1973, the arid and semi-arid reaches of Sudan suffered as severe a drought hit the countries of the West African Sahel, from Senegal to Chad. Three factors helped to lessen the impact on Sudan, compared to its neighbours, Chad to the west and Ethiopia to the east: (1) Sudanese herdsmen and their animals moved south, (2) domestic relief supplies were available from the surplus of Nile Valley agriculture, and (3) there was a certain degree of awareness and preparedness among policy makers of the necessity of combating desertification.

A detailed and well-thought out plan was drawn up under the sponsorship of the Sudanese Research Council and presented to the United Nations Conference on Desertification (UNCOD) convened in Nairobi from 29 August to 9 September 1977. The plan entailed (a) an inventory of the forms and extent of soil degradation and erosion, and (b) a pilot programme for soil conservation and desert control. Unfortunately, Sudanese efforts to engage the industrialised countries and oil-rich neighbours in a common cause against desertification fell on deaf ears. Even the conference planned to be held in Sudan in 1978 had to be cancelled due to lack of interest among the invited countries. Nevertheless, Sudan started, with its own funds and probably support from United Nations organs and bilateral assistance, several successful pilot projects that have shown that soil conservation is possible even in areas of extreme aridity. These projects include windbreak plantations along the western fringes of the Nile Valley bordering on the Sahara. Sweden also supported plantations near the town of Atbara.

In essence, the need to conserve basic resources like water, productive soil and vegetation in Africa cannot be overstated and is greater now than ever. Soil erosion is one of the most serious threats to the health and welfare of Africans today, especially marginalised groups, who are forced to live on the fringes of arable land. Traditional forms of land use can no longer support them. There is no place left for them to move should their present land be debased or destroyed. Soil conservation for long-term productivity must become a more central concern in the US's development assistance programmes than has been the case to date.

Global Warming

In June 2006, the government of Niger requested that its citizens pray and fast so that it would rain. The country had had three consecutive years of drought and the situation was getting desperate. Could anyone in the US imagine three years without a drop of rain? This is commonplace in parts of east and southern Africa.

The major reason for this and other deleterious effects that have resulted from global climate change, according to Dr Sama Banya, Honorary President of the Conservation Society of Sierra Leone, is the reckless manner in which some developed countries are misusing the earth's natural resources and polluting the atmosphere with greenhouse gases. He suggests that while Africans have no control over the way the industrialised countries are causing climate change leading to global warming, Africans can minimise the effects of those changes by the way they treat their local environment.

That the effects of global warming are being felt on the continent of Africa is hardly disputable. As Godwin Obasi (in Ramsay and Edge 2004:241) points out, global meteorological observational records show that Africa is now warmer than it was 100 years ago. Warming through the 20th century was at the rate of about 0.05 degrees centigrade per decade, with slightly greater warming from June to August and from September to November than at other times. The five warmest years in Africa have all occurred since 1988, with 1988 and 1995 being the two warmest years. Africa's rate of warming has mimicked that of the rest of the world. Obasi adds that a comprehensive characterisation of regional climate change projection for Africa in the 21st century is that future annual warming will be from 0.2 to more than 0.5 degrees centigrade per decade – i.e. ten times the rate during the 20th century. Warming is expected to be greatest over the interior semi-arid margins of the Sahara and central and southern Africa.

According to Science base Section News (2006), researchers from University College London found that the fabled equatorial icecaps in the Rwenzori Mountains will disappear within two decades because of global warming. The Rwenzori Mountains, also known as the 'Mountains of the Moon', are on the border between the Democratic Republic of Congo and Uganda. The mountains are home to one of the four remaining tropical icecaps outside of the Andes and are well known for their spectacular and rare Afro alpine flora and fauna. The legendary status of these mountains can be traced back to the 2nd century when Greek geographer Ptolemy proclaimed that the River Nile was supplied by snow-capped mountains at the equator of Africa. In his words, they were 'The Mountains of the Moon whose snows feed the lakes, sources of the Nile' (Science base Section News 2006).

The glaciers were first surveyed a century ago, and glacial cover over the entire range was estimated at the time to be 4.3 square miles. Recent field surveys and satellite mapping of the glaciers conducted by University College London, Makerere University and the Ugandan Water Resources Management Department reveal that some glaciers are receding tens of yards each year and that the area covered by glaciers halved between 1987 and 2003. The researchers also found that since the 1960s, there have been clear trends toward increased air temperature around the Rwenzori Mountains without significant changes in precipitation.

If present trends continue, then less than one square mile of the remaining glaciers will disappear within the next twenty years. It is not clear, however, how the projected loss of the glaciers will affect tourism and the traditional belief systems of the BaKonzo people. Nzururu, the BaKonzo word for snow and ice, is the father of the spirits who are responsible for human life, its continuity and welfare. The irony of global warming as it pertains to Africa is best stated by Richard Taylor, the lead researcher from University College London, as follows: 'Considering the continent's negligible contribution to global greenhouse-gas emissions, it is a terrible irony that Africa, according to current predictions, will be most affected by climate change. Furthermore, the rise in air temperature is consistent with other regional studies that show how dramatic increase in malaria in the East African Highlands may rise, in part, from warmer temperatures as mosquitoes are able to colonise previously inhospitable highland areas' (Science base Section News 2006).

Conclusion

Planting trees is one of the most important tasks facing Africans today and will require considerable efforts. A continent-wide reforestation programme would cost billions of dollars, but no other course of action offers the same advantages at that price. The value of trees cannot be overestimated: as mentioned earlier, trees shade the soil and crops against the scorching heat of the sun; they help retain moisture in the soil and mitigate the effects of seasonal drought; they inhibit erosion, a severe problem in Africa; they pump up nutrients from deeper layers of soil; they provide fodder for livestock and food, fuel and timber for people.

In order to stimulate such a reforestation programme, more money should be channelled directly to planting groups, so that more people can be activated in the projects. The problem is so serious that governments alone cannot solve it without mobilising the people. Bottlenecks in reforestation projects usually involve the supply of seeds and seedlings, shortages of cars for transport and implements and watering cans for use in planting. Seed collection and founding nurseries must get under way promptly.

The International Center for Research in Agroforestry (ICRAF) studies the co-cultivation of trees and crops to see what systems are best suited to different types of soil. It has found that over the years, Western agricultural practices, with large-scale monocultures that leave the earth bare from time to time, are poorly suited to African soils and climatic conditions. Combining agriculture and silviculture produces better yields, while combating erosion. This leads to better harvests and more trees, which is important inasmuch as food production is vital and should not be in competition with energy sources.

Energy must be used effectively in every phase, and there is a lot of room for improvement. Simple wood stoves, built with local materials, might increase the efficiency of wood use. It is vital, however, that the stoves be inexpensive, so that many people can afford them. An expenditure of any magnitude will not attract many users, even though households in many areas spend as much on wood as they do on food each year. A conceivable solution might be to introduce portable, effective kilns of the type developed by the Food and Agricultural Organization (FAO), the Cusab kiln. The kiln could be transported, making local purchases of wood. In the long run, alternative energy sources such as solar, wind and water will contribute to Africa's energy supply. But for the present, most people on the continent rely on wood. Hydro-power can be further exploited to provide more electricity for the modern sector. One problem with this energy source is that dams and reservoirs tend to clog with sift as a consequence of soil erosion. Therefore, hydroelectric power, too, is dependent on the success of reforestation and soil conservation efforts.

Geothermal energy has begun to be exploited in some areas of Africa. For example, in Olkaria, some 62 miles north of Nairobi, a hole was drilled 353 feet into the earth. Steam is produced and harnessed to drive the turbines of a generator to produce electricity. Drilling was done at several other sites, so that geothermal electricity can contribute approximately 11 percent of Kenya's electricity.

Bio-gas (methane), derived from the manure of livestock, can be produced and utilised on large farms, although it is unlikely to contribute on a large scale, as cattle are grazed sparsely scattered over vast areas. Ethanol, or ethyl alcohol, can be produced from molasses, a by-product of sugar refinery. Ten per cent ethanol can be mixed with gasoline to reduce Africa's need for imported gasoline. But efforts to increase ethanol production further will be at the expense of foodstuffs. Producing methanol (methyl or wood alcohol) offers greater promise.

Solar cells are used for telecommunications, to drive pumps in isolated places, and to electrify fences to keep animals out of cultivated fields. They are too expensive, however, to have a major impact on the total energy strategy. Solar radiation is used to heat water and to dry various crops. The prospects for expanding this type of energy are vast. The sun can heat water for schools, hospitals, institutions of various kinds, hotels and homes. It can also be used to dry coffee and tobacco. The drying of tobacco leaves today consumes vast quantities of wood – approximately thirty trees per hectare of tobacco. Thus, in the short term, only mass mobilisation to plant trees, coupled with more efficient use of wood fuels, can solve the energy crisis in the traditional sector.

References

Banya, Sama, 2006, 'Apart from Climate Change What Else?', Freetown, Sierra Leone: Concord Times, 6 July.

Blatt, Harvey, 2004, *America's Environmental Card*, Boston, MA: MIT Press.

Lapham, Nicholas P., 2004, 'A Natural Resource Conservation Initiative for Africa', in Walter H. Kansteiner III and J. Stephen Morrison, eds, *Rising U.S. Stakes in Africa: Seven Proposals to Strengthen U.S.-Africa Policy*, Washington, DC: Center for Strategic and International Studies Press.

Obasi, Godwin O. P., 2004, 'Embracing Sustainability Science: The Challenge for Africa', in F. J. Ramsay and W. Edge, eds, *Africa* (Global Studies, 10th ed.), Guilford, CT: McGraw-Hill/Dushkin Company.

Sciencebase Section News, 2006, 'Disappearing Equatorial Icecaps', 15 May, posted by <Africans_Without_Borders@yahoogroups.com>

Lovett, John, 2006, 'Impact of Climate Change in Africa', *Science Daily*, 27 November <http://www.sciencedaily.com/releases/2006/11/061126115458.htm>, accessed 7 May 2010.

Swedish International Development Authority, 1981/82, *Report, Theme: The Environment*, Stockholm: SIDA Information Division.

Vig, Norman J. and Michael G. Faure, 2004, *Green Giants? Environmental Policies of the United States and the European Union*, Boston, MA: MIT Press.

2

Environmental Communication and Sustainable Forest Governance Management in Cameroon

Victor Ngu Cheo

Introduction

The global environmental crises, and their associated consequences, are more than ever before a cause for concern not only to international and regional organisations but also at national and local levels. There is much debate on how best to sustainably exploit the various natural resources. Anxieties about forest decline are significant because forests provide a complex array of ecological, social and economic goods and services to humans. About 25 per cent of the world's people depend to some extent on forest resources for their livelihoods and subsistence (GFW 2000).

In much of sub-Saharan Africa, deforestation is the major environmental problem and much deforestation in Africa is attributed to timber companies whose trade in wood responds to international demand. The resultant effect is that high-value tropical timber is increasingly becoming scarce especially at the local level of economically impoverished countries (Wunder 2000). Household energy consumption outside larger African cities depends almost exclusively on wood sources, and cooking is the most energy-intensive activity (Goldemberg 1996). Population growth and unsustainable wood uses are causing an ever-increasing imbalance between firewood demand and supply, which then triggers deforestation. Given its current rate of expansion, Africa's population is expected to triple from 642 million in 1990 to 1.6 billion in 2025. This astronomical increase portends a greater disaster for an already crisis-ridden continent whose environment has been exploited and plundered for a long time (Lambi 2001). Furthermore, poverty and high population growth often induce land degradation and deforestation, which lead to growing food insecurity and loss of biodiversity. The severity of these mutually reinforcing constraints is compounded by low investment in human capital, which often forces individuals to continue to rely on their own unskilled labour and short-term exploitation of natural resources as the only way to survive (World Bank 1996).

Furthermore, poverty is linked to the environment in complex ways, particularly in African economies which depend on natural resources. It is also a factor in accelerating environmental degradation owing to the fact that the poor, with often less secured access to natural resources, are unable and often unwilling to invest in natural resource management (Mink 1993; World Bank 1996). This is compounded by the fact that about 80 per cent of forests in sub-Saharan Africa are state property, a tenure form that is usually exposed to severe degradation. State enforcement of forest tenure and access rules tends to be less efficient and more costly, and nationalisation can be disastrous for local management incentives. Insecurity of tenure promotes forest mining and discourages long-term timber management (Wunder 2000). Furthermore shifting cultivators, in many cases forest-dwelling ethnic groups, have traditionally been precluded from legalised forest tenure by an intentional state strategy towards forest colonisation (Wunder 2000). Government tenure and colonisation policies thus deliberately tend to favour deforestation activities over sustainable forest uses (Bedoya 1991; Rudel 1993). Last but not least, poor economic performance, together with colossal external debts, pushes African countries to exploit forest resources for short-term gains. Generally, economic crisis drives marginalised people towards the limit and forces countries to promote foreign exchange-generating primary export sectors, some of which are land-using (agriculture) or tree-consuming (timber) (Rowe et al. 1992; Wunder 2000). Increased primary product exports increase pressure on natural resources; and forest sustainability is part of the problem (Sedjo 2005). Concern over forest sustainability poses a serious challenge to Africa in general and Cameroon in particular.

The outcome of the composite research method employed in this study reveals a predominantly supportive and vertical or top-down communication approach adopted by MINFOF and collaborative partners, namely GIZ and ASSOFOMI. Hence, despite the use of multiple channels ranging from meetings, seminars/workshops, newspapers and television reports to the recognition and very frequent use of rural radio, as is the case in Bonakanda in the Mount Cameroon region, and community radio in the Mount Kilum region, the impact in enhancing sustainable forest exploitation has been minimal. This limited success is due to the fact that environmental communication ought to be a multi-stakeholder process involving information exchange, cooperation and participation, and consideration of the opinions of all key target groups, that is, local people, municipal state institutions, NGOs and the media. The rise of democratisation around the world clearly shows the growing desire of people to participate in decisions that affect them. In Eastern Europe, the former Soviet Union, Latin America, Asia, and Africa, news of the past two decades has been of people's increased control over their governments. Participation by local residents and stakeholders changes the nature of policy. It also makes policy more likely to be effective. The need for public participation is a prerequisite for sustainable forest management. As a result, environmental communication and education techniques can enhance the effectiveness of people or groups seeking to participate. Therefore, providing information to forest dependents about forest policies and laws, the global consequences of deforestation as well as education on better land use management is definitely a useful environmental communication strategy. But it is not enough to bring about the desired behavioural change or solve environmental problems as well as enhance sustainable development that is so badly needed (USAID 2000).

Meanwhile, despite their adoption, due to proximity and accessibility, rural and community radio stations and their potential for information dissemination in English, Pidgin English (a lingua franca) or local regional languages have not engendered maximum cooperation and participation of the various stakeholders. This is explained by the fact that rather than adopt a 'pull' environmental communication strategy to draw the target audience in, engaging them, involving them and enhancing a relationship with them in a more proactive way, dominant stakeholders indulge in a 'push' strategy, literally pushing information out to the target audience. This type of strategy is not effective in generating political pressure from below, which is particularly important in developing countries, as it contributes to the reversal of the structural weaknesses of environmental ministries and agencies, and institutions in general. The solution lies in the adoption of a horizontal communication approach, still using radio as the dominant channel but employing a more interactive or participatory model such as the consensus conference model approach, bringing together journalists, experts, stakeholders and local inhabitants to discuss issues of sustainable forest management.

Despite the advanced level of technology in media production and distribution, radio remains the key communication channel to reach a greater audience in the delivery of environmental messages. This conclusion is arrived at based on an analysis of the overall media context in Cameroon, and the area of focus in this study in particular: specifically how information (mainly on environmental matters) is delivered and through which channels stakeholders receive information and can be best approached. However, while radio remains the most frequently used medium of environmental communication in Cameroon in general, and in the Mount Kilum and Mount Cameroon areas in particular, it is necessary to also consider other traditional means of communication such as story tellers, local theatres, which are very influential in some rural areas, and annual cultural events, which are very popular in Cameroon, as key venues for active involvement and information sharing with those communities that cannot be fully reached through the modern media.

The evolution of the forest sector in Cameroon is related to the country's agricultural and political economy. Between 1950 and the early 1970s, with the blessing of the World Bank, the government encouraged the conversion of its moist tropical forests to small-holder coffee and cocoa agro forests. This yielded some positive economic growth, averaging about 5 per cent a year. Furthermore, due to the discovery of commercial oil fields, real GDP per capita increased by 7 per cent a year between 1978 and 1985. But a protracted decline in the terms of trade for its main agricultural exports actuated a dismal depression from 1986 through 1993. Per capita income and consumption fell by almost half and Cameroon's large external debt became unserviceable. In 1993, public-service employment and wages were drastically cut by 70 per cent followed by a 100 percent devaluation of the CFA franc in 1994. These measures seriously affected Cameroonians' income and expenditure potential, with a dramatic impact in the rural areas. Rural populations cleared additional forest for subsistence crop production while the government, on its part, granted more logging concessions. Impoverished city dwellers returned to the countryside to take up farming. The expansion of food crops, notably in remote forested areas, has accelerated deforestation. A decline in food imports during this period and the phasing out of agricultural input subsidies to farmers forced them to cultivate larger areas to maintain significant production.

Forests make a major contribution to export receipts with timber accounting for about 28 per cent of total export earnings, the second most important source of foreign exchange after petroleum (47 %). This figure excludes the considerable levels of revenues lost to illegal logging each year (DfID 2002). The economic compensation gained by government finances from timber revenue became more critical during the early 1990s due to the decline in economic productivity and the low prices of some of Cameroon's other major commodities. In the face of negative growth during the late 1980s and early 1990s, and a mounting debt burden, government identified timber as one sure means to mitigate the situation of inadequate finances (Tesi 2004; Geist and Lambin 2003; Essama-Nssah et al. 2002; GFW 2000).

Poverty in Cameroon is overwhelmingly concentrated in the rural areas. Approximately 86 per cent of the country's poor are rural. The entire rural population relies on forest products for food, medicine, fuelwood and construction materials. Also, non-timber forest products play an important role in the households of the urban poor and forest-dwelling communities. They are an important source of cash revenue for Cameroon's forest-dependent people. The majority of women in rural Cameroon are poor, often refused land ownership and not guaranteed access to forest resources (GFW 2000; Ndoye 1998).

In a bid therefore to bolster Cameroon's economic recovery process, the government initiated in the early 1990sa forest policy reform process in conjunction with a World Bank structural adjustment loan. The Bank sought to improve forest management in the region by using Cameroon as a model. This reform sought to address conflicting economic, social and environmental goals. Major innovations in the new forest management framework included community forestry, new pricing and taxing mechanisms, allocation of concessions through an auction system and the requirement of management plans. However, forests in Cameroon have continued to suffer degradation (DfID 2002; GFW 2000). Ndenecho (2005) attributes this perennial degradation to the fact that the indigenous people, in part, have not always respected forest legislation, especially when their livelihoods or interests are threatened, and also because, in most cases, protected area status has often been imposed with no prior consultation whilst ignoring the socio-economic and cultural situation of those whose survival depends on the forest. This approach has often provoked social tension and conflicts and has undermined the possibility of implementing and achieving sustainability objectives.

This chapter attempts an appraisal of the current approaches of environmental communication and forest management in Cameroon with the main objective of reconstructing a valid environmental communication and forest governance strategy for the mitigation of non-sustainable forest exploitation while enhancing sustainable development. The chapter illustrates that forest policies and laws are bound to be less effective unless accompanied by an auspicious implementation strategy. Lastly, the fact that effective environmental communication is an integral component of any effective sustainable forest management approach is underlined.

Environmental communication is defined as the 'planned and strategic use of communication processes and media products to support effective policy making, public participation and project implementation geared towards environmental sustainability' (OECD 1999b). It is therefore of prime importance as the foundation for establishing relationships between people and the environment and as a means for enhancing environmental literacy and sustainable environmental practices. However, despite its validity as an environmental management tool, it has not been effectively exploited in Cameroon.

According to Lambi (2007), a critical obstacle to the participation of rural people in sustainable natural resource usage and conservation is the lack of reliable and accurate information. Balgah (2007) attributes this to the lack of a viable environmental communication strategy which adequately addresses issues like deforestation and the loss of biological resources. Against this background, this section investigates the state of environmental communication in Cameroon with a focus on montane forest areas. Given that this is mostly practised by local and international institutions in collaboration with the Ministry of Forestry and Wildlife (MINFOF), officials from both the regional and divisional delegations of MINFOF, German Technical Cooperation, GTZ (now GIZ), Association of forest management institutions in Oku, ASSOFOMI, and journalists of two radio stations (Bonakanda community radio and Oku community radio) were interviewed. The reason for their inclusion is because the media, particularly radio, is the main channel for the dissemination of environmental messages. These interviews were backed up by personal monitoring and content analysis of the environmental slots on the various radio stations in question.

Cameroon and its Forests

Cameroon has one of the largest reserves of rainforest left in the world, which extends into neighbouring Congo Brazaville, Gabon and the Democratic Republic of Congo (Ndenecho 2005; Ngwa and Fonjong 2003). Forests resources are estimated to cover 22 million hectares (an approximate area of 200,000 km2), of which 14 million are tropical forest and 8 million are in the savannah biome. Cameroon has the second forest reserve in terms of surface area after the Democratic Republic of Congo as well as the second biodiversity reserve after Madagascar (Ndenecho 2005). The rainforest covers about 42 per cent of the country and contains trees of economic importance such as iroko, *mahogany, obeche,* ebony and many others. The highly diverse forests of Cameroon are representative of the biological diversity of forests in the Congo Basin which is home to about 80 per cent of Africa's moist forests and 20 per cent of the world's moist tropical forests. Biodiversity in the moist tropical forest ecosystems of Cameroon is among the most extensive and unique to be found, both in Africa and across the globe. Cameroon is also one of the few places in the world where tropical montane forest systems are found. The montane forest is unique with the highest levels of endemism in the whole of Africa, particularly among birds and vascular plants. These are particularly important centres for plant and faunal endemism. On Mount Cameroon alone, over 45 endemic plant species have been described (GFW 2000). However, their sustainability is highly threatened as Cameroon has the second highest annual deforestation rate in the Congo Basin, after the Democratic Republic of Congo (Ndenecho 2005). Hence the focus of this study is on the montane forests of Mount Cameroon and Mount Oku respectively.

Forest Governance Strategy and the Case of Mount Cameroon and Mount Kilum Areas

The concept of governance recognises and emphasises the role of interdependence between and among state agencies and society groups, and between public and private spheres. It can thus be defined as a governing model that is not produced exclusively by the state, but that involves social, economic, political and administrative actors that guide, steer, control or manage the society. This definition assumes that the relationship between state and non-state actors is non-hierarchical and therefore based on mutual dependence (Jachtenfuchs 1997).

The analysis of environmental governance is rather complex. It must consider not only the traditional setting of variables of the physical environment and the political, legal and administrative context, but also the set of variables which deal with stakeholders' cultural values, social norms, interests and socio-economic conditions (OECD 1999a).

In Cameroon, the evolution of forest policy reform in the post-1990s resulted in a certain degree of forest democratisation with a governance regime slightly more open to public consultation and transparency than the previous method of forest management prior to the 1990s. The overall objective of the forest reform is to improve practices of forest exploitation and management. Forest policy is meant to correct former non-sustainable practices in natural resource management. It assigns a high priority to the protection of the rich and important biodiversity of the country. In this regard, it seeks to eradicate institutionalised corruption, increase public participation in decision making, mitigate poverty, enhance socio-economic development as a measure of reducing livelihood dependence on forest exploitation, and improve accountability and transparency with respect to accrued revenue from forestry, particularly with respect to benefits sharing with beneficiary communities. But an assessment of the effective implementation of the above-mentioned forest governance strategies in the Mount Cameroon and Mount Kilum regions of the south west and north west regions Cameroon respectively reveals that very little has been accomplished.

Findings of the Investigation

The potential of Cameroon's forest policy to significantly mitigate forest exploitation has been compromised by inadequate logistics as well as incomprehensive and ineffective forest sustainability-oriented strategies. In fact, the much lauded 1994 forestry law, the 1996 environmental management regulation, as well as the concomitant institutional capacities and incentives to enforce them, have lagged behind in translating national policy into an effectively implemented forest strategy (Esama-Nssah et al. 2000).

Public Participation

In spite of the importance of effective public participation in enhancing forest sustainability, it is not yet a priority in Cameroon. It is therefore not surprising that more than half of the respondents, 64 per cent, agreed that there is no form of public consultation in terms of forest management decisions. Worse still, forest dependents in these areas are not incorporated in the forest management scheme. Those concerned about and making use of the forest should be actively involved in its management. One of the approaches to sustainable forest management, and which reportedly seemed to have most potential, is the joint forest management paradigm. The system involves participative management between the government and local communities. The incentives for the people to participate include collection rights of most of the non-wood forest product, increasing the stakes of communities in the management and utilisation of forests, and creating alternative sources of employment to reduce pressure on forests (Abdallah and Kaoneka 1999). Meanwhile, focus group discussion revealed that women are often marginalised when it comes to decision-making. There is also need for gender equity in public participation for decision-making. According to Tiani (2001) women represent more than 51 per cent of the Cameroonian population, and 80 per cent of them live in rural areas. They are important not only because of their numbers but more significantly because they are the actors most closely related to the forest. Hence, their indispensability to forest management that claims to be truly sustainable.

Government Partnership with Local Institutions

Another form of public participation is through partnership with local institutions. The emergence of local indigenous institutions in the form of a Common Initiative Group, for example, Mount Cameroon Prunus Management Common Initiative Group (MOCAP-CIG), working in collaboration with the government is proving to be an auspicious approach to sustainable forest resource management. A growing number of scholars and practitioners recognise the crucial role played by local people in natural resource management (Ostrom 1990; Ascher 1995). They also assert the need for local-level institutions considered better than central government institutions at providing, *inter alia,* rules related to access, harvesting and management. Local-level institutions can respond to conflict quickly and cheaply and implement monitoring and sanctioning methods that are effective. The problem with this approach is that it is not very well formalised; hence, maximum collaboration cannot be attained.

Partnership with International NGOs

In a bid to mitigate unsustainable forest practices in the country, the government has reached technical and financial agreements with international NGOs working in this domain. NGOs like Birdlife International, World Wildlife Fund for Nature (WWF) and Living Earth have been working with local forest dwellers, transferring technology and knowledge in the domains of agriculture, bee farming as well as other alternatives to livelihood (Ngwa and Fonjong 2003).This has greatly boosted Cameroon's sustainable management efforts.

Benefits-sharing Mechanism

The mechanism of benefits-sharing in state managed forest domains in Cameroon constitutes a serious disincentive for cooperation and collaboration from the forest adjacent communities, thereby jeopardising any sustainable management endeavours. This is the case in the Mount Cameroon region where more than 95 per cent of forest is state-owned. Here only 10 per cent of benefits are allocated to the community. Worst still, for the community to even access the meagre 10 per cent allocated to them, they must initiate a good project. And since the local people are poor at making project proposals, the council authorities, the custodian of this money, usually syphone it. Paradoxically, the government retains 50 per cent while the remaining 40 per cent is doled out to the council of the area. According to Tainter (2001) people are more likely to manifest stewardship towards forests from which they derive benefit. Hence, unfair distribution of benefits can stimulate the intentional retaliatory degradation of forest resources as well as other undesirable conflicts.

Transparency and Accountability

Besides the irrational benefit-sharing mechanism described above there is also overwhelming evidence from the respondents' viewpoints that the procedure is marred by lack of transparency and accountability. Considering the various percentages of responses about transparency and accountability in benefit sharing, it is evident that these constitute a serious cause for concern. However, given the pervasive nature of corruption in Cameroon, it is not surprising that only 10 per cent of respondents, exclusively in the Mount Kilum region (MKR), agreed strongly with the application of these variables while 14and 12 per cent in the Mount Cameroon region (MCR) and MKR respectively simply agreed. But of greater significance is the 59 and 31 per cent of respondents who disagreed in the MCR and MKR respectively, while another 19 and 35 per cent, respectively, also disagreed strongly. Respondents, meanwhile, attribute this vice to the corruption syndrome in Cameroon as reflected in their perception of corruption as an incentive for unsustainable practices. This seriously undermines policy implementation and good forest governance.

Poverty Alleviation

Poverty is an important determinant of the rate of forest exploitation. On average 60 per cent of respondents from the case study area attributed their reason for forest exploitation to poverty. Consequently, their primary objective of forest exploitation is to enhance human welfare by either direct usage (personal) or by monetisation (commercialisation) or both (personal and commercial). Each of these strategies either mitigate expenditure or supplement income or provide badly needed legal tender (Asanga 2001; Ndenecho 2007). This of course raises serious concerns given the relatively high degree of non conformity to policy requirements within a wider scope and intensity of forest exploitation. The challenge, therefore, is to reconcile forest exploitation with economic development and poverty alleviation. Empowered communities may focus more on accessing credits, creating community assets or investing in non-farm economic activities (bee-farming, snail propagation, mushroom cultivation). These economic benefits are often long-lasting and sustaining. McDougall (2001) seems to support this idea when he posits that contributing to human well-being makes a direct and significant contribution to sustainable forest management.

Socioeconomic Indicators

The status of certain socio-economic indicators as well as forest-dependents' access to them is crucial in dictating the pace and pattern of forest exploitation. Thus, in spite of the fact that over 65 per cent of the respondents in the MCR reportedly have access to drinking water and 60 per cent have access to good transport networks, they have continued to violate forest policies by invading the forest. In fact, the good road network in the MCR, rather than being an asset, is more of a liability as it facilitates the evacuation of illegal forest products (Tesi 2004). But these are no substitute for the limited access of other social welfare elements such as healthcare, education and micro credits. Unfortunately less than 40 per cent of respondents in the MCR have access to these. The scenario is worse in the MKR. In this part of the north west region, the majority of villagers rely heavily on traditional medicine. In fact the MKR is famous for its traditional medical practitioners and practices (Ndenecho 2005). However, despite the assiduity and industrious nature of the people of this region, the lack of any form of microfinance or concessional loan scheme is an obstacle to the economic endeavours of the people. Cases in point include the Oku Honey Cooperative with 209 registered members and the Kilum Craft Paper Group, the only one in the whole north west region. These two common initiative groups have contributed enormously to mitigating forest exploitation. The cooperative employs villagers and also facilitates the buying and selling of honey from bee farmers. However, due to the poor state of the road and high cost of transportation, dividends that members receive are seriously affected, and by extension, their wellbeing and also their families' wellbeing. Government subsidies could alleviate the effect.

Similarly, the absence of any government subsidies has caused this lone budding paper industry to stagnate. According to the manager, Solomon Chimtom, the resulting quality has remained poor. Ordinarily, government ought to encourage this lofty initiative as the local paper industry no longer debarks trees to produce paper, a factor which hitherto contributed to forest degradation and deforestation. The industry now uses corn stalks and the leaves of Indian bamboo. Hence, beyond the obvious environmental impacts, there are also socio-economic implications especially with regard to economic empowerment.

Road Map to Forest Sustainability and Sustainable Development

In view of mitigating non-sustainable forest exploitation and enhancing sustainable development in Cameroon as a whole, the government should provide the Ministry of Forestry, MINFOF, with all the necessary logistics and adequate financial resources to enhance the effective implementation of the forest policy currently in force. One pragmatic way of acquiring the required funds is through tourism in protected areas. Eco-tourism contributes to raising awareness of national and international visitors, as well as creating jobs, and sometimes leads to infrastructure development that contributes to poverty alleviation, provided the funds generated are managed in a transparent and accountable manner.

In place of the often empty threats and verbal rhetoric of ministry officials, corruption and all forms of illegal and unsustainable exploitation of forests should be severely sanctioned. Owing to the potential success of third party monitoring, international NGOs should also be involved in the fight against corruption which pervades the forestry sector in Cameroon. For instance, according to Essama-Nassah et al. (2002) Global Witness, an international NGO, was involved in monitoring corrupt practices and illegal logging in Cameroon from 2002 to 2005. The NGO registered significant results and impacted on some of the companies logging activities outside of agreed limits. And finally, as proposed by Nalini and Naresh (2001), there should be greater decentralisation and participatory and transparent sharing of forest management responsibilities with local communities as a means of minimising corruption.

Effective decentralisation by government and participatory sharing of forest responsibilities with local communities could be an effective and significant way of minimising corruption, enhancing forest governance and ensuring sustainable management and development. A good example is the delegation of responsibility to the Mount Cameroon Prunus Management Common Initiative Group (MOCAP-CIG) by government. The CIG which was created on the 31 July 2000 (in accordance with Law no. 92/006 of 14/8/92 and its Decree no. 92/455/PM of 23/11/92) has the global objective of contributing to poverty alleviation around the Mount Cameroon region through sustainable management and conservation of *Prunus africana* and other forest resources. This has drastically reduced the illegal exploitation of *Prunus africana*. Hence government should collaborate with various civil society groups which share similar or the same objectives.

There is equally a need for government to create a special trust fund dedicated to poverty alleviation to ensure long-term financial support for addressing the livelihood and employment needs of the forest-dependent poor, especially where the incidence of poverty is large. Access to economic alternatives to meet the social requirements of indigenous people is still a big challenge. One way of enhancing this is through integrated conservation and development projects (ICDPs) such as the improvement of road and school infrastructure, provision of support for educational training, healthcare and welfare services and investment in non-timber forest activities such as bee-farming, snail propagation, cultivation of *eru* (*Gnetum africanum*) and domestic livestock and fish farming. The fund, apart from promoting traditional income generating activities, should also be dedicated towards the promotion and support of creative and self-help initiatives. These notwithstanding, government should encourage the creation of technical schools and rural artisan centres in Cameroon to train young Cameroonians to be self-employed and hence divert their attention from natural resources. In this regard, there is need for greater cooperation with international NGOs, especially in the domains of participatory management activities in the field of training, technological dissemination and the training of women's group. The focus should be on building social capital. Above all, the government should create employment opportunities for Cameroonians and also reduce the high taxes levied on private businesses so that more people can be self-employed and the pressure on natural resources will reduce.

Benefit-sharing is a very sensitive issue as people are more likely to manifest stewardship towards forest from which they stand to gain. Fair and equitable revenue-sharing with local communities increases their stakes in sustainable management. Unfair distribution of benefits can spur intentional and retaliatory degradation of forest resources as well as other undesirable conflicts.

Given the indispensability of fuelwood in the short term, it is important to exploit all the potential byproducts of the timber industry such as sawdust and chipboards for use by locally designed cooking stoves oriented towards firewood reduction. The formation of briquettes from the dust of charcoal production such as in Kenya by a company called 'chardust' is not only energy efficient but also enhances the efficient use of woody biomass products. Government should further invest in both solar and wind energy, and in biogas and pellets production from the colossal amount of municipal solid waste generated in the area. And government should exploit the ubiquitous presence of rivers and waterfall in the area for purposes of hydropower, which could eventually be used both for domestic and industrial purposes. The inauguration of the Memve'le and Lom Panghar hydroelectricity dams by Paul Biya are steps in the right direction.

Meanwhile, since smallholder agriculture is a major source of forest degradation, an active policy-led effort to intensify perennial crop and food crop systems to deflect further encroachment on the forest edge is needed. Government should revive the loan and credit facilities available to farmers prior to the economic crises through structures such as micro- finance banks. The same holds true for other agricultural inputs or subsidies such as fertilisers. Public knowledge of soil management through conventional practices of organic manure, use of cover-crops and composting should be enhanced. Furthermore, the entrenchment of agroforestry practices through public education could supply part of the badly needed environmental services.

For purposes of more effective environmental communication, there is need for the adoption of the 'consensus conference model approach', whereby environmental communicators, local people and experts are engaged more equitably in the problem solving and management process. The idea here is a kind of public debate in which a consensus is reached, followed by agenda setting for policy makers and the general public. Last but not the least: in addition to the need for government subvention to sustain and promote the good work of the rural radios, government should also facilitate the public's access to the audio-visual media.

One of the most heinous push-factors of forest degradation is poverty. Given a sliver of financial opportunity, many forest dependents will resort to various options of eking out a living. Thus, there is need not only for government financial handouts but more importantly for a review of the loans and credit policies in both state and private banks to accommodate even the poor. Current lending conditions, *inter alia,* collateral security and high interest rates are inimical to socioeconomic development, the growth of small local and medium-size industries and entrepreneurship. Based on practical experience from Bangladesh, micro-credit accessibility by the poor could be a potential tool for mitigating forest degradation.

According to Muhammad Yunus, Nobel laureate and founder of the Grameen Bank in 1974, the poor are neither too stupid nor too passive to earn money. Instead, the struggle for survival has honed their innovative skills such that all they need is a little capital to get them going. Defying all his sceptics and continuing with his vision of providing loans to the poor, Muhammad reveals that 95 per cent of Grameen's loans are paid back. He further stresses that loans should be given on acceptable terms while condemning the issuing of handouts: 'Give someone a handout, he will feel and act like a helpless beggar. Give him a loan, and you treat him (or her) as a responsible business partner.'

Conclusion

The unsustainable exploitation and management of forest resources in Cameroon, and in the Mount Cameroon and Mount Kilum regions in particular, is inextricably linked to the rural poor's limited and unequal access to information and basic necessities. The government of Cameroon is primarily responsible for this state of affairs. It has failed to consistently articulate a vision of socioeconomic development compatible with poverty alleviation and forest sustainability. Government lacked the goodwill and logistics to implement reforms while the majority of local communities were left out of the process. Government agencies in the sector are weak while international logging companies that dominate the sector continue to have a free hand in the exploitation of forest resources due to widespread corruption.

Like the burgeoning democratisation process in Cameroon which was stampeded by the media, the sustainable management of forest resources in Cameroon will also depend to a great extent on effective environmental communications, particularly through the radio, which is the dominant channel of information dissemination. Information also brings education: a pathway out of poverty. When people are empowered educationally through training for capacity building, they can further empower themselves economically. Empowered communities may focus on accessing credit, creating community assets and investing in non-forest timber products (bee-farming, snail propagation, mushroom cultivation, fisheries and livestock breeding etc.), the economic benefits of which are often long lasting and sustaining.

As a veritable tool of sustainable forest management, environmental communication should not only supply policy related information and cosmetic livelihood survival education but also set an agenda for an effective forest governance strategy which includes economic empowerment and sustainable development.

References

Abdallah, R. and S. Kaoneka, 1999, 'Asia – Pacific Forests, Society and Environment', in P.Matti and U. Jussi, eds, *World Forests*, Vol. 1, Dordrecht: Kluwer Academic Publishers.

Asanga, C., 2001, 'Facilitating Viable Partnerships in Community Forest Management in Cameroon: The Case of the Kilum-Ijim Mountain Forest Area', in E. Wollenberg, D. Edmunds, L. Buck, J. Fox, and S. Brot, eds, *Social Learning in Community Forests,* Bogor: CIFOR/East-West Center.

Ascher, W., 1995, *Communities and Sustainable Forestry in Developing Countries*, San Francisco, CA: ICS Press.

Bedoya, E., 1991, *Social and Economic Causes of Deforestation in the Peruvian Amazon Basinnatives and Colonists*, New York, NY: Institute for Development Anthropology. Working Paper No.60.

DfID, 2002, *Cameroon Country Strategic Paper*, Yaoundé: DfID Programme Coordination.

Essama-Nssah B., J. Gockowski, and L. Kelley, 2002, 'A New Deal for Cameroon's Forest' in Lele Uma, ed., *Managing a Global Resource: Challenges of Forest Conservation and Development.*Vol. 5, New Jersey: Transaction Publishers.

Geist, H. and E. Lambin, 2003, *Forces Driving Tropical Deforestation*, ASB Policy briefs No. 6, Nairobi: ASB Programme.

Global Forest Watch, 2000, *An Overview of Logging in Cameroon*, Washington, DC: World Resources Institute.

Goldemberg, J., 1996,*Energy, Environment and Development*, London: Earthscan.

Jachtenfuchs, M., 1997, 'Democracy and Governance in the European Union', *European Integration*, <http://eiop.or.at/eiop/texte/1997-002a.htm>, accessed March 2011.

Lambi, C. M., 2001, 'Land Degradation in the North West Province of Cameroon', in Dunlop, J. and R. Williams, eds,*Culture and Environment: A Reader in Environmental Education*, Buea: University of Buea.

McDougall, L. C., 2001, 'Gender and Diversity in Assessing Sustainable Forest Management and Human Well-Being', in J. CarolandY. Byron, eds, *People Managing Forests*, Washington, DC: Resources for the Future.

Nalini, K. and C. Naresh, 2001, 'India's Forests: Potential for Poverty Alleviation', in Lele Uma, ed., *Managing a Global Resource: Challenges of Forest Conservation and Development*, Vol. 5, New Jersey: Transaction Publishers.

Ndenecho, E., 2005, *Biological Resource Exploitation in Cameroon*, Bamenda: Unique Printers.

Ndenecho, E., 2007, 'Integrating the Livelihoods of Forest-Adjacent Communities in Forest Conservation Projects: Case Study of Mount Oku Cameroon', *Journal of Applied Social Sciences* 6 (1 & 2): 56–78.

Ndenecho, E.N. and S. N. Balgah, 2007, *The Population-Resource Scarcity and Conflict Trinity*, Bamenda: Unique Printers.

Ndoye, O., 1998, *The Impact of Macro Economic and Agricultural Policies on Forest Conditions in Cameroon*, Yaoundé: International Centre for Forest Research.

Ngwa, N.E., and L.N. Fonjong, 2003,'Actors, Options and the Challenges of Forest Management in Anglophone Cameroon', *GeoJournal* 57(2):95–111.

OECD, 1999a, 'Environmental Communication, Applying Communication Tools TowardsSustainable Development', unpublished paper.

OECD, 1999b, 'Environmental Communication, Working Paper of the Working Party on 'Development Cooperation and Environment', unpublished paper.

Ostrom, E., 1990, *Governing the Commons: the Evolution of Institutions for Collective Action*, Cambridge: Cambridge University Press.

Rudel, T., 1993, *Tropical Deforestation: Small Farmers and Land Clearing in the Ecuadorian Amazon*, New York, NY: Columbian University Press.

Sedjo, R.A., 2005, *Macroeconomics and Forest Sustainability in the Developing World*, Washington, DC: Resources for the Future.

Tainter, J.A., 2001, 'Sustainable Rural Communities', in J. Carol and Y. Byron, eds, *People Managing Forests*, Washington, DC: Resources for the Future.

Tiani, A.M., 2001, *The Place of Rural Women in the Management of Forest Resources: the Case of Mbalmayo and Neighbouring Areas of Cameroon*, Washington, DC: Resources for the Future.

Tesi, M. K., 2004, 'Cameroon's endangered environment: economic policy and forest loss', in K. Kalu, ed., *Agenda Setting and Public Policy in Africa*, Burlington: Ashgate Publishing Company.

USAID, 2000, *Environmental Education and Communication for a Sustainable World. Handbook for International Practitioners*, Washington, DC: Academy for Educational Development.

World Bank, 1996, *Toward Environmentally Sustainable Development in Sub-Saharan Africa*, Washington, DC: International Bank for Reconstruction and Development/ World Bank.

Wunder, S., 2000, *The Economics of Deforestation*, London: Macmillan.

3

Farmers' Perceptions and Adaptation to Climate Change: Evidence from Ghana

Henry de-Graft Acquah, Jacob Nunoo
and Kwabena Nkansah Darfor

Introduction

Climate change has gained increased attention in recent times due to its perceived negative repercussions on a range of activities, chiefly agriculture. These events are ample evidence of what climate change may unleash if attempts are not made to mitigate and adapt to its impacts. For instance, Dai et al. (2004) and Trenberth et al. (2007) point out that many third world countries have already experienced extreme weather events in terms of floods, droughts, heat waves and tropical cyclones that are more frequent and intense than previously. The resulting impacts point to the consequences for the environment, production systems, and livelihoods from future climate variability and change.

It is important that we shed light on what we mean by climate change in order to put things in the right perspective. The Intergovernmental Panel on Climate Change (IPCC) (2007) defines climate change as a change in the state of the climate that can be identified (e.g. using statistical tests) by changes in the mean and/or the variability of its properties, and that persists for an extended period, typically decades or longer. It refers to any change in climate over time, whether due to natural variability or as a result of human activity.

Agriculture contributes about 35 per cent of Ghana's GDP, generates 30 – 40 per cent of foreign exchange earnings, and employs about 55 per cent of the population. It is envisaged that climate change will pose a serious threat to the environment, agricultural production and food security of most developing countries including Ghana. In particular, rural farmers, whose livelihoods depend on the use of natural resources, are likely to bear the brunt of adverse consequences. This is largely because most developing countries experience high poverty incidence and as a result are incapable of adapting to climate change. However, the extent of the impact of climate change on agriculture can be ameliorated by the perception and level of adaptation of farmers. Studies have shown that African perceptions and understandings of climate change are poor. For instance, Taderera (2010) reported that South Africans' awareness of climate change was literally interpreted as 'changing weather' and this may influence the extent of adaptation. Adaptation is widely recognised as a vital component of any policy response to climate change. It is a way of reducing vulnerability, increasing resilience, moderating the risk of climate impacts on lives and livelihoods, and taking advantage of opportunities posed by actual or expected climate change.

The way farmers perceive climate change is important for their choice of adaptation and hence their willingness to pay for climate change mitigation action. Perceptions are however influenced by other factors. Gbetibouo (2009) observed that fertile soil and access to water for irrigation decrease the likelihood that farmers will perceive climate change. However, education, experience and access to extension services all increase the likelihood that farmers perceive climate change.

Much as perceptions and adaptations to climate change are important, it is however instructive to note that very few studies have examined farmers' perceptions and adaptation and the consequent effect on willingness to pay for climate change mitigation policy action in the Ghanaian context. This study therefore considers how farmers perceive and adapt to climate change and their willingness to pay for climate change mitigation policy. In investigating this research problem, the following objectives were pursued:

- examine the socioeconomic characteristics of the farmers;
- analyse their level of awareness of climate change;
- analyse farmers' perception of climate change;
- examine the various choice of adaptation measures among the farmers;
- identify the barriers to adaptation among the farmers; and
- analyse the socio-economic determinants of farmers willingness to pay for climate change mitigation policy.

In response to perceived long-term changes in climate, farm households have implemented a number of adaptation measures to reduce their vulnerability to climate change impacts. Analysis of the impacts of climate change and adaptation on food production in Ethiopia by Yesuf et al. (2008) revealed changing crop variety, soil and water conservation, water harvesting, planting of trees and changing planting and harvesting periods as the choices of adaptation measures by the farmers. Among these methods of adaptation, planting trees was the dominant measure adopted by most of the farmers. However, about 42 per cent of the farmers did not use any adaptation method for climate change impacts. Using two separate models to examine the factors influencing farmers' decision to adapt to perceived climate changes, Yesuf et al. (2008) confirmed that household wealth, represented by farm and non-farm income and livestock ownership, increases the likelihood of climate change awareness and adaptation. Deressa (2008) identified age of head of household, wealth, information on climate change, social capital and agro-ecological settings as having significant impact on farmers' perception of climate change. Farmers in areas with a higher annual mean temperature over the period of survey were more likely to adapt to climate change.

Numerous factors have been identified as barriers to adaptation: lack of information on choice of adaptation options, lack of financial resources, shortage of land, poor potential for irrigation and labour constraints (Deressa et al. 2008). However, lack of information on choice of adaptation options was the major barrier. Madison (2006) and Nhemachena and Hassan (2008) have shown that access to information through extension increases the chance of adapting to climate change.

Climate mitigation strategies must be viewed as a collective concern for the sustainability of agricultural production and livelihoods of many people, especially those in developing countries. Consequently, individual willingness to contribute to climate issues is vital in such endeavour. As a result some studies have analysed willingness to pay for climate change mitigation policy using different models. The impact of uncertainty associated with climate change on individual decisions regarding support for climate change policy was first examined by Cameron (2005). That study used a Bayesian information updating model in a single bounded contingent valuation framework to estimate an individual option price for future climate change using a convenience sample of college students. Empirical results revealed a quadratic relationship between expected future temperature changes and individual support for climate change policy. Thus, the respondents were willing to pay more as expected future temperature change increased but the amount increased at a decreasing rate.

Maddison (2006) reviewed studies on adoption of new technologies and identified farm size, tenure status, education, access to extension services, access to market and credit availability as the major determinants of speed of adoption in Africa. Minimising the impacts of climate change requires perception and adaptation. Farmers' ability to perceive climate change is a key precondition for their choice of adaptation. Maddison (2006) further revealed that adaptation to climate change requires farmers to first perceive that the climate has changed, then identify useful adaptations and implement necessary adaptation responses.

Akter and Bennett (2009) analysed the determinants of households' willingness to pay for the Carbon Pollution Reduction Scheme (CPRS) in Australia. Willingness to pay for climate change mitigation was found to be significantly reduced by uncertainty associated with the expectations of future temperature increases. Furthermore, willingness to pay for the CPRS was found to be negatively affected by respondents' lack of confidence in the scheme being effective in slowing down climate change.

Analysis of the perception and willingness of graduate students to pay a gas tax (Viscusi and Zeckhauser 2001) revealed that a major factor that may influence willingness to pay, holding risk estimates constant, is whether a respondent feels scientific uncertainty motivates a more aggressive or less aggressive approach to climate change policy. Han et al. (2010) estimated willingness to pay for environmental conservation by tourists in China, using a contingent valuation method. The results indicated that willingness to pay increases with income, education level and age.

Bamidele et al. (2010) analysed the factors affecting farmers' ability to pay for irrigation facilities in Nigeria. Empirical results from the logistic regression analysis in the paper revealed age of the farmers, education level acquired, farm household income and size of farmers' household as the major factors explaining farmers' ability and willingness to pay for an irrigation scheme.

The study was based in the Dunkwa in the Shama Ahanta East Municipality and the Bawku Municipality of Ghana. These districts are well known farming areas contributing significantly to the food basket of Ghana. The Dunkwa in the Shama Ahanta East Municipality is one of the sixteen districts/municipalities in the Western Region of Ghana. Fante, and Ahanta are the main ethnic groups living in the district. It is bordered to the north by the Mpohor Wassa East District, to the south by the Gulf of Guinea, Sekondi-Takoradi Metropolitan Assembly to the west (all in the Western Region), and Komenda Edina Eguafo-Abirem District to the Erst in Central Region. Its geographical coordinates are 50 7' 0"north and 10 37' 0" west. Relatively mild temperatures are experienced in the district ranging between 22 and 28 degrees centigrade.

The administrative capital is Shama and is located on the West Coast, about 15 kilometres from Sekondi, the regional capital, 130 kilometres east of the Côte d'Ivoire boundary and 280 kilometres west of Accra, the national capital connecting economic activities to the central region. The predominant occupation of the people in the district is farming. The district covers a land area of 215 km2 with an estimated population of 88,314 (2000 census) of which over 1,500 are farmers. Thus 78 per cent of the active labour force in the district is engaged in agriculture with the remaining 22 per cent found in industry, services and commerce. The major agricultural crops cultivated in the district include cassava, oil palm, maize, coconut and vegetables. The district lies within the tropical climatic zone and experiences two rainy seasons with an average annual rainfall of about 138 cm, with peak rainfall in July.

The Bawku Municipality, on the other hand, is one of the nine districts/ municipalities in the Upper East Region of Ghana. The district is bordered by Burkina Faso to the north and Togo to the east. Kusasi, Mamprusi, Bissa and Mossi are the main ethnic groups living in Bawku District. To the south, the municipality is bordered by the Garu-Tempane District and to the west by Bawku West District (Zebilla). It lies between latitude 110 and 110 151 north of the equator and longitude 10 301 and 00west of the Greenwich meridian.

The administrative capital town of the municipality is Bawku which is about 880 kilometres from Accra the national capital and vibrant commercial business centre, connecting economic activities between other West African states such as Togo, Burkina, Niger and Mali. The Bawku Municipality has a total land area of about 1,215.05 km2 and an estimated population of 216,271, an annual growth rate of 3 per cent, with an average of 7 persons per household (2000 census). Agriculture is the dominant occupation in the district with tomatoes, soya beans and onions being the main crops cultivated. The average annual rainfall of the municipality is 700mm, with peak rainfall in August.

The target population was farmers in Dunkwa and Bawku. A random sampling technique was used to select 193 farmers in Dunkwa and Bawku where every farmer was given an equal opportunity to be selected in the sample. An interview schedule was the main tool of data collection while descriptive statistics and logistic regression analysis were the main analytical techniques. Data was analysed using the SPSS and Stata tools.

The basic model of the log it estimation is as follows:

$$P_i = \operatorname{Prob}(Y_i = 1) = \frac{1}{1+e^{-(\beta_o+\beta_1 X_{1i}+.......\beta_k X_{ki})}} \quad\quad ......(1)$$

$$= \frac{e^{(\beta_o+\beta_1 X_{1i}+.......\beta_k X_{ki})}}{1+e^{-(\beta_o+\beta_1 X_{1i}+.......\beta_k X_{ki})}}$$

Similarly,

$$P_i = \operatorname{Prob}(Y_i = 0) = 1 - \operatorname{Prob}(Y_i = 1) \quad\quad ......(2)$$

$$= \frac{1}{1+e^{(\beta_o+\beta_1 X_{1i}+.......\beta_k X_{ki})}}$$

Dividing (1) by (2) we get

$$\frac{\operatorname{Prob}(Y_i = 1)}{\operatorname{Prob}(Y_i = 0)} = \frac{P_i}{1-P_i} = e^{(\beta_o+\beta_1 X_{1i}+.......\beta_k X_{ki})} \quad\quad ......(3)$$

Where Pi is the probability that Y takes the value 1 and then (1-Pi) is the probability that Y is 0 and e the exponential constant.

This research uses information criteria as a technique for providing the basis for model selection. Most commonly used information criteria such as Akaike Information Criteria (AIC) are employed. The idea of AIC (Akaike 1973) is to select the model that minimises the negative likelihood penalised by the number of parameters as specified in the equation (4):

$$AIC = -2\log(L) + 2p$$

$$........(4)$$

Where L refers to the likelihood under the fitted model and P is the number of parameters in the model. Specifically, AIC aims at finding the best approximating model for the unknown true data generating process and its applications draw from Akaike (1973), Bozdogan (1987)and Zucchini (2000).

Socioeconomic Characteristics of Farmers in Dunkwa and Bawku

Socioeconomic characteristics of the farmers in Dunkwa were investigated and the results are presented accordingly. Cereals, vegetables and root/tubers are the main crops grown by the farmers in the area; the majority, 73.5 per cent of the sample, are cereal farmers. Almost four-fifths of the respondents, 79.6 per cent, were male; while 20.4 per cent were female. The average age of the farmers interviewed was almost 45 years; 37.8 per cent were in the age range of 34-41 years; 20.4 per cent 42-49 years; and 14.3 per cent 58-65 years. Only 5.1 per cent of the farmers were in the age range of 66-73 years. A tenth of the farmers interviewed had obtained senior high school education; 48 per cent had obtained junior high school education; 35.7 per cent had obtained basic education; while only 6.1 per cent had no formal education. The average annual income of the farmers was GH¢1403.0612, with 48 per cent earning between GH¢100-GH¢1000, 33.7 per cent between GH¢1100-GH¢2000, 10.2 per cent between GH¢2100-GH¢3000; only 8.2 per cent of the farmers had an annual income of between GH¢3100-GH¢5000. Given the farmers' relatively low annual incomes, their adaptation and willingness to pay for mitigation policy may be low. The distribution of years of farming experience revealed an average of 17.816 years of farming with 33.7 per cent having between 1 and 10 years' experience, 32.7 per cent having between 11 and 20 years' experience, 23.5 per cent having between 21 and 30 years' experience, and 10.2 per cent having between 31 and 40 years' experience. The average household size of the farmers was about seven persons, with 88.8 per cent having a household size between 4 and 9 persons; 8.2 per cent having between 10 and15 persons; while only 1 per cent had a household size of between 21 and 25 persons. However, the distribution of farm size revealed an average of 4.306 acres with the majority of the farmers (69.4 %) having 1-4 acres of farmland' 16.3 per cent having 5-9 acres; 9.2 per cent 10-14 acres; and only 5.1 per cent had 15-19 acres of farmland.

From Bawku, the socioeconomic characteristics are presented below. Of the respondents interviewed, males dominated with 82.1 per cent while the remaining 17.9 per cent were females. Of the respondents interviewed 23.2 per cent were between the ages of 24 and 30 years; 45.3 per cent were between 31 and 40; 21.1 per cent were between 41 and 50; 8.4 per cent were between 51 and 60; and 2.1 per cent were between 61 and 70. Of the respondents 64.2 per cent were heads of their families while the remaining 35.8 per cent were not. Though educational levels of the respondents ranged from no formal education through to tertiary level, the number of years spent at these levels differed with the respondents. Of the respondents 23.2 per cent had no formal education; 12.6 per cent had obtained basic education; 12.6 per cent had obtained middle/junior high school education, 17.9 per cent had obtained O'level or senior high school education and 33.7 per cent had obtained education up to tertiary level. Of the respondents 41.1 per cent had a household size of between1 and 5 persons, 43.2 per cent had between 6 and 10 persons; 12.6 per cent had between 11 and 15 persons; 2.1 per cent had between 16 and 20 persons; and 1.1 per cent had between 21 and 25 persons.

With regard to their farming experience, 20 per cent had 3-10 years of farming experience, 47.4 per cent had 11-20years; 20 per cent had 21-30years; 7.4 per cent had 31-40years; and 5.3 per cent had 41-50years' experience. Of the respondents interviewed, the majority, constituting 55.8 per cent, had farmland size between 1-5 acres, 36.8 per cent had farmland size of 6-10 acres, 3.2 per cent had farmland size between 11-15 acres, 3.2 per cent had farmland size between 16-20 acres and 1.1 per cent had farmland size between 21 and 25 acres. 64.2 per cent of the respondents had other income generating activities, while for 35.8 per cent their only source of income was farming usually done at subsistence level. The majority, constituting 56.8 per cent of the respondents interviewed, earned an annual income ofGH¢800-GH¢2000; 18.9 per cent earned GH¢2100-GH¢3000; 12.6 per cent earned GH¢3100-GH¢4000; 7.4 per cent earned GH¢ 4100-GH¢5000; 2.1 per cent earned GH¢5100-GH¢6000; and 2.1 per cent earned GH¢6100-GH¢7000.

From the socioeconomic characteristics of farmers in Dunkwa and Bawku, the majority of the farmers had some form of education. More than two-thirds had more than a decade of experience in farming. Again, the majority of the farmers had small farmlands to work on in both areas. Even though general income accrued from agriculture in the country is generally low, the study reveals that those in the northern region have relatively higher incomes than their southern counterparts.

Figure 3.1: Perception of climate change (Bawku)

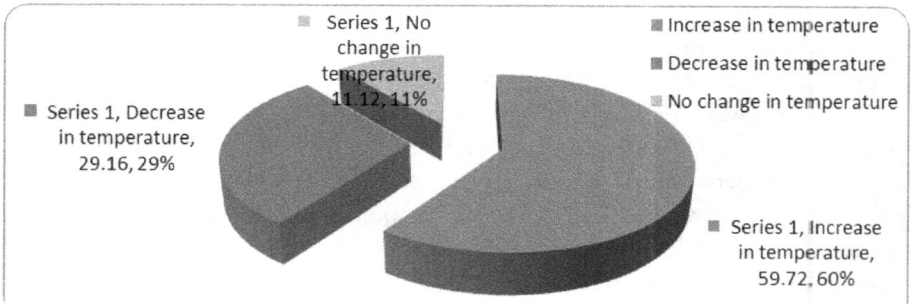

When asked about the perception of changes in temperature, the majority, constituting 60 per cent of the total respondents, perceived an increase in temperature. Of the respondents 29 per cent indicated a decrease in temperature while the remaining 11 per cent went contrary to this opinion and perceived no change in temperature.

Farmers' Perception of Temperature Changes in Dunkwa

About 49 per cent of the farmers perceived increases in temperature whilst 33 per cent perceived a decrease in temperature. However, 18 per cent did not perceive any change in temperature.

Figure 3.2: Farmers' perception on temperature changes in Dunkwa

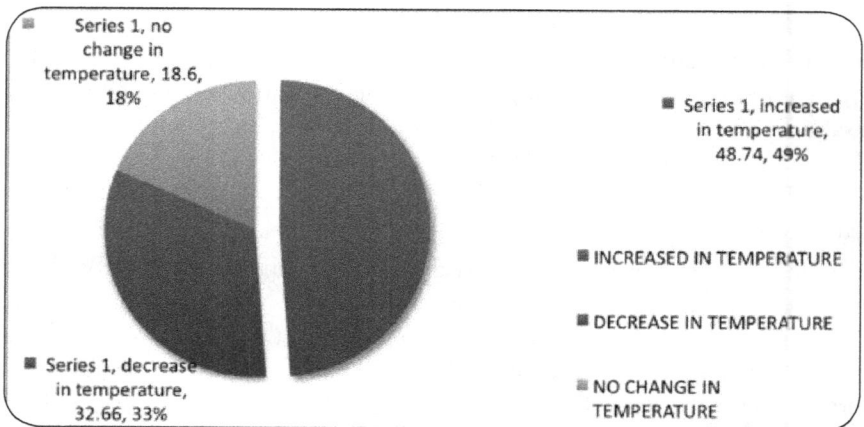

Perception of Changes in Rainfall in Bawku

Of the farmers interviewed, 24 per cent perceived an increase in rainfall. Up to 49 per cent of the total respondents perceived decrease in rainfall. Although 16 per cent of the total respondents perceived no changes in rainfall, up to 11 per cent were contrary to this view since they perceived irregular rainfall pattern.

Figure 3.3: Perception of changes in rainfall in Bawku

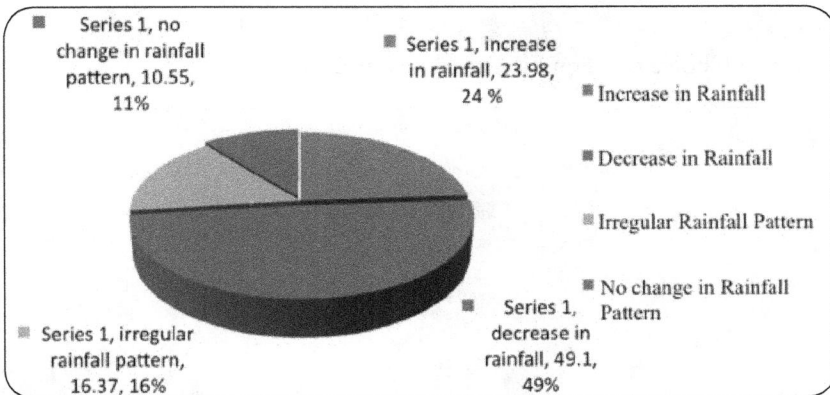

Farmers' Perception of Changes in Rainfall Pattern in Dunkwa

The distribution of farmers' perceptions concerning changes in rainfall pattern revealed that 22 per cent perceived an increase in precipitation; 37 per cent perceived a decrease in precipitation; 30 per cent perceived an irregular rainfall pattern. Despite the higher perception of the farmers interviewed on changes in rainfall pattern, 11 per cent of the farmers interviewed did not see any change in rainfall pattern.

Figure 3.4: farmers' perception of rainfall pattern in Dunkwa

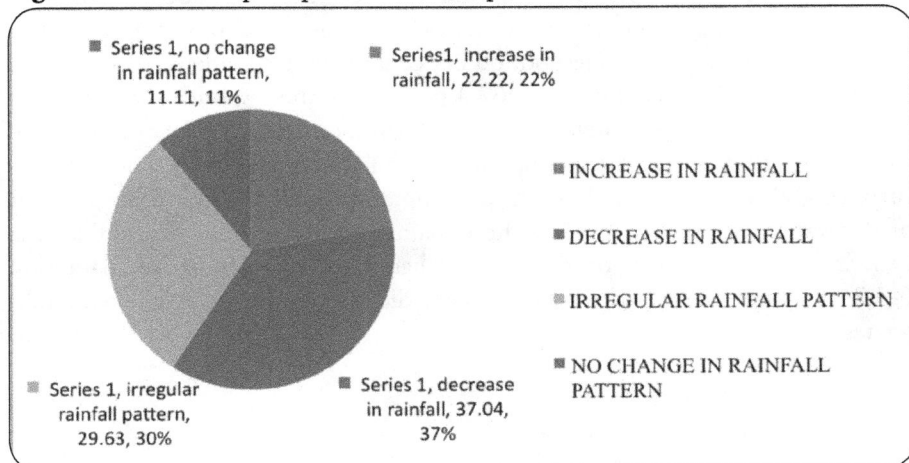

Choice of Adaptation Methods in Bawku

When asked if these farmers had introduced adaptation methods due to the perceived changes in climate, the majority, forming 87.4 per cent of the total population, had adapted methods while the remaining 12.6 per cent had not. Changing planting dates, soil conservation and using different crop varieties were the major methods. The other methods included planting trees, prayers and irrigation, with water harvesting being the method least adapted despite its numerous benefits.

Figure 3.5: Choice of adaptation methods in Bawku

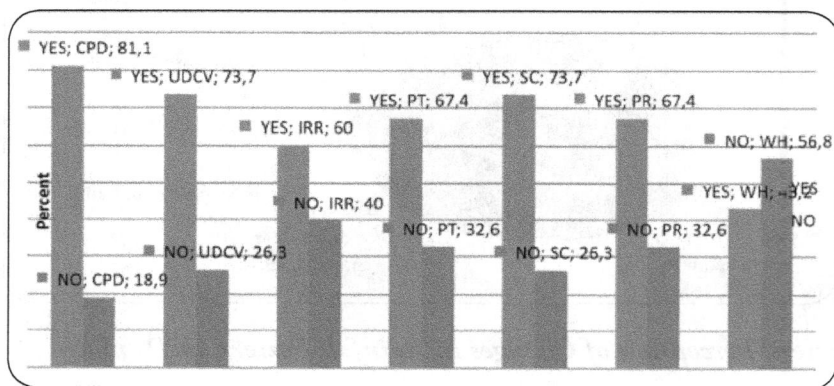

Note: CPD = *Changing Planting Dates*; IRR = *Irrigation*; UDCV = *Using Different Crop Varieties*; PT = *Planting Trees*; PR = *Prayers*; SC = *Soil Conservation*; WH= *Water Harvesting.*

From Figure 3.5, 81.1 per cent of the respondents interviewed adapted changing planting dates while 18.9 per cent did not. Of the respondents, 73.7 per cent adapted using different crop varieties while the remaining did not. With irrigation as an adaptation method, 60 per cent of the respondents used it while the remaining 40 per cent did not. 67.4 per cent of the respondents adapted to planting trees while the others did not. Most respondents (73.7 %) adapted to soil conservation during changes in climate while the remainder did not. Prayers surprisingly gained in popularity as an adaptation method with 67.4 per cent of the respondents using it while the remaining 32.6 per cent did not see the benefits. Water harvesting on the contrary had a lower percentage of adaptation (43.2 %) while the majority 56.8 per cent did not employ it as an adaptation strategy.

Choice of Adaptation Methods in Dunkwa

Attempts were made to find out whether the farmers used some climate change adaptation measures and subsequently the types and reasons for their choice of adaptation. Of the farmers interviewed, 60.2 per cent used some form of climate change adaptation options, whilst 39.8 per cent did not use adaptation measures. Changing planting dates, using different crop varieties, tree planting, irrigation practices, soil conservation, water harvesting and prayers were the main adaptation measures used by the farmers. Of the farmers interviewed, 92.9 per cent used changing planting dates as their method of adaptation whilst 7.1 per cent did not use this method. Of the farmers 93.9 per cent used different crop varieties to reduce climate change impacts whilst 6.1 per cent have never used this measure before. 73.5 per cent of the farmers use water harvesting as an adaptation measure whilst 26.5 per cent do not use this method.

With regard to irrigation and tree planting, 23.5 per cent of the farmers interviewed use irrigation to adapt to climate impacts whilst 76.5 per cent do not use this method; 33.7 per cent of the farmers use tree planting as an adaptation measure whilst 66.3 per cent do not use this measure. Soil conservation was used by 30.6 per cent of the farmers interviewed to adapt to climate change impacts. However, 74.5 per cent of the farmers used prayers as a measure of adaptation. Figure 3.7 depicts the distribution of various measures of adaptation used by farmers in Shama in the Western Region of Ghana.

When asked why they preferred their choice of adaptation over the other options, 67.8 per cent indicated that their choice of adaptation was most economical or less costly to use; 16.9 per cent said their choice of adaptation improved land fertility and prevented erosion; 10.2 per cent said their choice was environmentally friendly; only 5.1 per cent said their choice led to early maturity of crops.

Figure 6: Choice of adaptation methods in Dunkwa

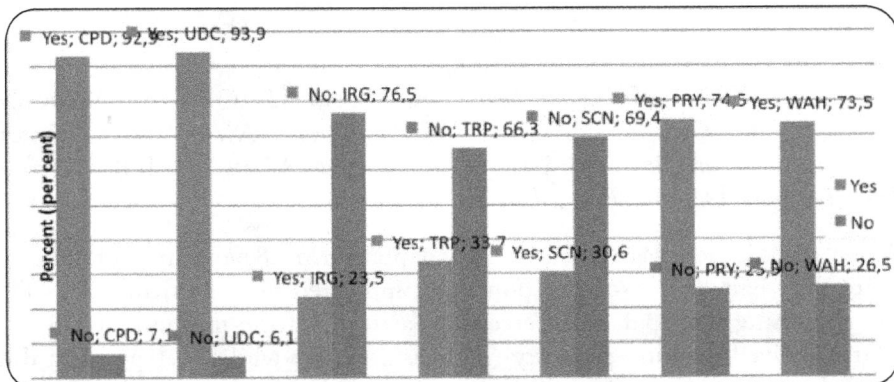

Note:CPD= *Changing Planting Dates;* UDC= *Use of Different Crop varieties;* IRG= *Irrigation Practices,* TRP= *Tree Planting,* SCN= *Soil Conservation,* PRY= *Prayers,* WAH= *Water Harvesting.*

Barriers to Adaptation Methods in Bawku

With regards to barriers to adaptation methods, insufficient access to inputs, lack of knowledge about adaptation options and no access to water dominated the responses. Other constraints included expensive changes, insecure property rights, lack of credits and lack of information about climate change. From Figure 7, 78.9 per cent of the respondents perceived lack of information about climate change to be a barrier to adaptation while 21.1 per cent went contrary to this opinion. 87.4 per cent of the respondents attributed lack of knowledge about adaptation options to be a barrier to adaptation methods while 12.6 per cent did not. While 85.3 per cent of the respondents interviewed attributed lack of credit and poverty as a barrier to adaptation methods, the remaining 14.7 per cent did not perceive that to be so. The majority (87.4 %) indicated no access to water as an important barrier to adaptation method while the remaining 12.6 per cent did not perceive that. Of the respondents 77.9 per cent affirmed changes are expensive while 22.1 per cent perceived otherwise.

Figure 3.7: Barriers to adaptation methods in Bawku

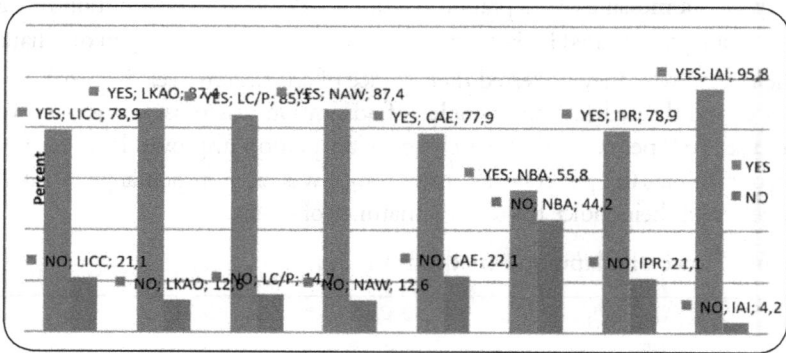

Note: LICC = *Lack of Information about Climate Change;* LKAO = *Lack of Knowledge about Adaptation Options;* LC/P = *Lack of Credit/Poverty* ; NAW= *No access to Water;* CAE = *Changes are Expensive* ; NBA = *No Barriers to Adaptation* ; IPR = *Insecure Property Rights* ; IAI= *Insufficient Access to Inputs.*

When asked if there were no barriers to adaptation, 55.8 per cent, representing more than half of the total respondents, indicated in the affirmative while the remaining 44.2 per cent perceived barriers. Of the respondents 78 per cent perceived insecure property rights as a barrier while 21.1 per cent did not. Most (95.8 %) attributed insufficient access to inputs as a major barrier to adaptation methods while only 4.2 per cent of the total respondents (95) did not perceive that.

Barriers to Adaptation Methods in Dunkwa

Barriers preventing farmers from adapting to climate change in Dunkwa were investigated. Results as shown in Figure 8 identified lack of information on climate change impacts and adaptation options; lack of knowledge about adaptation measures; lack of access to credit; no access to water, high cost of adaptation; insecure property rights and insufficient access to inputs as the major barriers inhibiting their ability to adapt to climate change impacts.

With regard to lack of information, 77.6 per cent of the farmers identified this as the main barrier to effective adaptation to climate change; whilst 22.4 per cent did not think that was the case. 71.4 per cent of the farmers identified lack of knowledge regarding adaptation measures whilst only 28.6 per cent were aware of adaptation options. 93.9 per cent of the farmers interviewed indicated that access to credit was very low and this had constrained many of them from effective adaptation of climate impacts.

No access to water for irrigation and other farming activities was identified by 41.8 per cent of the farmers as a barrier to adaptation; however, 58.2 per cent did not see access to water as a problem. Cost involved in adapting to climate change impacts was identified by 82.7 per cent of the farmers as the reason explaining their poor adaptation ability whilst 17.3 per cent disagreed. Insecure property rights over land constrained about 87.8 per cent of the farmers from using any adaptation measure. About 91.8 per cent of the farmers indicated that inadequate access to inputs was a barrier to adaptation. This was attributed to lack of access to credit as well as the expensive nature of adaptation measures.

Figure 3.8: Barriers to adaptation methods in Dunkwa

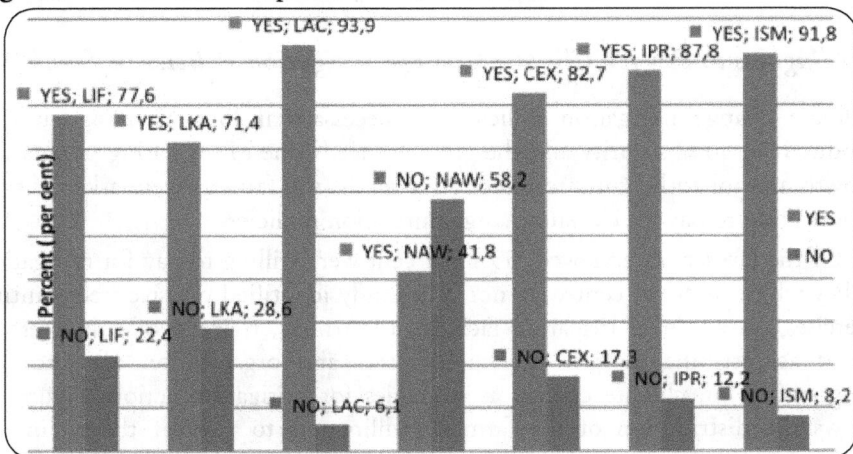

Note: LIF= *Lack of Information on Adaptation Options*; LKA= *Lack of Knowledge on Adaptation options*; LAC= *Lack of Access to Credit*; NAW= *No Access to Water*; CEX= *Changes are Expensive*; IPR= *Insecure Property Rights*, ISM= I*nsufficient Access to Inputs*.

Willingness to Pay for Climate Change Mitigation Policies in Bawku

Of the respondents interviewed 71.6 per cent were willing to pay for climate change mitigating policies while 28.4 per cent, despite the associated benefits of these policies, were unwilling to pay. From Figure 9, the respondents were willing to pay for four mitigating policies at a total amount of GH¢ 5,073. Out of the total respondents, 32 per cent were willing to pay GH¢1,618 for massive tree planting (MTPE), 27 per cent were willing to pay GH¢ 1,351for provision of irrigation facilities to farmers (PIFF), 22 per cent were willing to pay GH¢ 1,117 for training volunteers (TV) to guard against unauthorised cutting of trees and 19 per cent were willing to pay GH¢ 987 for organising an annual education programme for the farmers (OEP).

Figure 3.9: Willingnesstopay for climate change policies in Bawku

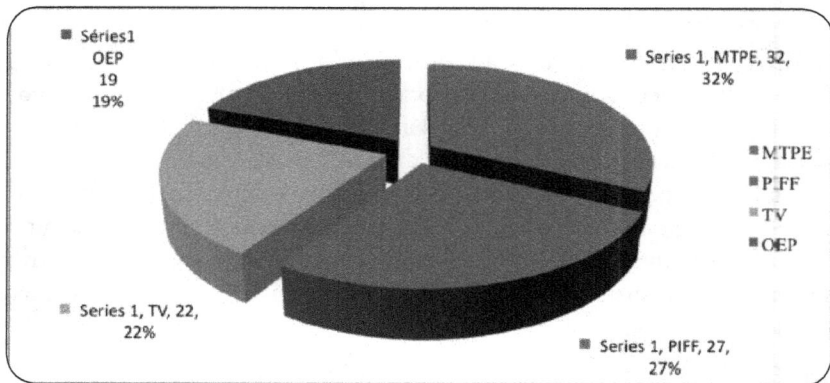

Willingness to Pay for Climate Change Mitigation Policies in Dunkwa

Climate change mitigation policies are necessary if long term agricultural productivity, food security and the growing needs due to increasing population growth are not to be compromised. As a result, the farmers were asked if they were willing to pay for climate change mitigation po.licies.

Of the farmers interviewed, 55.1 per cent were willing to pay for mitigation policy whilst 44.9 per cent were not. The study identified massive tree planting exercises, provision of irrigation facilities to farmers, training of volunteers to guard against unauthorised cutting of trees and organisation of education programmes on climate change as strategies for mitigation action. Figure 10 shows the distribution of the farmers' willingness to pay for these climates mitigation policies. From the data, it is obvious that farmers' willingness to pay for tree planting was high (35.68 %); followed by provision of irrigation facilities to farmers constituting about 30 per cent of the farmers. About 17 per cent of the farmers interviewed were willing to pay for training of volunteers whilst about 17 per cent were willing to pay for climate change education programmes.

Figure 3.10: Willingness to pay for climate change mitigation policies in Dunkwa

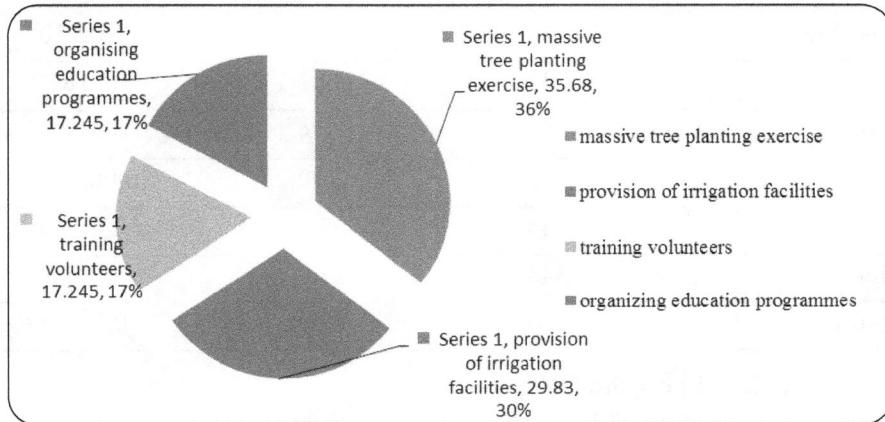

Table 3.1: The statistics of willingness to pay (WTP)

N=61	
Mean	12.3519
Median	9.00000
Std. Deviation	9.60573
Skewness	1.840 (std. error 0.325)
Kurtosis	2.915 (std. error 0.639)

Table 3.1 shows the summary statistics of the willingness to pay responses of farmers. The mean and median were GHS 12.3519, GHS 9.00 respectively. The median was lower than the mean, indicating that the majority of the farmers were willing to pay less than the mean willingness to pay, and that the response distribution was skewed by a limited number of high bidders.

Model Estimation Results of the Logistic Regression Analysis

A logistic regression analysis was employed to analyse the socio-economic factors that influence farmer's willingness to pay for climate change mitigation policy. The Akaike Information Criteria (Akaike 1973) provided the basis for selecting the model that provided the best fit to willingness to pay for climate change mitigation policy.

Table 3.2: Parameter estimates of the logistic model

Robust

Variables	Coef.	Standard Error	P>z
age -.338	.123	-2.75	0.006***
hhs .066	.044	1.51	0.132
edu .073 .	031	2.37	0.018**
exp.003	.001	2.54	0.011**
ofl1.065 .	357	2.99	0.003***
fs -.013	.044	-0.30	0.766
oinc .577 .	344	1.68	0.094*
cons6.784	2.838	2.39	0.017**

***1 per cent; ** 5 per cent; * 10 per cent

Note: AGE= Age of Respondent; HHS= Household Size; EDU= Years of Education of Respondent; EXP = Farming Experience in Years; OFL= Own Farmland; FS = Farm Size; OINC= Other Income Generating Activity.

The model specification, with willingness to pay for climate change mitigation policy as the dependent variable and age, years of education, years of farming experience, ownership of farm land, farm size and other income as the covariates provided the best fit with AIC of 244.95.

Empirical results from the logistic regression analysis reveals that age and farm size negatively influence willingness to pay for climate change mitigation policy whilst household size, years of education, years of farming experience, ownership of farm land and other income generating activity positively influenced willingness to pay for climate change mitigation policy. The regression analysis finds age, years of farming experience, ownership of farm land and other income as significant predictors of the probability to pay for climate change mitigation policy.

The parameters of years of farming experience, and other income were significant at 5 per cent and 10 per cent levels respectively while age of the respondent and ownership of farm land were significant at 1 per cent. It should be emphasised that a negative sign of a parameter indicates that high values of the variables tends to decrease the probability of the willingness to pay for climate change mitigation policy. A positive sign implies that high values of the variables will increase the probability of willingness to pay for climate change mitigation policy. The results of the odds ratio are presented below in Table 3.3.

Table 3.3: Parameter estimates of the logistic model with odds ratio

Variables	Odds Ratio	Robust Std. Err.	z	P>z
age	.713	.088	-2.75	0.006***
hhs	1.068	.047	1.51	0.132
edu	1.075	.033	2.37	0.018 **
exp	1.003	.001	2.54	0.011**
ofl	2.899	1.034	2.99	0.003***
fs	.987	.043	-0.30	0.766
oinc	1.781	.613	1.68	0.094*

***1 per cent, ** 5 per cent, * 10 per cent

Conclusion

Farmers' adaption to climate change is crucial to combating food insecurity and related problems. Against this background, this paper assessed farmers' perception and adaptation to climate change. Specifically, the study investigated farmer perception of changes in temperature and precipitation, choice of adaptation methods, barriers to adaptation and socio-economic determinants of willingness to pay for climate mitigation policies.

Results from the descriptive analysis of farmers interviewed revealed that the farmers were characterised by comprising an active labour force, small farm sizes, low income distribution, high farming experience, large household size, and low levels of formal education. With regards to farmers' perception and methods of adaptation, the majority of the farmers perceived increases in temperature and decreases in rainfall pattern. Farmers' level of adaptation was found to be relatively high with the majority of the farmers using changing planting dates, different crop varieties and soil conservation methods as the major adaptation measures to climate change impacts. However, access to water, high cost of adaptation, lack of knowledge on adaptation, insecure property rights and lack of credits were identified as the major barriers to adaptation. Results revealed high level of willingness to pay for mitigation policies among the farmers. However, the majority of the farmers supported massive tree planting exercise.

Logistic regression estimates finds age, years of farming experience, ownership of farm land, and other income as significant predictors of the probability to pay for climate change mitigation policy. Implications for policy will be to implement a public education programme on climate change adaptation strategies. There is the need for government to embark on massive implementation of mitigation policies since most farmers are willing to pay for these policies. Additional income generating activities should be encouraged among farmers since it is a positive and a significant predictor of their willingness to pay.

References

Akaike, H., 1973, 'Theory and an Extension of the Maximum Likelihood Principle', in B.N.Petrov, and F. Csaki, eds, *2nd International Symposium on Information Theory*, Budapest: Akademiai Kiado.

Akter, S. and J. Benett, 2009, 'Household Perceptions of Climate Change and Preferences for Mitigation Action: The Case of the Carbon Pollution Reduction Scheme in Australia', *Environmental Economics Research Hub Research Reports*.

Bamidele F. S., I. Ogunlade, O. Ayinde, and P. Olabode, 2010, 'Factors Affecting Farmers' Ability to Pay for Irrigation Facilities in Nigeria: A Case of Oshin Irrigation Scheme in Kwara State', *Journal of Sustainable Development in Africa*, 12 (1): 334–49.

Bozdogan, H., 1987, 'Model Selection and Akaike's Information Criterion (AIC): The General Theory and its Analytical Extensions', *Psychometrika* 52(3): 345–70.

Cameron, T. A., 2005, 'Individual Option Prices for Climate Change Mitigation', *Journal of Public Economics* 89 (2–3):283–301.

Dai, A., K. E. Trenberth and T. Qian, 2004, 'A Global Dataset of Palmer Drought Severity Index for 1870-2002: Relationship with Soil Moisture and Effects of Surface Warming', *Journal of Hydrometeorology* 5:1117–30.

Deressa, T. T., R. M. Hassan, C. Ringler, T. Alemu, and M. Yesuf, 2008, *Analysis of the Determinants of Farmers' Choice of Adaptation Methods and Perceptions of Climate Change in the Nile Basin of Ethiopia*, Washington, DC: International Food Policy Research Institute.

Gbetibouo, G.A., 2009, *Understanding Farmers' Perceptions and Adaptations to Climate Change and Variability*, Washington, DC: IFPRI, Discussion Paper 00849.

Han, F., Z. Yang, and X. Xu, 2010, 'Estimating Willingness to Pay for Environment Conservation: A Contingent Valuation Study of Kanas Nature Reserve, Xinjiang, China', *Environmental Monitoring Assessment* 80:451–9.

Hassan, R., and C. Nhemachena, 2008, 'Determinants of African Farmers' Strategies for Adapting to Climate Change: Multinominal Choice Analysis', *African Journal of Agricultural and Resource Economics* 2(1): 83–104.

Maddison, D., 2006, *The Perception and Adaptation to Climate Change in Africa*. CEEPA (Centre for Environmental Economics and Policy in Africa, University of Pretoria) Discussion paper No. 10.

Trenberth, K. E., P. D. Jones, P.Ambenje, R. Bojariu, D. Easterling, T. A.Klein, D. Parker, F. Rahimzadeh, J. A. Renwick, M. Rusticucci, B. Soden and P. Zhai, 2007, 'Observations: Surface and Atmospheric Climate Change', in S. Solomon, D. Qin, M. Manning, Z. Chen, M. Marquis, K. B. Averyt, M. Tignor and H. L. Miller, eds, *Climate Change: The Physical Science Basis. Contribution of the Working Group I to the Fourth Assessment Report of the Intergovernmental Panel on Climate Change*, Cambridge: University Press.

Viscusi, W. K. and R. J. Zechauser, 2006, 'The Perception and Valuation of the Risks of Climate Change: A Rational and Behavioral Blend', *Climate Change* 77:151–77.

Yesuf, M., S. Di Falco, T. Deressa, C. Ringler, and G. Kohlin, 2008, *The Impact of Climate Change and Adaptation on Food Production in Low-Income Countries: Evidence from the Nile Basin, Ethiopia*, Washington, DC: International Food Policy Research Institute and Ethiopian Development Research Institute.

Zucchini, W., 2000, 'An Introduction to Model Selection', *Journal of Mathematical Psychology* 44:41–6.

4

Communities, Surrounding Environments and Dam-generated Hydroelectric Power Projects in Cameroon

Emmanuel Yenshu Vubo and Kometa Sunday Shende

Introduction

By the end of the twentieth century, the dam industry had choked more than half of the earth's major rivers with more than 50,000 large dams (Gujja and Perrin 1999). The consequences of these massive engineering programmes have been devastating. The world's large dams have wiped out flora and fauna species, flooded huge areas of wetlands, forests and farmlands and displaced tens of millions of people (International Commission on Large Dams 1998). The damming of a river creates a reservoir upstream from the dam and the reservoir waters spill out into the surrounding environments, flooding the natural habitats that existed before the dam's construction. Dam projects, which are useful in meeting the demand for water in desired times and in regulating stream regimes, have been important in economic development. Their benefits include controlling stream regimes, consequently preventing floods, providing domestic and irrigation water and generating energy. However, dams have also had some negative effects on the environment.

Wherever a dam is located, its ecological effects are the same, albeit by different magnitudes. According to recent studies, reservoirs contribute to greenhouse gas emissions as well (World Bank & United Nations Development Programme 1990). The initial filling of a reservoir floods the existing plant material, leading to the death and decomposition of carbon-rich plants (shrubs, grass and trees). The rotting organic matter releases large amounts of carbon into the atmosphere.

The decaying plant matter itself settles on the non-oxygenated bottom of the stagnant reservoir and eventually releases dissolved methane. This situation has led Uyigue (2006) to affirm strongly that 'dams are [non-renewable]'. There is therefore always a concern with balancing their economic against their negative effects. These conflicting perceptions of dams evidently illustrate the fact that dams are a mixed blessing.

The World Commission on Dams (WCD) (2000) reported that 60 per cent of the world's rivers have been affected by dams and diversions. The construction of dams may also result in the emission of greenhouse gases (GHG) from reservoirs due to rotten vegetation and carbon inflow from the catchments. It was estimated that the gross emissions from reservoirs may account for between 1 and 28 per cent of the global warming potential of GHG emissions (WCD 2000). This challenges the conventional wisdom that hydropower produces only positive atmospheric effects such as a reduction in emissions of carbon dioxide, nitrous oxides, sulphuric oxides and particulate when compared with other power generation sources such as fossil fuels (Bosi 2000; Ugigue 2006:5–7). Dams also alter the natural distribution and timing of stream flow. Flood timing, duration and frequency are all critical for the survival of communities of plants and animals living downstream. This may lead to the loss of aquatic biodiversity, forest and wildlife habitat, and species population and composition.

The lives of many people and societies have been negatively affected by dams. By 2000 an estimated 40–80 million people worldwide had been physically displaced by dams (WCD 2000). In China alone, 10.2 million people were displaced between 1980 and 1990 (Asian Development Bank 1999). It has been extensively documented that there are gender inequalities in access and control of economic and natural resources within dam project areas. In Asia and Africa, women may have the right to use land and forest but are rarely allowed to own or inherit the land they use (Mehta and Srinivasan 1999). For affected communities, dams have widened gender disparities by imposing a disproportionate share of social costs on women. Dams adversely affect the cultural heritage of many communities through loss of cultural resources (temples, shrines, sacred elements of the landscape, artefacts and buildings). The other cultural impacts of dams include the submergence and degradation of archaeological resources (plants and animals remains, burial sites and archaeological elements).

Environmental change and social disruption resulting from the construction and operation of dams and the associated infrastructure development such as irrigation schemes can have significant adverse health outcomes for local populations and downstream communities (Sleigh and Jackson 2001). Among the resettled, access to drinking water, health services and ability to cope with the new social and physical environment affect health conditions. Numerous vector-borne diseases are associated with reservoir development in tropical areas.

Beyond policy preoccupations, this chapter attempts to locate the new challenges facing communities around dam projects in the context of uncertain climatic developments (assuming they persist). It considers how the government is coping with these unexpected developments, with, for example, punctual often politicised assistance as opposed to long-term measures to permanently overcome problems triggered by old as well as new projects. The issues addressed include the negative consequences, which question environmental impact assessment, the passive rather than the active participation of communities in projects within their ecosystem, hazard vulnerability and finally the situation of existing projects in the light of the new projects launched. The methodology adopts a holistic approach that integrates analysis from geography/environmental science, sociology and policy studies. We systematically reviewed the literature with an emphasis on the recent floods in Cameroon over the past few years, on any form of water resource development, operation and its impact on the population and environment.

Hydroelectric Dams in Cameroon

The construction of dams for hydro-electricity generation dates as far back as the 1970s with the Lagdo and the Bamendjin dams (Figure 4.1). The Lagdo dam (Figure 4.2) was built between 1977 and 1982. The Lagdo dam constructed on the River Benue in the Northern Region (Region here refers administratively to the French *région* which, since the law on decentralisation, replaces the former Provinces) was built between 1977 and 1982 and is situated 50 kilometres south of the city of Garoua. Its reservoir is a lake which covers an area of 586 km². Its construction was intended to supply electricity to the northern part of the country and, by extension, allow the irrigation of 15,000 hectares of crops downstream. The dam is 308 m long, 40 m in height and 9 m thick. The Maga Dam (Figure 4.2), situated some 85 kilometres East of the town of Maga, was constructed in 1979 as part of the second SEMRY (Société d'expansion et de modernisation de la riziculture, a subsidiary of the Ministry of Agriculture) project, with the objective to expand and improve the cultivation of rice. The scheme that was constructed comprised a 7,000 hectare rice plantation irrigated with water supplied by the Maga reservoir, which, with its associated flood protection dikes, also served to protect the plantation against annual floods from the River Logone. The scheme was constructed at the onset of a prolonged drought. The dam extends from the village of Guirvidig in the west to Pouss in the east with associate dikes along the left bank of the Logone, extending for 100 kilometres from Yagoua to Tekele upstream and Pouss downstream respectively.

The Maga Dam has a full storage level of 312.5 m with a minimum operational level of 310.8 m. This dam covers a surface area of 400 km² with a direct catchment area 6,000 km². However, the volume at full storage level is 680 mm³ while at minimum it is 280 mm³ (SEMRY and Mott MacDonald 1978).

Ephemeral streams known as *mayos* drain the catchment area with peculiar ones being the Tsanaga and the Boula, whose catchments extend as far as the Mandara Mountains to the west. These *mayos* flow from August to October and are dry from November until July. Water flows into the reservoir from the Logone through three connections: the Mayo Gouerlou, the Djafga canal and the spillway. Inflows to the reservoir via the Mayo Gouerlou and the spillway are uncontrolled. The Maga Dam it should be noted was not designed with internal filters.

Figure 4.1: Map of Cameroon showing administrative regions and the location of some dam sites.

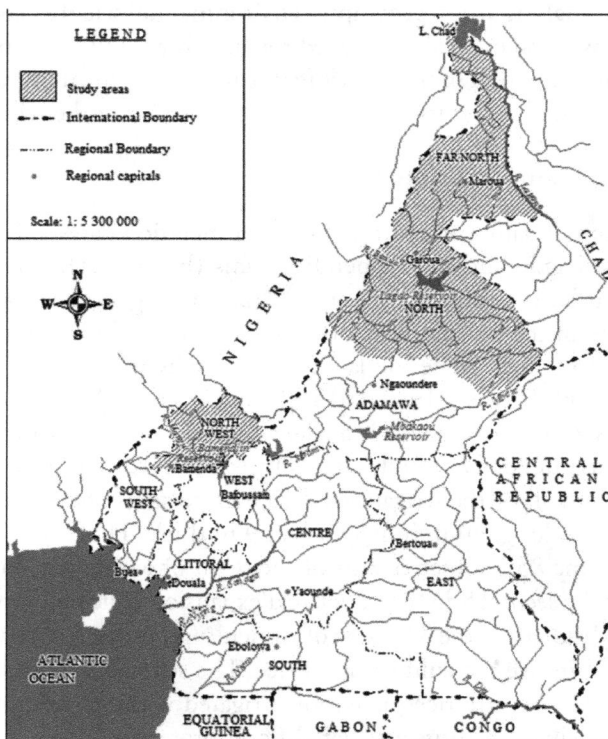

The Bamendjin Dam (Figure 4.3) was constructed in the early 1970s on volcanic lava across the mouth of the River Nun which drains the upper Nun Valley region. Surrounding the extensive lowland which makes up the Upper Nun Valley are volcanic hills and mountains such as the Mount Oku, Sabga chains of hills, the Mbam and the Nkogam. Given that the water level of the Sanaga needs to be maintained high enough to turn the turbines at Edea for example, the Bamendjin reservoir therefore acts as a regulator of the volume of water in the Sanaga. The first filling-up of the dam started in 1974 and the first partial release occurred from January to February 1975. At full capacity, this reservoir contains

over 1,847 km³ of water and in principle extends over a surface area of 333 km²
although most often it attains 442 km². The impact of this dam was so negative
that Boutrais (1974) questioned whether its construction was necessary. His
argument was based on the fact that the drainage basin of the Nun was too small
(2000 km²) as compared to that of the R. Djerem at Mbakaou (20,000 km²) and
so could not sufficiently contribute as a regulator of water flow in the Sanaga.

Figure 4.2: The Maga and Lagdo dams

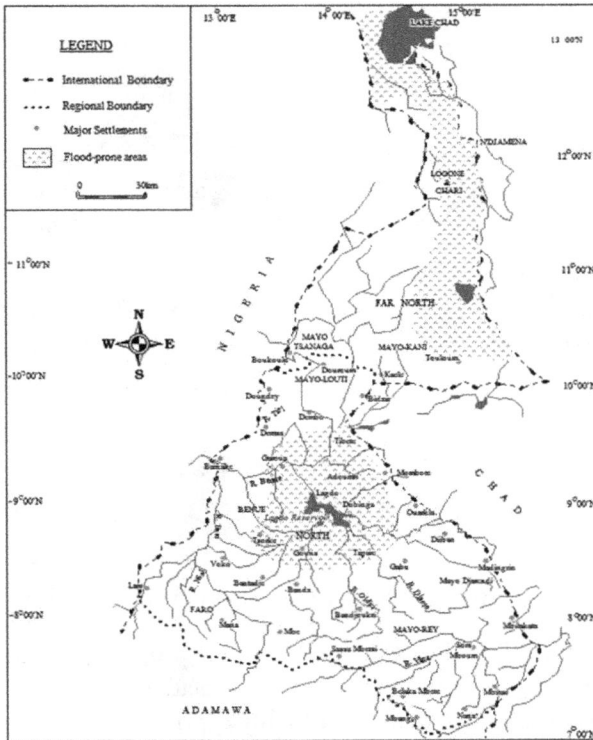

Dams were also subsequently created on the Mbakaou on the Lom on the Djerem
on the Adamaoua Plateau and Mape to the east of the same plateau to boost the
Sanaga after the Bamendjin had been completed (African Development Bank
1997:7). Within the perspective of enhancing the hydro-electricity capacity of
the Sanaga based Song Lulu complex at the time of writing a new dam to produce
a reservoir of 540 km² was being created at Lom Panga (Electricity Development
Corporation 2012).

Figure 4.3: The Bamendjin dam

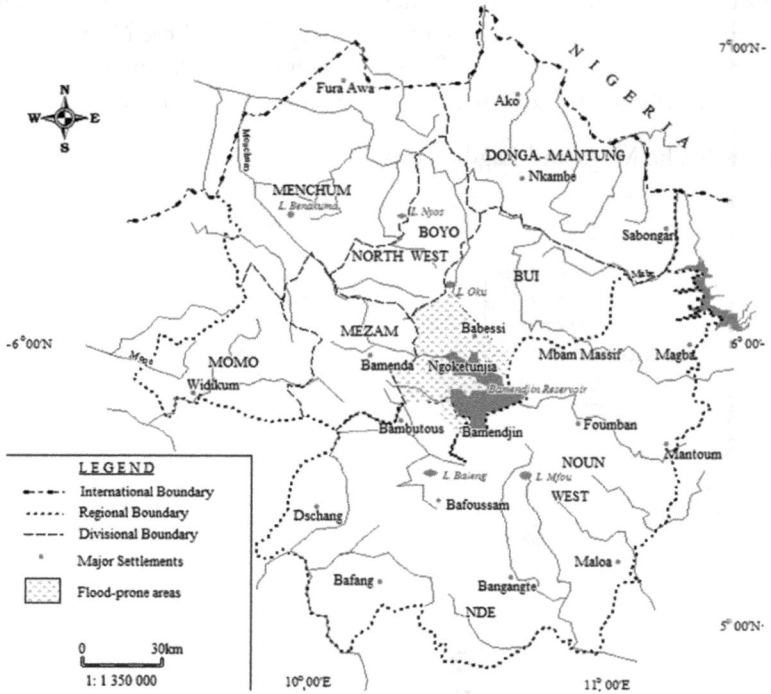

Surrounding Communities and Dam Projects

Most communities located adjacent to dam projects in Cameroon have experienced varying negative effects of dam related projects. This has come about especially as a consequence of a highly capricious climatic situation. The Logone basin of Cameroon constitutes one of the natural risk zones because of the constant rise and fall in the water level. The period from mid-August to mid-October is usually characterised by a drastic increase in the water levels because of heavy torrential rains. In an attempt to control the water level and avoid flood situations and droughts, the government of Cameroon constructed in the early 1970s a dike of about 85 kilometres on the left flank of the River Logone. This dike that runs from Yagoua to Pouss serves as a control mechanism to regulate the flow of the Logone on which the dam was built. By the end of the same decade, the government had built a 27 kilometre long dam at Magba. About forty years later, these constructions have considerably depreciated and worn out due to age and lack of adequate maintenance.

The total population living around the Maga scheme is estimated by SEMRY to be 20,000. However, many of these people live far away enough from the dam and would not necessarily be at risk in the event of a dam failure. Because the area downstream of the dam is so flat, the escaping water would spread over a large area with relatively low velocities and depth. Therefore it is reasonable to suppose that only the people living close to the dam would be at risk. Clearly the most vulnerable population is that of Maga village, because apart from the fact that they live close to the dam, the dam is higher adjacent to the village than elsewhere. Furthermore, there is no formal warning system in the area.

The construction of the Bamendjin dam brought about floods which affected a number of villages in the Bamboutos, Nun and Ngoketunjia Divisions (A Division being equivalent of the French-Cameroon département). Large proportions of some low-lying villages were submerged by flood waters with Mbissa, a ward in Bambalang, becoming an island. The negative dimensions of this dam provide evidence that it does not represent a success story. Indeed, this dam was not designed to provide electricity to the Upper Nun Valley which it occupies. Rather, its function was as a dry season reservoir for Cameroon's major hydro-electric installation hundreds of kilometres downstream on the River Sanaga at Edea, of which the River Nun is only a tributary. Like in many parts of the world which have experienced the construction of such monumental edifices, these are sometimes referred to as 'planning mistakes' or 'ecological disasters' (Lambi 1999).

It is true that the shear spread of floods and the consequent deposition of silt increases the amount of usable land. The alarming invasion of the lowlands and flood plains by water has increased areas of land under rice cultivation in the Far North and North West regions. Prior to the construction of the dams, rice cultivation was an entirely unknown farming practice (Lambi 1999). The dam thus encouraged, and also reinforced, an agricultural innovation that eventually proved to be a major cash cow for many farmers. This region is one of the areas in Cameroon with a high population density at 99.9 persons per square kilometre (Bureau Général de Recensement 2005). With such a population, far-reaching changes and adjustments came into play with regards to their economic and socio-cultural setting. This new physical environment then called for changes in land use pattern. From this perspective, rice cultivation and fishing were a welcome innovation. On the other hand, the flooding considerably altered former traditional farming and land holding traditions. Besides, everybody in the flooded area was compelled to adjust to the seasonal fluctuations incumbent on the changes in water level. Agricultural practices no longer depended on known seasonal fluctuations in climate, which could be predicted and managed by local peoples, but were dictated by flood patterns that could not be controlled by them. Such changes in the natural environment were compounded by the absence of an environmental impact assessment before the construction of the dam. Indeed only one study was ever conducted on this and limited to the prospects of rice cultivation (SEDA 1978) which itself did not arm the people against the likely outcomes of the project.

These dams have occasioned definite negative effects that are being replicated in new projects. Some of these are: the permanent loss of fertile farming lands to the artificial creation of a vast expanse of water, the permanent and irreversible loss of biodiversity, the creation of a new micro-climate, a change in the socio-economic diversity of the surrounding environs, and the introduction and spread of water-borne diseases. The latter are very well known to constitute a health risk to the inhabitants of the settlements within the vicinity or neighbourhood of these dams where the standing water from the floods provides a breeding habitat for vectors of malaria, schistosomiasis and onchocerciasis (Atangana et al. 1979; Audibert et al. 1990; Ripert 1985).

It is worth noting that the construction of dams in Cameroon is done principally with the motive of improving the provision of energy in response to the needs of communities. These projects which are well-intentioned are unfortunately poorly executed, seldom maintained and often do not account for the environmental repercussions that adjacent communities might face. Cameroon as a country has often been taken aback by a number of floods, disease outbreaks and other environmental hazards which plague communities closer to such giant water projects. This makes planning and disaster risk management very difficult.

Moreover, appraisals of impact on communities are always optimistic. In its evaluation report on the Mape Dam, the African Development Bank (1997:17) held that the socio-economic impact was satisfactory because 'two villages within the [dam] area [had been] electrified...A dynamic economic area [had been] established, comprising fishermen, traders and artisans'. Very often these villages are makeshift camps occupied by occasional migrants who, not being within the resettled areas, are the most vulnerable to the disasters. In the older dam project areas such as with the Mape the additional problem is that 'the financing mechanism of people related activities had not been planned at the time of project implementation' (African Development Bank 1997:17). It was therefore rare to find any concerns about the welfare of resettled people or vulnerable groups in project documents or impact assessment exercises. In this regard, no substantial transformation in livelihoods could be observed beyond incidental activities atunsustainable levels. In the case just cited the African Development Bank reported that in the resettlement area, 'the project had contributed to the development of productive activities generally undertaken by women, namely market gardening as well as fish salting, drying and smoking' (African Development Bank 1997:17). These activities are evidently not engineered by the dam project but are incidental fallouts in terms of precarious coping mechanisms as compared with real losses in terms of farmlands and other assets as a result of resettlement. Moreover, such projects took for granted that communities could be displaced with little option to resist because the projects were created in the name of development. That is why reference to resettled areas and communities do not feature in the assessments. This was evidently a period of a tough top-down administration within the authoritarian regime, which did not pay attention to the interests of local people and was when the World Bank had not yet introduced the conditionality of environmental impact assessment (EIA) or at least it was not yet a universal precondition.

In order to assess the real impact on surrounding communities we may need to revisit the 2012 flood events. On September 6 of that year, the water level was on the rise within the Maga Dam. The retaining dike at Maga, with a critical point of 312.50, went above this point to about 312.76. All valves in this dam were open to send out the excess water. The population was asked to evacuate the area. By 6 September 2012, 3,000 persons were homeless in Maga and twelve deaths were reported. In addition one person was missing and 4,500 were at risk. The situation forced the authorities of SEMRY, based in Yagoua, to open a number of its turbines to release the excess water. However, the canal at Virick was blocked by grass and sand forcing the water to over-flow its beds or banks flooding adjacent villages. Despite efforts made by SEMRY to clear this canal, the situation did not improve. Instead more water flowed in the Maga Dam increasing its level. The population of Maga, to protect their homes, used bags filled with sand offered by the government. This however did not solve the problem.

In the Logone and Chari Division, more than 1,000 people were made homeless. In all, 31,013 people were affected by the floods in this administrative division. In the Mayo Danay Division, flooding occurred between 15 and 23 August and several families faced adverse consequences. In the camp of Gaya in Pouss there were 300 families made up of about 2,500 persons.

In the North Region, four localities were affected in Mayo Rey and Benue Divisions. In Kaikai sub-locality, the people of Sokomai and its environs and some 15 victims from Vele were moved to schools. In this area ten dikes were threatening to give way. SEMRY offered these riverine populations 10,000 empty bags which they filled with earth to temper the advancing waters. In Garoua, 14 people were reported dead, six missing and several houses and property destroyed. Some localities along the bank of River Benue on the way to Mayo Rey Division remained in darkness for weeks following the floods. The heavy rains that affected most of the region completely cut-off access roads to areas such as Poli Sub-Division in Faro Division and the Ray Bouba in Mayo Rey Division from Garoua. In Benue Division, 118 villages were affected by the floods. Apart from several houses that were submerged, school children had to be relocated as water and flood took over their schools.

In 2012, water released from the Lagdo dam flooded surrounding areas including Adamawa State in Nigeria. The flooding resulted in more than ten deaths and loss of properties worth thousands of dollars. A bigger effect of the flooding was however in the lower River Benue region where more than 10,000 homes were submerged for more than two weeks. This left more than 10,000 hectares of farm land flooded and the streets of Makurdi town in Nigeria's Middle belt area were occupied by crocodiles amongst other dangerous aquatic animals. This is not the first time these problems have occurred. Uyigue (2006: 9)reports that the 'Obudu Dam spillway was damaged by storm in July 2003 which resulted in fatal disaster that claimed over 200 houses, several farmlands, settlements and business concerns. The disaster was allegedly caused by the release of excess water from the Lagdo Dam in [Cameroon] which overflowed the Benue and Niger River Banks'.

The floods from the Bamendjin affected the Babessi area where on 9 September 2012. 95 people from 26 families lost their homes while 59 houses and farmlands were totally destroyed.

Official Mitigation Efforts

The initial reaction of government to the affected people of the northern regions during the 2012 crisis was the disbursement of 550 million CFA francs for the acquisition of food, medication and provision for schools and resettlements (Table 4.14). Overall, the amount of relief funds from government amounted to CFA 1.5 billion. In the North Region, the government promised 30 million CFA francs as assistance to victims to take care of their immediate needs. Regional committees for the management of the crisis were set up. Basicrelief health care services were set up by the Ministry of Public Health in Pouss where medicines and health relief personnel were dispatched. A thousand improved housing facilities were provided by MINEPDED. The Ministry of Livestock made medication available for cattle while the defence ministry gave tents, medicine, school equipment, basic food items, bed covers and trunks to transport aid to the victims. Non-governmental organisations also assisted the people affected by this ecological catastrophe. Financial and material assistance for the floods in the North and North West Regions came from the President of the Republic, the Ministry of Territorial Administration and Decentralization (in-charge of disaster mitigation), the United Nation High Commission for Refugees and the Government of Morocco. Military engineering corps and health personnel were mobilised to erect tents, dig bore holes and provide basic sanitary facilities and dispensaries. As a result of the severity of the problem in Babessi, about 40 hectares of land was carved out for resettlement by government authorities.

Table 4.14: Distribution of financial assistance according to surrounding communities

Sub-division	Empty bags	Tents	Financial assistance (CFA)
Kousseri	6,000	100	120,000,000
Blangoua	3,000	0	42,400,000
Logone Birni	3,000	0	54,000,000
Hile-Alifa	2,000	04	64,600,000
Goulfe	2,000	02	63,600,000
Makary	4,000	06	68,900,000
Fotokol	2,000	02	25,500,000
Waza	1,000	02	27,500,000
Zina	2,000	04	27,500,000
Darak	5,000	0	54,500,000

Source: Cameroon Tribune No 10207, 25 October 2012, p. 5.

Beyond these immediate relief measures we need to understand permanent measures taken to mitigate possible problems of this nature occurring in future. It is understood under Cameroon Law that dam owners are responsible for the safety of their dams. In the case of the Maga Dam, this is ultimately owned by the Ministry of Agriculture through their subsidiary SEMRY. Although there is no formal safety plan at Maga, daily records are kept of the reservoir level and periodic inspections of the embankment are done. Warning systems work best when they provide local people with advance notice of a possible emergency so that they can retreat to a safe-haven on adjacent high ground. The only crude method of monitoring is the vigilance of the local people. To make matters worse, there is no adjacent high ground to which people can retreat. The construction of the 85 kilometre dike and the 27 kilometre long dam at Maga to control floods in the 1970s had temporarily mitigated the effect of the problem for some time. However, about forty years later, these buildings have considerably depreciated and become dilapidated due to age and lack of adequate maintenance. The dike on the River Logone is made up of three sections:

- the first section built with compact soil at a distance of 45 kilometres from Diguim to Begue-Palam;
- the second section built with non-compact material over a distance of about 30 kilometres from Begue-Palam to Pouss;
- the third section, built in the 1950s, goes from Pouss to Tekele over a distance of 29 kilometres.

Three factors explain the yearly rise in water levels be it in the River Logone or the Maga Dam. These include the high amounts of rainfall which were recorded here in the past year, the early arrival of heavy rains and the building (by neighbouring

Chad) of a parallel dike on the right bank of the River Logone. Consequently
the rising waters of the Logone naturally discharge part of their surplus on the
Cameroonian side, with the Chadian side being well protected. The seriousness
of the floods partially due to the obsoleteness of the aforementioned defects
necessitates action. This includes strengthening the dike along the River Logone
from the extreme northern part of Cameroon (from Maroua to Kousseri), the
rehabilitation of the dike at Maga, the dredging of the Mayo Vrick, and in the
medium term the dredging of the Maga Dam. These flooded areas will provide
fertile land for agriculture and this certainly augurs well for the rice, wheat, and
other crop farms in this region. On the other hand, when the floods occur, water
sources are polluted. Given the fact that cholera has created much desolation
during the last two years in the northern part of Cameroon, it is feared that the
recent floods could easily leave behind the same situation. The flood prone areas
may also provide breeding grounds for mosquitoes with malaria as an attendant
consequence.

The annual budget available for the maintenance of all ten dams managed by
the Ministry of Agriculture in Cameroon is CFA 200 million. The exact amount
allocated to Maga, Lagdo and Bamendjim Dams was not available to us at time
of this study but assuming that all their dams face similarly acute problems, it
should approximate to CFA 20 million or US$27,000. Funds allocated are not
sufficient and there seems to be no monitoring system on the effect of climatic
variations. There are two main threats facing the integrity of the dam. These
are continued erosion of the upstream face and crest of the embankment due to
wave attacks at high reservoir levels. If this continues unchecked it may result
in one of the following: overtopping, sliding (failure) of the downstream slope,
piping failure and overtopping of the embankment by a severe flood which would
probably result in a breach of the dam.

It is important to note that the creation of these dams has been paid for
with special development funds whose beneficiaries should have been the affected
people. In principle, these special development funds can be critical resources
for social development programmes in the communities affected, which are
essentially poor. However, in practice, the situation is a far cry from that. There
were reports of misappropriation of funds and non-compensation of some of
the flood victims in the case of the Bamendjin dam. Human victims of dam
projects are the unfortunate people whose homes are flooded and are forced to
live a new way of life in their newly created resettlement areas as experiences from
Cameroon show (Diaw 1990).

When the rains become too heavy and intense, as has been the case in recent
years in the northern regions of Cameroon where a fragile ecological system has
regularly caused rivers and other waterways to outflow their banks, there are tales
of hardship including loss of life through drowning or of villages swept being

away by running water. The region is, for the most part of the year, exposed to drought, and farmers and stock-breeders have to rely on the few months of the year when there are rains, to carry out their sustenance activities. However, when rains come at the same time, as in 2012, the rivers become a source of real danger. This often leads to humanitarian crises given the number of people affected and the contingency measures put in place which are far from adequate to properly address the problems. This is therefore the most propitious moment to take durable measures to pre-empt dangers to the environment and communities in the event of a failure of such structures. It is not enough to resettle people. Governments need to take steps to protect communities through measures they cannot afford themselves and educate them about the risks of living in dangerous zones. In that way, they can take ownership of their new environments, understand the real dangers and avoid a situation wherein, every year, governments rush in to provide temporary measures. The new projects are factoring these into their implementation programmes, as in the case of the Lom Pangar project, which has projected its GHG net emissions as against the ability to save the same and concluded that it is in its favour 'especially considering that its construction opens the door to a larger resource mobilization on the Sanaga' (EDC 2012: 17). It is also definitely aware of some permanent negative impacts such as 'increased pressure on land, increased land clearing, agricultural intensification and soil degradation' (African Development Bank 2012: 12). The few families that have been resettled have been so 'with their consent' (ibid.). A 'Local Community Development Support Plan' (involving 8000 people) is also envisaged (ibid.: 13). While their outcomes are expected, this is just what was lacking with previous projects.

The Ministry of the Economy, Planning and Regional Development has come up with its own emergency plan to address the immediate needs of the embattled people of the flooded areas in the North and Far North Regions. A number of measures have been envisaged to control the situation. It must be noted that no durable system had ever been used to ensure that the waters of the River Logone and Lake Maga are kept under control. Rudimentary technology has often been used to keep the waters away by the use of mud which could only but cede under pressure from mounting water. The dangers posed by the rising level of water can only be grasped by looking at other parts of the world where similar situations have caused considerable harm to human settlement and real humanitarian concerns.

A critical examination of policies executed so far reveals their shortcomings and the need for redress. There is an urgent need to integrate durability as a cornerstone of any attempt to correct the situation and plan for the future. Structures such as dykes should have a life span long enough to avoid keeping policy makers or local administrative and political authorities constantly on the alert. It is necessary to take measures that physically endure in the long term; just as it is also necessary to be more proactive in all other approaches. In a bid to contain flood threats, the Ministry of the Economy, Planning and Regional Development announced work on the protection dikes on Lake Maga in Mayo Danay Division of the Far North Region in 2012. It is still too early to say whether this will pre-empt the type of disaster witnessed in 2012. In the short term, funds have been disbursed for the treatment of the critical points of the protection dyke on the shores of the Logone River. Also, funds have been allocated for the clearing of the bed of the River Vrisk that evacuates water from Maga retaining lake. As a medium term measure, the protection dike along River Logone and the Maga dam wall are being stabilised using appropriate techniques.

Conclusion

Although dams are critical to the supply of hydropower, their adverse effect on environments and surrounding communities calls for action. One way is to think about the need to exploit other options of energy supply that are more environmentally friendly than dams. These alternative options may include wind power, solar energy, biomass and wave energy systems. The older dams need to be assessed for their environmental impact and certainly rehabilitated if they are to continue to operate. In these re-evaluations, the vulnerability of communities must be factored in. There is also need for early warning and monitoring systems to forestall catastrophes of the type that result from climatic vagaries. Lastly, more viable resettlement schemes must be developed, even for the older projects.

References

African Development Bank, 1997, *Cameroon-Mape Dam: Project Performance Evaluation*, Abidjan: Operations Evaluation Office, African Development Bank.

African Development Bank, 2012, *Summary of the Environmental and Social Impact Assessment*, Tunis and Yaoundé: Energy, Environment and Climate Department, African Development Bank.

Asian Development Bank, 1999, *China Resettlement Policy and Practice: Review and Recommendations*, Manila: Asia Development Bank.

Atangana, S., J. Foumbi, M. Charlois, P. Ambroise-Thomas and C. Ripert, 1979, 'Epidemiological Study of Onchocerciasis and Malaria in Bamendjin Dam Area (Cameroon): Malacologic Fauna and Risks of Schistosomian Introduction', *Médicine tropicale* 39:53–43.

Audibert, M., R. Josseran, R. Josse and A. Adjidji, 1990, 'Irrigation, Schistosomiasis, and Malaria in the Logone Valley, Cameroon', *American Journal of Tropical Medicine and Hygiene* 42:550–60.

Bosi, M., 2000, *An Initial View on Methodologies for Emission Baselines: Electricity Generation Case Study*, IEA Information paper, International Energy Seminar, Paris.

Boutrais, J., 1974, *Etude d'une zone de transhumance: La Plain de Ndop (Cameroun)*, Paris: ORSTOM.

Electricity Development Corporation (EDC), 2011, *Lom Pangar Hydroelectric Project: Environmental and Social Assessment (ESA)*, Yaoundé: Electricity Development Corporation.

Gujja, B. and M. Perrin, 1999, *A Place for Dams in the 21st Century*, Geneva: World Wildlife Fund for Nature.

International Commission on Large Dams, 1998, *World Register of Dams*, Paris: ICOLD.

IUCN, 2000, *Rehabilitation of the Waza-Logone Flood Plain: Proposals for the Re-inundation Programme*, Yaounde: IUCN.

Diaw, K., 1990, 'Exodus, But No Promised Land: Resettlement in Ghana's Volta Plain', *Development & Cooperation* 5: 14–16. Electricity Development Corporation (EDC), 2011.

Lambi, C., 1999, 'The Bamendjin Dam of the Upper Nun Valley of Cameroon: No Human Paradise', in J. Dunlop and R. Williams, eds, *Culture and Environment*, Glasgow: University of Strathclyde.

Mehta, L. and B. Srinivasan, 1999, *Balancing Pains and Gains: A Perspective Paper on Gender and Large Dams*, Paper for WCD Thematic Review.

Mott MacDonald, 1999, *Logone Flood Plain Model Study Report*, Cambridge: Mott MacDonald Group.

Ripert, C., 1985, 'Epidemiological Study of Malaria in the Rice-Growing Regions of Yagoua and Maga (North Cameroon)', *Bulletin de la Société de Pathologie exotique et de ses filiales* 78: 191–204.

Sleigh, A. C. and S. Jackson, 2001, 'Dams, Development and Health: A Missed Opportunity', *Lancet* 357: 570–1.

The World Commissions on Dams (WCD), 2000, *Dams and Development: A New Framework for Decision Making*, London: Earthscan.

Uyigue, E. 2006, *Dams are Unrenewable: A Discussion Paper*, Benin City: Community Research and Development Centre.

World Bank & United Nations Development Programme, 1990, *Irrigation and Drainage Research: A Proposal*, Washington, DC: World Bank.

5

Transforming African Agriculture: Challenges, Opportunities and the Way Forward in the Twenty-first Century

Ntangsi Max Memfih

Introduction

Africa remains the continent with the greatest unexploited agricultural potential and yet is home to the highest proportion of hungry and malnourished people. Statistics from various sources show that, of the 900 million people suffering from chronic malnutrition in the world, about 240 million are from Africa, constituting more than 25 per cent of the continent's population. About 35 million children go to sleep malnourished and hungry every night. Africa is one of the poorest and least developed regions of the world. There is widespread concern at the continuing and indeed deepening poverty situation particularly in the sub-Saharan region. To compound this, there is the lack of rapid and broad–based economic growth to combat the situation despite many international discussions on the issue. This is largely an outcome of a neglected agricultural sector even though statistics reveal that this sector constitutes the mainstay of sub-Saharan economies. It contributes about 40 per cent of GDP and provides employment to about 70 per cent of the labour force. The sector equally provides about 35 per cent of export earnings. In addition, it supplies food to meet the ever-increasing population, savings and capital accumulation and finances the development of other sectors through tax revenues. The average growth rate of agricultural production stands at less than 1.8 per cent since 1960 as against more than 2.5 per cent growth in population. This reflects a decline in per capita terms.

Why has the agricultural sector performed so poorly in Africa compared to other developing regions of the world? What are the opportunities particularly in this era of globalisation that Africa can tap to transform its agriculture in a sustainable manner? How can the best of science and technology be harnessed to help Africa increase its agricultural productivity, profitability and sustainability, thereby contributing to improved food security for all? How, precisely, can we produce higher crop yields and more nutritious foods from thinning soils, making food both affordable and accessible to increasing numbers of people? What are the larger socio-economic and political conditions necessary for the effective use of science and technology in both the public and private sectors?

This chapter is conceived accordingly and is structured to provide answers to the above research questions. Specifically, it examines constraints to agricultural development in Africa since independence on both domestic and external fronts, assesses the potentials and opportunities that are inherent in the Twenty-first century global arena and speculates on what needs to be done to target agriculture for the continent's development in order to achieve the much cherished Millennium Development Goals, as time is running out. The main premise of the chapter is that agriculture constitutes the foundation for an industrial revolution in Africa. In order to achieve the above objectives, a descriptive approach is used with information drawn from secondary sources particularly from the FAO, IITA, IFPRI, CAADP, AGRA, CGIAR and World Bank databases.

Background

Agricultural transformation means a situation where a substantial number of rural households (1) have incomes exceeding the poverty level, (2) operate farms commercially (selling a substantial portion of the value of their output), (3) specialise in production at the farm level, (4) invest more heavily in the farm, (5) purchase commercial inputs, including hired labour, in significant quantities, and (6) adopt new technologies on a regular basis. At this point a dynamic growth process can be said to be in place, with the agricultural sector modernising, continuing to produce food cheaply, and releasing labour to the non-agricultural economy.

Agriculture provides food for the ever-increasing population, revenues from foreign exchange and taxes that finance both agricultural and other sectors, raw materials for industries, and most importantly, employment for a majority of the people. The average growth rate of agricultural production has stood at about 1.7 to 1.9 per cent per annum since 1960. Population growth on the other hand has increased from 2.5 per cent per annum during the period 1960-1980 to about 2.7 per cent since 1980 due to marginal improvements in health care services. This reflects a decline in per capita agricultural output, which in turn is mirrored in a decline in per capita food production of about 6 per cent between 1980 and 2002. The results have been low food intake per capita in Africa which is estimated at below 75 per cent of required levels since the 1980s. To this deplorable agricultural and food situation there is additionally substantial evidence of environmental degradation including rapid deforestation and loss of soil fertility. In these circumstances, domestic policies combined with international concerns have fared badly in Africa. Current development problems of food insecurity and increasing poverty at all levels remain in the continent.

Africa has abundant arable land and labour which, with sound policies, could be translated into increased production, incomes and food security. This has not materialised because of lack of consistent policies and/or effective implementation strategies. Thus, despite agriculture accounting for 70 per cent of the labour force, over 25 per cent of GDP and 20 per cent of agribusinesses in most countries, it continues to be given low priority. Agriculture also has a high multiplier effect, which means that agricultural investment can generate high economic and social returns and enhance economic diversification as well as social development. Strategies for transforming African agriculture need to address such challenges as low investment and productivity, poor infrastructure, lack of funding for agricultural research, inadequate use of yield-enhancing technologies, weak linkages between agriculture and other sectors, unfavourable policy and regulatory environments, and climate change.

African agriculture has a unique set of features that make it very different from Asia, where the Green Revolution has had a pervasive impact. These include among others:

- lack of a dominant farming system on which food security largely depends;
- predominance of rain fed agriculture as opposed to irrigated agriculture;
- heterogeneity and diversity of farming systems and the importance of livestock;
- key roles of women in agriculture and in ensuring household food security;
- lack of functioning competitive markets; under-investment in agricultural research and development, and infrastructure;
- lack of conducive economic and political enabling environments;
- large and growing impact of human health on agriculture;
- low and stagnant labour productivity and minimal mechanisation;
- predominance of customary land tenure.

A combination of factors has led to this deplorable situation which range from external shocks to internal policy weaknesses. Externally, agricultural support through subsidies and tariffs in developed countries has led to drastic falls in prices and makes products from Africa uncompetitive. The constant depreciation of the US dollar also made things more difficult for African agriculture. On the domestic front, inadequate attention is given to the sector as most governments continue to allocate less than 10 per cent of total expenditure to agricultural development. Following the Maputo Summit, African countries agreed to devote at least 10 per cent of their public expenditure to agriculture (AU 2003). But according to a validation workshop organised by NEPAD in December 2008, only 19 per cent of African countries were allocating more than 10 per cent of their national expenditure to agricultural development. Many countries hardly reach 4 per cent of GDP and have depended on overseas development aid for funding agriculture and other sectors.

This has led to low technology, poor infrastructure and above all low productivity. There is clearly a need for governments to increase agricultural investment in order to enhance food production and accelerate economic transformation, given the strong multiplier effect of agriculture.

The traditional land tenure system limits women's access to land contrary to the fact that they play significant roles in food production decisions. The fiscal systems do not encourage agricultural development. The vagaries of climate have not been helpful. Above all the poor governance that characterises the region sets a mediocre pace. Given the direct relationship that exists between agricultural performance and economic growth, it is of paramount importance that the performance of the sector be improved.

As a result of these difficult economic realities, several initiatives launched to develop African agriculture have failed. The dilemma for scholars, policy makers and development specialists now is how to isolate and explain Africa's economic dislocation and disarticulation so as to bridge the gap with other societies. It is in this light that the New Partnership for Africa's Development (NEPAD) was created in July 2001 in recognition of Africa's responsibility to create the conditions for economic recovery in the continent. NEPAD recognised the challenges of agricultural development and food security and proposed measures to revamp the sector. It focused on increasing investments in the three mutually reinforcing pillars of agricultural development in Africa, which include extending the area under sustainable land management and reliable water control systems, improving rural infrastructure and trade related capacities for improved market access, and increasing food supply and reducing hunger. In addition to the three pillars, NEPAD proposed measures to ensure peace and security, technological and infrastructural developments, human resource development, good governance, and other measures which all have relevance to agricultural development. Ten years have passed since NEPAD introduced such good ideas.

Performance of the Agricultural Sector

Agricultural Production

The overall picture of the agricultural sector shows that its performance between the 1960s and the first decade of the Twenty-first century fell below expectations even though there has been some recorded progress in the volume of production, trade, value added and diversification. Per capita output has recorded serious declines. The situation has been particularly bad for sub-Saharan countries. The total volume of agricultural production grew at an annual rate of 0.8 per cent during the 1960s; -0.9 per cent during the 1970s; 1 per cent during the 1980s; -1 per cent during most of the 1990s; and 0.8 per cent during the period 2000 to 2009. Between 1960 and 2009, agricultural production recorded a 0.1 per cent growth rate. For North Africa, agricultural performance was better. During the 1960s, these countries recorded agricultural production growth of about 1.2 per cent, dropping to 1 per cent during the 1970s, and then rising by 2.7 per cent during the 1980s and 1990s. During the period 1960 to 2009, these countries recorded average growth of 2.1 per cent.

In per capita terms, marked declines occurred in both food and non-food production. During the 1960–1965 period, per capita output declined by 0.9 and 1.1 per cent for agricultural and food production respectively. These negative per capita values persisted throughout the period 1960–2001. However, in a handful of countries, including Cameroon in West Central Africa, Côte d'Ivoire in West Africa, Mauritius in the Indian Ocean area, Egypt and Morocco in North Africa, and Malawi in southern Africa, per capita agricultural and food production indexes recorded slight improvements during this period. In sharp contrast, large countries such as Kenya, Tanzania, Sudan, DRC, Ethiopia and Nigeria recorded substantial declines.

Agricultural Trade

In view of the heavy reliance on exports of primary products, the performance of African agriculture has significant implications for the countries' foreign exchange earnings, as the trend in export volume and market share of Africa's major export cropsindicates. There were substantial declines in the growth rates in the volume of virtually all agricultural exports particularly during the 1970s and early 1980s. During the late 1980s, the 1990s and the first decade of the 21st century, export performance improved particularly due to the structural adjustment measures of the 1980s and 1990s. Because of this poor performance, Africa recorded significant losses in market shares. Particularly noticeable were the losses for cocoa (from 80 % to 60 % market share), groundnuts oils (54 % to 26 %), shelled groundnuts (85.5 % to 18 %), oilseed cake (10 % to 2 %), palm kernel oil (55 % to 21 %), palm oil (55 % to 6 %) and bananas (11 % to 5 %). In the few cases where gains were achieved, such as coffee, tea and sugar, these were marginal.

African economies remain largely tied to a narrow range of exports crops. In the mid-1980s, African countries derived 75 per cent of their agricultural export earnings from only six commodities: coffee, cocoa, cotton, sugar, tobacco and tea. Coffee and cocoa accounted for more than half of the total earnings. World market trends for the traditional export crops, on which the region depends, have not been favourable since the early 1970s. Among Africa's leading commodity exports, the growth rate of imports in industrial countries over the period 1970–1990 was negative for two commodities (sugar and cotton) and less than 0.5 per cent for two others (tea and tobacco). Much of the expansion in import demand for these commodities came from developing countries, to which Africa directs only a small proportion of its exports. During the 1980s, the real prices of five of the traditional export crops fell by an annual average of 4 to 9.7 per cent, while their yearly prices exhibited high coefficients of variations (about 15.9 to 52.5 %). Market prospects for this narrow range of crops are unlikely to improve.

Africa's agricultural growth record worsened in the 1980s and the region's food self-sufficiency declined. The incremental demand for food had to be met increasingly by commercial imports and food aid. As far back as the 1960s, Africa's imports of food and other agricultural products had grown rapidly in both volume and value. Between 1960 and 1965, agricultural imports into the continent grew at the rate of 9.4 per cent, increased to 11.9 per cent during 1975 to 1980 and reduced to 5 per cent during the 1980s. In the 1990s and the first decade of the 21st century, the growth of agricultural imports further reduced to 2.5 per cent. On aggregate, between 1960 and 2009, agricultural imports grew at the rate of 6.8 per cent.

At a regional level, agricultural and food imports growth was highest for countries in the southern African region, recording a rate of above 10 per cent between 1960 and 2001. By contrast, the Central African region experienced the lowest growth of about 3.3 per cent during the same period. The West African region recorded a remarkable drop from about 19 per cent during the period 1975–1980 to less than one per cent between 1990 and 2001. To finance these imports over the period, countries had to set aside between 10 to 40 per cent of their export earnings.

Although agricultural imports (particularly food) doubled in volume between 1960 and 2009, African countries also received substantial amounts of food aid over the same period. The growth rate of food aid into Africa between 1960 and 2009 stood at above 15 per cent. At a regional level, food aid grew at about 30 per cent in the southern region and less than five per cent in the west and northern regions. The trend of food imports and food aid in Africa shows that the continent depends significantly on an external supply of food. This is dangerous for poor countries with already precarious food security situations.

Agricultural Diversification

There have been few cases of export diversification into high-value products such as fish, meat and horticultural products. In domestic food markets, government food security strategies in most countries have focused on increasing maize and rice production with other cereals, legumes, roots and tubers being relatively neglected in terms of official support services and marketing. Many African countries have potential comparative advantages in the production of fresh and processed horticultural products as a result of their agro-ecological conditions, location and relatively low labour costs. Very few countries, notably Kenya, Côte d'Ivoire and South Africa, have effectively translated these resource advantages into competitive and profitable trade in horticultural trade with the outside world.

The traditional export crops including coffee, cocoa, cotton, sugar, tobacco rubber and tea have another weakness, and this is of inflexibility. With the exceptions of sugar and cotton which can be transformed into several other products using relatively small scale equipment, other crops are low value bulk goods that offer few processing possibilities, provide limited scope for new product development and have severely limited local or regional markets. The beverage crops have another element of inflexibility being a long gestation period for production, which increases market risks and financing problems. With the exception of coffee, each of the other commodities requires lumpy investments in large processing facilities to produce derivative products that meet international quality standards.

Another major issue of agricultural diversification is trade. Africa continues to depend on colonial ties and therefore still focuses on trade with former colonial powers. This therefore limits markets for agricultural products from Africa as well as for cheap imports from the non-ex-colonial powers. This situation has worked against intra-African trade. Over the past four decades, official trade among African countries has stagnated. Recorded African imports from the region increased in nominal terms from about US$ 2.15 billion in 1980 to US$ 2.71 billion in 1995, representing a decline in real terms. In 1990, only 7.4 per cent of imports to Africa originated from other African countries. A majority of African countries conducted less than 10 per cent of their external trade within the continent. Up to an additional estimated US$ 5 billion of Africa's current imports from the rest of the world could be supplied by African countries already exporting similar products outside the region. Only 2 per cent of Africa's beverage crop exports (e.g. coffee, tea and cocoa) were traded within the region. The major exports, of which 10 per cent or more was traded within the region, were live animals (59 %), tobacco (21 %), sugar (17 %), and fruits and vegetables (11 %).

Value Added in Agriculture

One major component of agricultural performance that current literature neglects concerns the value added in agriculture. This indicator translates the structural transformations or changes that have taken place in the sector. Agricultural value added during the period 1960–2009 grew on average at 1.4 per cent for all of Africa. However, during the period 1985–1995, this growth was about 3 per cent whereas it was 0.5 per cent during the period 1960–65. On a regional basis, agricultural value added grew at 2 per cent and above in Central and North Africa during the period 1960–2001. During the same period it grew at 0.3 per cent in the southern region (excluding South Africa), 1.5 per cent for East Africa and 1.3 per cent for West Africa. The low growth rate of value added in African agriculture indicates that there has been less vertical and horizontal integration, which translates as low structural transformation of agriculture. Agricultural exports remain largely unprocessed primary products. A majority of countries are therefore natural resource based economies.

Agricultural Performance and Food Security

Food security can be defined as the abilities of countries, regions or households to meet their required levels of food consumption at all times. Although the agricultural sector provides the bulk of food in Africa, the overall food security situation in the continent has not been encouraging. According to recent FAO estimates, the total number of people around the world suffering from severe malnutrition was between 800 and 900 million over the last twenty years but is declining gradually. Africa, particularly the sub-Saharan region, has been a notable exception in this world-wide trend. There has rather been an increase in malnutrition over the same period, with the number of malnourished increasing from about 100 million to more than 200 million. About 35 million children go to sleep malnourished and hungry every day.

Agricultural production in Africa will remain the most important element ofaddressing food security and poverty in the continent since most of the poor and the food insecure are rural people. Essentially, food security can be analyzed from the point of view of physical supply and economic access. These two aspects constitute supply and demand and are the two main factors that affect food security. Supply side factors are concerned with food availability, which involves the natural resource endowments of a society, available technology and its dissemination (for food production, storage and preservation), prices, market opportunities and the ability to augment one's own production with external supplies. Demand side factors on the other hand determine the degree of access to available food. These include household incomes, assets, prices, demographic factors such as numbers, age, composition of households and gender; and socio-cultural factors like health, educational level, cultural norms and food consumption habits. Food security can therefore be regarded as an income problem. In Africa, food security and agricultural development are two sides of the same coin. Both concepts centre on increasing agricultural productivity and incomes of a large majority of the population, which remains poor and derives its income from agriculture and related activities.

Constraints to Agricultural Development in Africa

Constraints on the External Front

External factors that have contributed to the dismal performance of the agricultural sector in Africa concern principally the falling prices of agricultural products on the world market and the depreciation of the US dollar. The prices of Africa's major agricultural exports have exhibited a generally downward trend in real terms since the early 1970s, meaning a substantial loss in terms of trade. There was a sustained decline in world market prices from 1980 to 1991. These prices fell to the lowest level in 50 years during the early 1980s. Between 1980 and 1982 alone, this loss was estimated at 1.2 per cent of GDP for all sub-Saharan countries.

The main cause of the sustained declines in international prices is the heavy subsidisation of agriculture by developed countries. Each year, over US$300 billion is given in support to agricultural producers, roughly six times the amount they spend on aid. To put this figure in context, it is more than the total income of the 1.2 billion people in the world living on less than a dollar a day. The EU and US are the 'subsidy super powers', accounting for over 60 per cent of developed countries' agricultural support spending. Europe spends more in absolute terms but the US spends more per farmer. They justify agricultural support by reference to social objectives. High levels of agricultural support translate into increased output, fewer imports, and more exports than would otherwise be the case. In most situations, subsidised export dumping is practised. This is very damaging to agricultural development in Africa.

The US dollar, a major currency against which commodities are traded on world markets, recorded the highest depreciation rate in recent times (more than 40 %) during the early 1980s. The depreciation of the dollar reflects an automatic fall in producer prices for the various exports measured in domestic currencies. This therefore had the same effect as falls in world market prices. The combined effects of the depreciating dollar and falling world market prices had markedly negative repercussions on the performance of the agricultural sector during the 1980s in countries within Africa.

There is an irony, too, that the peoples who have done the least to cause climate change are the ones who are worst affected by its impact. It is Africa, not the large carbon emitters like America, Europe, and now China, which experts forecast will be hit hardest. We are already seeing this impact in Africa as rains fail and previously fertile land turns into desert. Climate change will further increase pressure on water resources and degrade bio-diversity. But while this must be the start of our discussion, it is only half the story for there is also considerable potential within Africa for agricultural growth.

Constraints on the Domestic Front

Although African leaders attribute the dismal performance of agriculture to harsh international environments, internal policies have played a leading role. When comparisons are made with other developing areas particularly in Asia and Latin America, it is clear that African governments do not give adequate attention in terms of needed assistance to the agricultural sector. Even though the sector contributes more than 25 per cent to GDP, most African governments still allocate less than 10 per cent of total expenditure to the development of agriculture. African governments allocated on average only about 7.7 per cent of total expenditure to the agricultural sector between 1960 and 2009. Only countries in the East African region consistently allocated about 10 per cent on average to agricultural development during the period 1960–2009. Governments in the Central and West African regions allocated on average only about 6.4 per cent of total expenditure to agricultural development. This explains the low level of agricultural infrastructure prevalent in most countries.

A review of the existing literature on domestic constraints to agricultural development in Africa reveals that the sector has been heavily taxed. The various ambitious industrial development plans launched during the 1970s and early 1980s were constructed on the assumption that funds for their financing would be generated from agricultural surpluses. In addition, many countries depend heavily on taxes from trade as a source of government revenue. Since agricultural exports account for such a large proportion of total export earnings, it is inevitable that agriculture would bear a heavy tax burden. For these and other related reasons, governments in most African countries are playing a leading role in determining producer prices for all major crops through the use of para-statal commodity marketing boards. As export taxes increased through the 1970s and early 1980s, marketing boards' margins also widened whereas producer prices fell far below international levels.

Oyejide (1993) using nominal protection coefficients (NPC) for some categories of crops showed that between 1969 and 1989, farmers did not receive up to 75 per cent of the border prices for their products in sub-Saharan Africa. Similar results are obtained for the period 1990–2009. These NPC estimates used by Oyejide (ibid.) show that sectoral pricing, marketing and trade policies are generally unfavourable to agriculture. The NPC for all crops remained below one throughout the whole period. This shows that government's sectoral policies towards agriculture during the period 1969 to 2001 did not provide incentives for more agricultural production.

The rate of relevant technological innovation has been slow, providing only limited technology, which African farmers can adopt. This is caused by weak agricultural research and extension. Irrigated areas, which are excellent users of new agricultural technologies in Asia and Latin America, have not been developed significantly in Africa; and where they have been developed are nearly universally poorly managed. Inherent soil and water constraints to expanded agricultural production using imported technology are not sufficiently considered.

There is inadequate transport infrastructure. African countries recognised the importance of transport infrastructure in general and regional transport infrastructure networks in particular to their development prospects as far back as the 1960s just after most of them attained independence. As a result, several transport infrastructure development initiatives have emerged over the years. One of the most ambitious of these initiatives is the Trans African Highways (TAH) network, conceived in the early 1970s. However, several years after its conception, missing links still exist in the network, especially at border areas. An analysis of 103 cross-border TAH links (TAH sections leading to border posts) shows that 33 per cent are unpaved roads in various conditions – good, fair and poor; 16 per cent are paved roads in poor condition; and 38 per cent are paved roads in good or fair condition. This clearly illustrates the poor state of physical integration between African countries. Generally, using the missing TAH links as a measure of road integration, the ECA (2004) ha shown that there is a disparity in the level of physical integration across the continent. Overall, the road sub-sector in Africa is in a deplorable state. The total length of roads in the region is 2,064,613 kilometres out of which only 29.7 per cent is paved, the remaining portion being either earth or gravel roads. In addition to its low density, distribution, and the fact that a large proportion is unpaved, a sizeable chunk of Africa's road network is in a state of disrepair. For instance, 34 per cent of paved roads and 55 per cent of unpaved roads in CEMAC were in poor condition in 2005. Similarly 34 per cent of paved roads and 68 per cent of unpaved roads in COMESA were in poor condition in the same period. The poor state of roads, telecommunications and ports throughout sub-Saharan Africa has created high transport costs.

Inadequate provision of social amenities like rural health care centres, rural water, family planning units and educational establishments have resulted in a high incidence of unhealthy, poorly educated people in rural areas. Most of these persons cannot therefore understand the need for the application of modern farming practices and improved varieties of crops. An increasing number of youths leave for urban areas in order to attend schools or to look for jobs. The overall consequence has been the depletion of human capital for agriculture in rural areas. This is generally characterised by schools without teachers or structures, and health centres without personnel, equipment and medicines.

Ill-conceived public agricultural projects have contributed to the stagnation of the sector. Even well-conceived projects are badly implemented. This explains the high rate of abandoned or uncompleted agricultural projects after heavy capital commitments. The inefficient management of para-statals has led to frequent heavy budgetary deficits in most African countries. Autonomous farmers' organisations and cooperatives and farmer participation in the management of agricultural development have not been encouraged.

Traditional African land tenure systems provide considerable security of tenure on land brought into farming through customary rules of community land ownership. Considerable migration (rural-rural, rural-urban, urban-urban) has occurred within and between countries. Migrants often come with conflicting traditions of land allocation. In addition, many governments have nationalised land. Some of this land is distributed for other uses such as plantations owned by the state or by private enterprises and farms owned by elites. Both these phenomena have reduced the traditional security of land tenure. Farmers who are unsure that the land they farm will belong to them or can be used by them in future are less likely to invest in or conserve it. This accelerates environmental problems. A more severe problem manifests itself in the form of a majority of the agricultural population not having access to land, thereby being forced to rent it out or work under landlords; and some work on marginal lands. Primitive farming practices also contribute to degrading farmlands.

Another major constraint to agricultural development in Africa involves the role of women in society. African women traditionally bear most of the responsibilities for food production, fuel wood gathering, water collection and other household related activities. In traditional societies, this works well but with increasing population pressures in townships; access to land by women has become very difficult. The role of women particularly in areas dominated by Islamic tradition is not facilitated due to a number of socio-economic restrictions. Increased work burdens on women make it difficult for them to apply the labour needed to intensify agriculture. Research in African agriculture has paid little attention to the gender element in farming and many extension systems appear to neglect women altogether.

The problem of poor governance exacerbates agricultural development constraints in Africa. The lack of will and commitment by government officials and agents is mired by the prevalence of poor governance. This has created a bureaucracy that holds back everything. Private sector participation in agriculture has not been facilitated by these delays. Studies undertaken in a number of countries (e.g. Cameroon, Côte d'Ivoire) show that an investor takes about two years to get authorisation from the government to undertake an investment activity. This therefore discourages mechanised agriculture. Industrial Free Zones established during the early 1990s are yet to have any impact on agricultural production since most of the investors are still to get authorisations after so many years.

Over-dependence on rain fed agriculture has proven dangerous for agricultural development. During the last twenty years, rainfall has considerably declined and the duration of rainfall has significantly reduced in many areas, making rain-fed agriculture highly risky. Frequent locust attacks have been recorded in the continent particularly in the West and Central African regions during the 1980s. Worse still, only 7 per cent of arable land is irrigated (and barely 3.7 % in sub-Saharan Africa) while the corresponding percentages for South Africa, East and South-East Asia, and South Asia are 10 per cent, 29 per cent and 41 per cent respectively. Furthermore, in Africa 16 per cent of all soils are classified as having low nutrient reserves while in Asia the equivalent figure is only 4 per cent; moreover, fertiliser productivity (expressed in terms of maize yield response) is estimated at some 36 per cent lower in Africa than in Asia and 92 per cent lower than in developed countries.

Conflicts and wars were a major threat to agricultural production and food security in the continent during the 1980s and 1990s. These ranged from inter-ethnic wars within countries to boundary problems between countries. A majority of these are politically motivated. Even where there is no outright war, conflict has made it impossible for farmers to achieve anything like full production potential.

Fiscal and monetary policies have not always been helpful to farmers and agricultural development in general. Most governments in the continent have lacked strict discipline in relation to money supply. The volume of money in circulation is usually increased at rates that have proved harmful to the economy. The supply of money has contributed significantly to the observed level of inflation, which encourages consumption over savings. This restricts the abilities of various economies to mobilise investments, which are prerequisites to agricultural development. Credit policies have not been helpful to farmers. The available evidence about credit provision to different economic activities in Africa shows that the smallholder sub-sector has been marginalised, even when credit projects have been relatively successful (Tshibaka 1994; 1998).

Opportunities to Transform African Agriculture

The greatest opportunity for transforming African agriculture is the recognition by African leaders of the need for concerted action. This has resulted in a number of initiatives being taken during the first decade of the Twenty-first century. These include the CAADP Process, FARA, and AGRA. The Comprehensive Africa Agriculture Development Program (CAADP) was adopted at the AU Assembly of Heads of State and Governmentin Maputo in 2003 as a framework to spearhead and accelerate agricultural and rural development in Africa. AU heads of state and governments have continued to reaffirm their political commitment to CAADP as demonstrated by the adoption of relevant decisions and declarations, including most notably, the Sirte Declaration on the Challenges of Implementing Integrated and Sustainable Development on Agriculture and Water (adopted in 2004) and more recently, the Sirte Declaration on Investing in Agriculture for Economic Growth and Food Security (adopted in July 2009).

While CAADP implementation is driven primarily by country level stakeholders – government, private sector, civil society and development partners

– regional and continental institutions also play an important role in supporting the process. CAADP support institutions help implement core CAADP objectives such as:

- leveraging African institutions for advocacy;
- technical backstopping and capturing regional and continental spillovers;
- ensuring mutual responsibility and accountability through joint analysis, ownership and peer review;
- and promoting alignment of government, development partners and private sector around agreed national agendas.

AUC works with all other CAADP support institutions – NEPAD agencies, RECs and pillar or other technical institutions – in order to facilitate their role in CAADP processes.

The process for establishing FARA was started in 1997 and ratified in 2001 with the first General Assembly meeting in July 2002 in Maputo. Main objectives are:

- to promote pan-African agricultural research for development through enhanced support by national governments, development partners, and private sector;
- to facilitate the exchange of agricultural technologies, knowledge and experience by building mutual partnerships between various institutions, the private sector, farmers and producers in Africa;
- to support relevant and cost-effective African regional research programmes;
- and to catalyse the process of agricultural technology dissemination and knowledge dissemination relevant and appropriate for Africa.

These are to be achieved through:

- advocacy of the role of agricultural research;
- promotion of functional partnerships and strategic alliances;
- accelerating sharing and exchange of knowledge;
- stimulating the development and dissemination of new technologies and methodologies in natural resource management, genetic resource management and biotechnology;
- andstimulating policy and market development.

The Alliance for a Green Revolution in Africa (AGRA), created in 2006, works to achieve a food-secure and prosperous Africa through the promotion of rapid, sustainable agricultural growth based on smallholder farmers. AGRA aims to ensure that smallholders have what they need to succeed: good seeds and healthy soils; access to markets, information, financing, storage and transport; and policies that provide them with comprehensive support. Through developing Africa's high-potential breadbasket areas, while also boosting farm productivity across more challenging environments, AGRA works to transform smallholder agriculture into a highly productive, efficient, sustainable and competitive system, and concurrently protect the environment.

Advances in science and technology constitute a huge opportunity for Africa to transform its agricultural base. Science and technology has contributed to Africa's agricultural development in at least four areas: direct agriculture, transport and communication, energy, human and animal health, education and the environment. African agriculture has witnessed considerable transformation in several respects. Crops that were formally alien to the continent such as wheat, barley, rice, maize, tomatoes and apples have been successfully introduced and adapted to different countries in Africa. Many research results from agricultural research institutions on the continent have been successfully disseminated to farmers. This dissemination has transformed plant breeding, agronomy, physiology and horticulture. The impact of these results has been manifested in higher yields, the introduction of disease- and pest-resistant varieties and the production of crops of higher nutritional value. However, much more needs to be done in this domain.

The continent is blessed with abundant land and natural resources. Africa's population is growing rapidly. But in comparison with India, for example, it has twelve times the land area and less than two-thirds of its people. Working with Africa's army of small-holder farmers, the continent can transform its rich agricultural resources to grow enough food to meet its own needs, and produce a surplus to meet the growing demands across the globe. Consistent increases in food prices during the first decade of the twenty-first century offer Africa prospects for agricultural development. Huge global demand for bio-fuels constitutes leading opportunities for agricultural development in Africa.

ICT hold some level of promise. The role of ICT is recognised in Millennium Development Goal 8 (MDG8), which emphasises the benefits of new technologies, especially information and communications technologies in the fight against poverty. This has created a new generation of services aimed to boost to agricultural development in Africa. Mobile phone technologies are presenting Africa's smallholder farmers with an unprecedented opportunity to run their operations more productively and to increase their own income levels. One of the largest challenges traditionally experienced by Africa's smallholder farmers has been lack of transparent information about market prices of crops. A number of new mobile phone-based services are however addressing this problem by giving farmers access to market prices, enabling them to negotiate better deals with traders and improve the timing of getting their crops to market. These services typically include a function whereby famers can send a SMS text message to a specific number which then gives them wholesale and retail prices of crops.

Another aspect of the new generation of services includes access to insurance. Mobile phones are also being used to distribute agricultural insurance products to farmers, most of whom cannot afford conventional insurance. A product called Kilimo Salama, Swahili for 'safe agriculture', enables smallholder farmers in Kenya to insure their agricultural inputs against adverse weather conditions, such as drought or too much rain. Developed by UAP Insurance, the Syngenta Foundation for Sustainable Agriculture and mobile operator Safaricom, Kilimo Salama allows smallholder farmers to insure as little as one kilogramme of maize, seed or fertiliser. To be covered under the scheme, farmers only need to pay an extra 5 per cent for a bag of seed, fertiliser or other inputs.

The rising concern over global food price volatility has put agriculture at the centre of international diplomacy. But unlike in the 1950s when food aid became a major tool in international relations, modern interactions among states are being defined by trade and knowledge transfer. A new field – agricultural diplomacy (Agro Diplomacy) – is emerging as countries learn more about their shared ecological experiences and agricultural trade interests. The prospects for building such relations are evident in the rise in cooperation between Africa and Latin America. This constitutes another dimension of opportunity for agricultural development in Africa.

The increasing interest is shown by the G20 in improving agricultural productivity of smallholders. In June 2011, the G20 agriculture ministers promised to give 'special attention' to improving the productivity of smallholder farmers who provide 80 per cent of the food in the developing world. These farmers, who typically own fewer than 2 hectares of land and maybe a cow or two, must be kept at the centre of the G20 agenda. FARA, together with the GFAR platform, is advocating that by listening to the farmers and recognising their needs, the barriers that prevent the use of required innovative technologies can be overcome and opportunities in agribusiness expanded.

Conclusions and Recommendations

A number of conclusions are discernable. Firstly, agricultural development efforts in Africa have not been at all rosy. The performance of the sector has deteriorated significantly from pre-1980 standards. Various countries' and the international community's intensification of effort at improving productivity has resulted in negligible progress because of a lack of real commitment and political will. Paper rhetoric alone cannot overcome scarcity and institutional constraints. Secondly, agricultural development in Africa continues to face the same problems as in the past with falling prices, a mounting debt burden, conflict, insecurity, poor governance and weak institutions, with poor infrastructure topping the list. Thirdly, African leaders are largely to blame for the poor state of agriculture and food security in the continent. However, a collection of ideas provides the basis of hope for the African people. Most important are agricultural productivity, peace and security, infrastructure, trade and investment, and the expansion of information technology.

Fourthly, although various initiatives have been well received within the governing elite community, they lack foresight in many respects.

Governments need to increase capacity to support farmer productivity. They should review their national research and extension systems and implement the reforms required to improve national research capacity and efficiency. Extensive reviews and analyses of national agricultural research systems in Africa over the past twenty years indicate that funding for agricultural research will need to double in the next ten years from the current allocation of US$1 billion annually. Additional funding is required to train scientists, rehabilitate and restructure research institutions, strengthen extension services and subsidise agricultural inputs.

Establishing a strong partnership between public and private sectors for increased investment, promoting the collaboration between the public and private sectors in post-harvest management, storage, distribution, processing and marketing, should all be given serious support and emphasis by various governments. Public and private sectors should be encouraged to share costs and risks to assists smallholders in the adoption of new technology through poverty reduction programmes and debt relief. Increased attention should be given to national food security programmes during discussions regarding poverty reduction and debt relief. Provision of farm tools at subsidised rates should constitute a fundamental aspect of partnership between the public and private sectors.

There is an urgent need to invest significantly in both physical and social infrastructure with emphasis on rural areas so as to stimulate the smallholder sub-sector. Various governments need to increases the efficiency and use of water supply for agriculture. Establishing small-scale irrigation facilities, improving local water management, and increasing the exchange of information and technical knowledge with other countries in the region could achieve this.

The security of land tenure for traditional and modern farming needs should be improved. This requires in particular that land ownership by women and the poor should be guaranteed through reviewing existing land laws.

There is a need to enhance agricultural credits and financial schemes. This can be achieved through improvements in credit access by small-scale farmers and in some cases women. Governments could also open agricultural development banks to assist these vulnerable groups as used to be the case in the past.

Continental Level

In order to strengthen the enabling environment for agricultural development and food security at the continental level, a number of issues need to be addressed. In the domain of infrastructural development, the institution of regional support programmes for regional infrastructure can facilitate overall infrastructure breakthrough in the continent. These should target particularly agriculture and communication.

To strengthen economic recovery at the level of economic groupings, there should be provision for some consistency between national economic reform programmes and regional policy objectives. The duplication of membership of countries in many economic groupings and the proliferation of RECs in Africa contradicts reality. It is often suggested that the integration process would be more effective if there were fewer RECs and if member states were limited to membership in only one.

Apart from wringing their hands, endorsing development goals and promising more aid, governments in developed countries should get serious about reforming farming policies. They should reduce the rate at which they are subsidising agriculture to meet WTO standards. In addition, efforts must be made to develop new partnership to address donor fatigue for individual high profile agricultural projects; to promote co-operation with developed countries carrying out and developing research and development capabilities in agriculture; and to promote access to international markets by improving the quality of African produce and agricultural products, particularly processed products, to meet the standards required by those markets; support African networking with external partners in the areas of agricultural technology and know-how, extension services and rural infrastructure; support investment in research in the area of high yielding crops and durable preservation and storage methods; and provide support for building national and regional capacity for multilateral trade negotiation including food sanitation and other agricultural trade regulations.

References

African Development Bank Group, 2010, *Small Holder Agriculture in East Africa: Trends, Constraints and Opportunities*, Tunis: ADB Working Paper Series No. 105.

African Development Bank (ADB), 2002, *Selected Statistics on African Countries*, Tunis: ADB Statistics Division.

FAO, 2008, State of Food and Agriculture: World Food and Agriculture in Review, Rome: Food and Agriculture Statistics, <www.fostat.org>

NEPAD, 2004, *Implementing the Comprehensive African Agriculture Development Programme and Restoring Food Security in Africa: The Roadmap*, Addis Ababa: African Union.

Oyejide, Ademola, 1993, 'Effects of Trade and Macroeconomic Policies on African Agriculture', in Romeo M. Bautista and Alberto Valdes, eds, *The Bias Against Agriculture: Trade and Macroeconomic Policies in Developing Countries*. San Francisco: ICS Press.

Tshibaka, B.T., 1994, 'Policy Imperatives for Agricultural Development in Africa', in IITA, *Sustainable Food Production in Sub-Saharan Africa: Constraints and Opportunities*, Ibadan: IITA.

Tshibaka, B.T., 1998, *Structural Adjustment and Agriculture in West Africa*, Dakar: CODESRIA.

6

Land Grab and the Viability of Foreign Investments in Sub-Saharan Africa: The Nigerian Experience

Justitia O. Nnabuko and Chibuike U. Uche

Introduction

In recent times, foreign farmers from all over the world have become increasingly interested in African land and agriculture. Over the past few years, investors from high – and medium-income countries, including state agencies, have started to lease large areas of land in lower-income countries for commercial agricultural production. The pattern is likely to continue due to increasing demand for food in emerging super-economies such as India and China, rising oil prices and scarcity of water and land. Both the numbers of land deals and the size of landholdings being leased or purchased have significantly increased over the past five years. According to the World Bank, the rights to some 50 million hectares in Africa alone have either been acquired since 2006 or are under negotiation, while NGOs like GRAIN estimate that a far greater area is affected. Countries selling or leasing farmland to investors are primarily low-income countries in Africa, and to a lesser extent Asia and Latin America. In Africa, countries selling or leasing very large areas of land include Sudan, Mozambique, Mali, and Ethiopia, and many other countries have seen smaller deals. The Agricultural Investment Agency in Ethiopia is reportedly considering offering foreign firms three million hectares of land over the next two years (Huggins 2010; see also Silver-Greenberg 2009). All across the continent, governments are now selling what is arguably the only factor of production that is under their control and the very basis of their nationhood: land under various guises. 'Land is at the heart of social, political and economic life in most African economies, which continue to rely heavily on agriculture and natural resources for a significant share of GDP, national food needs, employment [and] export revenue' (Toulmin 2008:10). So intense is this movement that an international conference was recently organised in Groningen Netherlands to address this issue.

From the above, it is clear that although Africa doubtless has food security issues especially given its expanding population, it is not the initiator of these mega land deals currently being struck all around the continent and championed by countries rich in natural resources but with poor agrarian land like Saudi Arabia. The Gulf States (Bahrain, Kuwait, Oman, Qatar, Saudi Arabia and the United Arab Emirates) have neither the water nor the soil to produce food. But they have plenty of oil and money. Because they depend on food imported mainly from Europe, and their currencies are pegged to the US dollar, the simultaneous rise in food prices on the world market and the fall in the US dollar have boosted their import bill from US$8 billion to US$20 billion within the past five years. Given that water is already in short supply, the Saudi government has decided to stop growing wheat, their main staple, by 2016, and instead to grow it elsewhere and ship it back (Mae-Wan Ho 2010). China and India, arguably because of their large population, are also increasingly becoming interested in this market. These investments are principally driven by three key motives. First, investors are attracted by the increasing and shifting demand for food, animal feeds and bio-fuel, which is likely to continue should fuel prices remain above historical levels. Second, due to its relative scarcity, the value of agricultural land is increasing and Africa is the only continent that still has vast unexploited agricultural land. This offers the potential for both intensification and extensification. At the global level, the price for agricultural land increased by about 16 per cent in Brazil, 31 per cent in Poland and 15 per cent in the US Mid-West in 2007 (von Braun 2008). Agricultural land prices in Africa have not increased on a comparable scale. Third, governments in countries that do not have enough land and water to feed their populations are making investments in their quest to secure food supply (Castel and Kamara 2009:1).

The essence of this chapter is to explore the possible consequences of foreign investments in the African agricultural sector. Although the African continent has a long history of foreign dominance of its economic space, the rise in interests of foreign businesses and governments in the African agricultural industry is a relatively new phenomenon. In the light of the above there is a need for more studies to help our understanding of the possible dynamics and consequences of such foreign investments in African agriculture. This chapter presents a case study of what is arguably the biggest foreign involvement in Nigerian agriculture to date: the Shonga Farms experiment in Kwara State. Drawing lessons from such an existing scheme is intended toreduce the potential minefields for foreign investors in African agriculture and enhance the utility value of such investments for both the foreign investors and the concerned African countries. The remainder of this chapter explores the dynamics of food security in Africa; critiques the Shonga Farms experience in Nigeria; and attempts to draw lessons and conclusions from the above experience for local and foreign interests in African agriculture.

Food Security in Africa and India

Agriculture has always been central to the economic and social wellbeing of most African countries. It is both the dominant economic sector and the highest employer of labour in such African countries.

Agriculture, providing 60 per cent of all employment, constitutes the backbone of most African economies; in most countries, it is still the largest contributor to GDP; the biggest source of foreign exchange, still accounting for about 40 per cent of the continent's hard currency earnings; and the main generator of savings and tax revenues. The agricultural sector is also still the dominant provider of industrial raw materials with about two-thirds of manufacturing value-added in most African countries being based on agricultural raw materials. Agriculture thus remains crucial for economic growth in most African countries. The rural areas, where agriculture is the mainstay of all people, support some 70-80 per cent of the total population, including 70 per cent of the continent's extreme poor and undernourished. Improvement in agricultural performance has potential to increase rural incomes and purchasing power for large numbers of people Thus, more than any other sector, agriculture can uplift people on a mass scale. With greater prosperity, the consequent higher effective demand for African industrial and other goods would induce dynamics that would be a significant source of economic growth (NEPAD 2002).

Exploiting and advancing the above advantages has however proved to be difficult for many of these countries. In fact, in most post-independence African countries, the agricultural situation has been getting worse (Reij and Smaling 2008:410).

The consequence is that despite its dependence on agriculture, Africa now has serious food security issues. It has for instance been noted that the continent has more countries with food security problems than any other continent in the world:

> One of the most striking phenomena is the gradual marginalisation of sub-Saharan Africa in international agricultural export markets. Even though SSA possesses 12 per cent of the world's arable land, the region's share of global agriculture exports have declined gradually from almost 10 per cent four decades ago to around 2 percent today. .... On the import side, the opposite pattern emerges: sub-Saharan Africa is the only developing region that has seen its share of world agricultural imports increase rather than decrease (Webber and Labaste 2010:3).

In fact, more than 60 of all countries with food security problems are in Africa. Furthermore, of the 44 countries with poor or critical food security, 30 are in Africa. Also of importance in this equation is the fact that Africa has the highest population growth rate of all the continents in the world. It has therefore been estimated that should present trends continue, the number of constantly malnourished persons in sub-Saharan Africa would rise from 180 to 300 million by 2010. Sub-Saharan Africa has one of the world's fastest growing human populations, with a rate of increase of 2.6 per cent per annum (Otte and Chilonda 2002:1 ; see also Pelum Association and Practical Action 2005).

The major reason is that land in Africa is under-utilised both in reference to the size being cultivated and the yield from such cultivations. Most African countries have been unable to take advantage of their enormous lands, arguably their greatest developmental asset. The preponderance of game reserves across the entire continent is clear evidence of this fact. Even on the limited portion of the African arable land being cultivated, the yields are relatively low.

Large parts of agricultural lands in Africa remain unexploited despite the fact that many countries on the continent face unsustainable food import bills. They suffer from low intensification of agricultural production systems. Sub-Saharan Africa records the lowest milk and meat production per animal (6.8 kg of meat and 24.8 kg of milk per animal and per year in the highland mixed system), the highest crop land area per tractor of 773.8 ha/tractor (against 58 at the global level), the lowest use of fertiliser in the world at 11.1 kg/ha (against 89.6 at the global level), and the lowest share of irrigated area (3.7 % of the total cropped land, compared to a global average of 17.9 %). Sub-Saharan Africa also records the lowest yield for major cereals, which are about a third of global averages. Given this low performance, foreign investment may offer a way of revitalising agriculture in Africa (Castel and Kamara 2009:1). In the case of Nigeria, it has also been similarly noted that:

> Nigeria's agriculture therefore points to a gross record of under-performance. A recent FAO estimates shows that the average yield for maize in Nigeria is between 0.9 to 1 tonneper hectare. In India, the yield is 1.8 per hectare; in Zimbabwe, 3.0; Pakistan, 1.7; China, 4.7; and the USA, 8.5 tonnes per hectare. Whereas the average yield for rice in Nigeria is 1.2 tonnes per hectare, in India, it is 2.9; Pakistan, 3.0; China, 6.3; Egypt, 8.1; Vietnam, 4.2 and U.S.A, 7.0. The yield per hectare for groundnut in Nigeria is 1.08; whereas in China, it is 3.1 and in the U.S.A, 3.2 tonnes per hectare. Apart from yield per hectare, Nigeria performs poorly in overall level of crop production when compared with many other countries. While Nigeria's annual rice production stands at an average annual of 3,219,333 metric tonnes (paddy rice), Vietnam's is at 31,949,000; Bangladesh produces an annual average of 35,021,000; Thailand, 24,933,000; and China, 190,577,000. This means that Nigeria produces only 10 per cent of Vietnam's rice; 9 per cent of Bangladesh's; 12.9 per cent of Thailand's and 1.68 per cent of China's annual rice production (Saraki 2006).

The consequence is that Africa remains a net food importer. Despite its deficiencies, it is important to note that the current alarm over food security in the world has not emerged from the continent. Rather, it has emerged from countries with concerns about the rising global food prices which have at least in part been occasioned by the global warming (see Food and Agricultural Organisation 2010:15). Since Africa is arguably the continent with the freest under-utilised and, most importantly, cheapest arable land, it has become an instant attraction for countries worried about the possible economic consequence of rising food prices for their various economies.'Investor interest is focused on countries with weak land governance', a draft report said. Although investment deals promised jobs and infrastructure 'investors failed to follow through on their investment plans, in some cases after inflicting serious damage on the local resource base'. The report also flagged that 'the level of formal payments required was low, thereby fuelling speculative investment' (The Guardian (UK) 2010). Ideally, this would provide an opportunity for African economies to benefit from rising global food prices. This has however not been the case. Most countries interested in African agriculture are simply interested in setting up agricultural enclaves for feeding their home communities. Cheap African labour and cheap African land have the potentials of making it far cheaper for such countries to produce food for their home communities in Africa rather than at home. More worrying however is the fact that such an arrangement may not enhance the food security situation of the African continent. As already stated, most of the countries currently interested in African agriculture are also concerned about their food security position at home. India is no doubt a classic example. Despite the laudable goals of the 2008 India-Africa Forum Summit with respect to all aspects of economic development, the fact remains that India is increasingly worried about its food security at home because of rising production costs and declining land quality (India-Africa Forum 2008). This no doubt influenced the agricultural content of the agreement (Vashisht 2010). Other factors at play include the fact that with falling poverty in India, concerns over food security has been increasing. The country's experience with hunger in the past has made it extremely sensitive to food security issues. In 1943, for instance, the Bengal famine claimed more than two million lives (Chakraborty 2005:1).

It is therefore not surprising that Indian farmers with explicit state support have been increasingly interested in exploiting the cheapness of land on the African continent for agricultural purposes. From 2008, Indian and Indian-owned companies have been part of a new global trend of buying agricultural land in African and South American countries for cultivation. India's participation has so far been concentrated in African countries, but South America is seen as a growing new destination for agri-investment, while integrated Indian oilseeds firms already have operations in south-east Asia from plantation cultivation to processing of edible oils and export. Companies and agri-business groups that have leased or purchased land in Africa include Allied Chemicals, AVR Engineering (construction), BP Jewellery, Kankaria group (manufacturing and textiles), Karuturi Agro Products, Kommuri Agrotech (floriculture and horticulture), KSR Earthmovers, Nelvo International (minerals) and Surya Electrical (electrical products). According to one estimate, more than 80 Indian and Indian-owned companies have invested in large tracts of land and huge plantations in Africa, particularly in Ethiopia, Kenya, Madagascar, Mozambique and Senegal (Goswami 2010). Jaswinder Singh, an Indian farmer commented thus:

> The offer from Africa basically means a farmer can take a large tract of land on lease for 50 years, and in some cases even up to 99 years. With land prices in Africa much lower than those in Punjab, farmers can think of doing agriculture on a scale that's unimaginable in the state. ... The land lease rate in Punjab's Doaba region is a minimum of Rs 40,000 per acre. In most African nations, land lease rate in terms of Indian currency comes to Rs 700 per acre. This means that for every one acre in Punjab, we can own 60 acres in Africa. With a per capita land holding of 1.5 acres in Punjab, agriculture is ceasing to be a sustainable activity. During my trip to Africa recently, I saw our farmers owning tracts as large as 2.5 hectares (Vashisht 2010).

It is not however sufficient to dismiss the entire interest in African agriculture by foreign companies and states. Irrespective of the problems such investments may have, the fact remains that African lands for a variety of reasons have remained under-utilised. By increasing the yield per acre of land, Africa will also gain from such cooperation. At the very least, they will earn valuable foreign exchange from the export of such crops. At another level, African countries will benefit from the employment of labour that such investments in agriculture, which is labour intensive, will generate. For this to happen however, foreign businesses and governments that are interested in African land and agriculture must not simply regard this as an opportunity to solve their employment problems at home. Densely populated countries like India and China will no doubt be tempted to exploit this opportunity. Unfortunately, most African countries are content with burying their heads in the sand without proactively dealing with foreign businesses on the rules of engagement. It is for instance not surprising that China, which got a head start in this scramble for agricultural investment in Africa, actually runs such farms on the risible ratio of one African to one Chinese worker. Unfortunately some scholars have actually praised this:

> These investments may benefit local farmers by giving them access to technology, connecting them to market opportunities, and enabling them to benefit from fo- reign experience. The 'Baoding' villages, for example, employ locals and Chinese at a one-to one ratio to ensure local support. Such investments are a potential source of employment, government revenue, and foreign exchange. Castel and Kamara (2009:2).

This surely cannot be acceptable in an industry that is labour intensive. Given the divergent interests of foreign agricultural investors and their African host communities, it is important that from the very beginning, African governments should make clear their preferences which should essentially be driven by the need to transfer agricultural skills to Africans. African countries should also be interested in developing the value chain in the agricultural sector rather than just producing and marketing primary products. Interestingly, some foreign farmers having failed at this in their home countries, with regrettable consequences, will be eager to exploit such opportunities in Africa. According to Gunbir Singh, head of the Punjab chapter of the Confederation of Indian Industry:

> The mistake that we committed in Punjab should not be repeated there. We succeeded in increasing the yields but failed to set up the relevant food processing industry or infrastructure such as cold storage. This means that agriculture in Punjab is not as remunerative as it used to be (Vashisht 2010).

This however may not be easy. The lack of infrastructure in the entire African continent will no doubt complicate matters for such foreign farmers. To overcome these problems, however, African governments must be proactive and provide more infrastructure. Foreign investment in African agriculture can therefore not be the whole solution to addressing African food security issues. The next section, a case study on the Shonga Farms project in Nigeria, will highlight some of the social, political and developmental complexities and difficulties of such foreign investments in African agriculture.

The Shonga Farms Project in Kwara State Nigeria

On the surface, Nigeria does not look like an agricultural country. This is especially so given the role its national oil wealth has played in its social, economic and political development in the past three decades. Prior to 1970, agriculture formed the bedrock of Nigerian foreign exchange earnings. And it virtually dictated and conditioned the economic development of the nation. But suddenly, in the last decade or so, the oil industry eclipsed the economic importance of agriculture and its production has been declining. For instance, the country used to be one of the world's leading exporters of palm oil and groundnuts, but now the production of these crops cannot even satisfy local demand. Similarly, cocoa, an important foreign exchange earner in the 1960s, has dropped by nearly 70 per cent since 1971 (Akinola 1986:224). Despite this, the fact remains that Nigeria is an agricultural community:

> Nigeria may be known to the outside world as a major oil producer, but the mainstay of its economy is actually agriculture. Although petro-dollars account for 98 per cent of national revenue, the agriculture sector employs more than 70 per cent of our population. Close to three decades of oil wealth has not changed this equation. With this huge percentage of our people engaged in agriculture, you may however wonder why Nigeria has over the years come to rely heavily on food imports. A simple overview of agricultural practices in Africa's most

populous nation will not only explain this paradox; it will also provide the clue
as to why most people in our oil-rich nation live below the poverty line. Nigeria
has a total land area of 92.4 million hectares and 91 million of this is suitable for
cultivation but only about half of it is put to use for both staple and industrial
crops. And because they rely on age-old practices, a majority of the people engaged
in agriculture are grossly under-employed and indeed under-productive (Saraki
2006).

Kwara State, where the Shonga Farms are located, is one of the 36 states in
Nigeria. It was created from the former Northern Region on 27 May 1967 by
the Government of General Yakubu Gowon. It was initially named West Central
State with Ilorin as its capital. The name of the state was however later changed
to Kwara, a local name for the River Niger. Over the years the land mass of the
state, which currently stands at 32,500 km², has been eroded as a consequence of
numerous state creations. The state, which has a population of 2.5 million people,
comprises rainforests in the southern parts and wooded savannah covering the
larger part of the state. The soil is fertile and the entire state is well serviced by the
various tributaries of the River Niger. It is therefore not surprising that agriculture
has always been the main economic activity in the state (Kwara State n.d.).

The Shonga Farms project in Nigeria started with the inauguration of Governor
Bukola Saraki as the Executive Governor of Kwara State in 2003. In his inaugural
speech, he made it explicit that one of the priority areas of his administration
was agriculture and agro-allied industries (Saraki 2003). This was perhaps not
surprising given the fact that his state is endowed with plenty of arable land. At
the very beginning of his administration, the governor experimented with the
'Back to Land Programme'. Under this scheme, the government provided credit
facilities to farmers in the form of seedlings, fertilisers and land cultivation. This
however was not very successful:

> Ultimately, the results were not as good as hoped for from this pilot programme. It
> did serve however, to underline the need for a more radical solution to overcome
> years of inertia and bad habits ingrained in the local sector. ... What was required
> was to groom a whole new generation of farmers skilled both in the techniques of
> modern farming and modern financing, capable of managing a farm as a business
> with a clear focus on profitability (African Business Series n.d.: 1).

In 2005, the expulsion of white famers from Zimbabwe provided a unique
opportunity for the governor to bring in experienced farmers into the state. He
subsequently reached an agreement with thirteen such farmers from Zimbabwe. It
was reported that under the terms of the agreement, the Kwara State Government
was to make available the following to the participating foreign farmers:
- 1000 hectares of land to each of the Zimbabwean farmers;
- good road network to the farms;
- domestic water supply from a borehole per farm;

- adequate security at the farm house of each farmer;
- electricity supply to all the farms;
- a loan of $250,000 to each farmer by the Kwara State Government;
- a loan of $250,000 to each farmer by a bank chosen by the farmer with the Kwara State Government as the Guarantor;
- procurement of entry visas, work and resident permits for the farmers and their families and employees;
- conducive bungalow house of up to 2,500 square feet complete with requisite amenities such as 200 KVA generator, adequate storage sheds; fencing of the farmlands;
- finally, the Kwara State Government is to help such companies secure: pioneer status; exemption from tax liabilities; duty free concession; and other exemptions for financial advantage from the appropriate Government Authorities /Agencies.Elombah Perspective (2010).

The above terms could not have been further from the truth. According to one of the thirteen farmers:

> He commended Governor Saraki, who he said made it a lot easier for them to start farming in the state by giving them all they needed for take-off. He said the state did the roads, cleared the farmland and built accommodation for them. He said the state also gave them money to start business, but added that the money was given as loan. He said they would repay the loans they took from banks as soon as they started making profit. Asked when that would be, he said in the next few years' (Nairaland 2009).

The thirteen farmers were all required to register their individual farms. In order to operationalise the above project, Kwara State guaranteed loans. Kwazimbo Enterprises became the operational vehicle for all thirteen farms. Kwazimbo Enterprises, with the guarantee of the Kwara State Government through an Irrevocable Standing Payment Order (ISPO), subsequently borrowed N650 million from the Nigerian Agricultural Co-operative and Rural Development Bank (NACRDB). The ISPO was duly registered with the Federal Ministry of Finance. In a letter sent to the Kwara State governor, Bukola Saraki, on 7 April, 2006, the federal finance ministry stated its support for the loan. The letter, signed by a director of the ministry, J. I Zarewa, said

> I am directed to refer to your letter dated March 3, 2006 on the above subject matter and to convey the approval of the Honourable Minister of State for Finance to your request for deduction at source from the State's monthly Statutory Revenue Allocation, in respect of the N650,000,000.00 loan granted to Zimbabwean farmers by the Nigerian Agricultural, Cooperative and Rural Development Bank, in the event of default. Consequently, in the event of inability to liquidate as and when due, any installment of the loan outstanding to NACRDB would be

deducted at source and credited to NACRDB, Kaduna, Account No 1030290146 (Next Newspaper 2009).

With the farmers unable to repay the loan and the banks threatening to execute the ISPO, the Kwara State Government quickly arranged a refinancing of the entire project with five banks: Guarantee Trust Bank, United Bank for Africa, FinBank, Intercontinental Bank and Unity Bank. The consequence of this was that this private sector enterprise was converted into a Private Public Sector Partnership. The Shonga Farm Holdings Company Limited was incorporated as a Special Purpose Vehicle to facilitate the conversion(Tell Magazine2009). Under the new arrangement, the Shonga Farms Holdings owns 60 per cent of the shares in each of the thirteen farms with the Zimbabwean farmers owning 40 per cent. The Shonga Farm Holdings itself is jointly owned by the five banks and the Kwara State Government at the ratio of 75 per cent to 25 per cent. The implication of the above financial structure is that each of the thirteen farms are jointly owned by the five banks (45 %), Kwara State Government (15 %) and the Zimbabwean Farmers (40 %) (Business Day 2010).

The entire project is centred around three clusters of farming activities namely: mixed farming, poultry farming and dairy farming. Four of the thirteen individual farms are in the mixed farms cluster, while another four and five farms are in the poultry and dairy farms clusters respectively.

There are no doubt clear advantages in having these farms arranged in clusters within the same proximity. The four poultry farms for instance have come together to jointly establish an all encompassing integrated processing plant:

> All the poultry farms, in order to be self-sufficient, jointly floated a processing plant which also includes an abattoir and a feed mill. The feed mill is designed to produce feeds for the birds being raised on the poultry farms. Each of the farmers is also into extensive cropping of maize, soya bans, etc. which are largely processed into the animal feeds. The feed mill is also being equipped with machineries for the production of ancillary products such as extracted oil from soya beans. After the birds are raised to maturity stage, they are then processed through the processing plant for sale to buyers. Each poultry farmer is expected to have a capacity of 60,000 birds at a time at the first and second phases of the project (Nation Newspaper 2010).

Such arrangement will no doubt have great economies of scale advantages for the participating farmers. The project is however not just about the Zimbabwean farmers. The government has rightly identified that the success of the project will to a great extent depend on its ability to transfer farming skills and techniques to Nigerians. This should occur at two levels. First, with the employment of locals in such farms, technical know-how is bound to be transferred with time. Unfortunately, the agreement signed by the government with these foreign farmers contained little about limiting their ability to import labour.

A second mechanism for transferring skills is through formal education. In this direction, the state government has already established the Malete Youth Farm as the vehicle for this skills transfer:

> The Malete Youth Farm is the vehicle through which the expertise of the Zimbabwean farmers will be passed on to the new generation of Nigerian farmers. … The course is aimed at young men and women in their twenties interested in pursuing a career in commercial agriculture. They are trained in a wide range of agricultural practices from soil and animal husbandry, irrigation and maintenance of farm machinery, to crop harvesting and storage. They are also thought the necessary skills in labour management, finance and marketing to keep the farms running efficiently. If the youth farm at Malete represents the future of farming in Kwara State, then the Zimbabwean expats (sic) are the bridge. Indeed the farm at Malete was originally managed by one of the Zimbabweans, who are now happy to go by the name New Nigerian farmers. Their techniques and knowledge has laid the foundation for the agricultural revolution… How the rest of the structure emerges will depend on those 100 young men and women that pass through Malete each year (Africa Business Series n.d.: 2).

It has also further been noted that:

> Due to large rates of unemployment across the state, we decided to engage youth[s] in farming. We have trained over 300 young school leavers and graduates in all aspects of commercial farming. The Malete centre is responsible for the transfer of technology and the training of this new Generation of Successor Commercial Farmers. Upon completion of training, these youths are provided cleared land and start up funds to establish their own farms. They have not only become self-employed on their own farms, but they have become self-sufficient agents of change and employers of labour (Saraki n.d.).

Another potential advantage of the project is the huge reductions in the importation costs of agricultural products. In the context of the Shonga project, the dairy milk cluster makes this point well. Up until now, Nigerians have been fixated with unhealthy imported milk which currently costs the country US$1.5 billion annually. 'Over the years, due to neglect of agriculture, Nigeria has been a country of powdered milk. Powdered milk is not healthy. If you go to America, it is a small percentage. You don't even see powdered milk in Europe. You don't see powdered milk in developed countries. If you compare the two, powdered milk is not as healthy as fresh milk but because you cannot import fresh milk, that is why powdered milk became the alternative. There is a law in Saudi Arabia. The country is not allowed to consume more than 10 percent of powdered milk' (NBF News 2010). This is so because, although 6.6 million litres of milk daily are consumed in Nigeria, only 5 percent of it is produced locally. The Shonga Farms Dairy project, which is the largest dairy farm in Nigeria, is however beginning to have a little impact in changing this process (Saraki 2010). It has already set up the West African Milk Company, arguably the country's biggest importer of milk to begin to source some of its milk locally. The farm is capable of producing 60,000 litres of fresh milk per day (Vanguard Newspaper 2010). The impact and future potentials of the Shonga Farms has been summarised thus:

> Do you imagine what it would look like if we have about 3,000 of this Shonga Farm scattered all over Nigeria? Here alone, they employ about 50 people per farm. If you talk about 3,000, it means you are already giving 150[000] people employment. Then you have factories processing the milk and you need about 100 of such factories at full production. We have about 600 cows at Shonga, that means you need 300,000 to meet the total demand. You have got to feed these cows. They need maize, soyabeans. You need farmers to produce maize and soyabeans for the cows. You are going to give people employment.If we have the right policy, which we are beginning to have. We can [give] the importers a five-year plan. Today, we are only doing five percent locally produced milk, and 95 per cent imported. Next year, let's go to may be, 15 per cent, then following year 30 per cent. Hopefully, within the five-year period, we will achieve our target. Once you have that in place, and it is abiding, it does not mean government intervention. It is going to be a business on its own (NBF News 2010).

> Such arrangements will also have positive national health implications. WAMCO's strict safety checks and controls also helps ensure that farms like Shonga adhere to very strict health standards. It is unlikely that traditional sources of milk supply in Nigeria regularly meet such high standards (Nation Newspaper 2009).

Despite the potential benefits of this programme, problems remain. Arguably the greatest threat to the entire project is the secrecy surrounding the entire agreement of the farmers with Kwara State Government. A former Commissioner for Agriculture in Kwara State once described the project as a fraud *(Tell Magazine 2009)*. The financial relationship between the two parties has been of great concern to critics of the project. It has, for instance been alleged that the entire project was designed for the benefit of the governor and his family:

> The Sarakis gave the first set of fifteen of their Zimbabwean employees $250,000 USD each and each also obtained $250,000 USD from Intercontinental Bank PLC/Guaranty Trust Bank PLC with the Kwara State Govt as the Guarantor. Not done, Saraki also used their rubber stamp, the Kwara State House Of Assembly, to pass a 'RESOLUTION' using the state monthly allocations from the Federation Account to guarantee another loan of N650,000,000.00 obtained by the Zimbabwean farmers in the name of KWA Zimbo Enterprises Ltd from the Nigerian Agricultural Cooperative and Rural Development Bank (NACRDB). KWA Zimbo Enterprises Ltd defaulted in the repayment of the principal and interest and when the NACRDB wanted to enforce the Irrevocable Standing Payment Order (ISPO) given by the Kwara state govt on the state monthly allocations, the Sarakis arranged and obtained a re-finance Loan from the First Bank Plc in the sum of N650,000,000.00, this time in the name of Shonga Farm Holdings Nig. Ltd. (Elombah News 2010).

Furthermore, it has been noted that both the initial government loan and government guaranteed loan totalling US$500,000 per farmer were all supposed to be paid back according to the agreement with the farmers, over a period of three years. But four years after take-off, the farmers have not only failed to pay back the money given to them by the state, they are also asking for more.

The farmers have explicitly admitted their indebtedness to the banks and have blamed Nigerian bureaucracy and import delays for this. Mr. Retzcaff, one of the farmers asserted that they:

> had to contend with delays in importation of raw materials and some of their machinery, which made it difficult for them to meet set target. You know we have delays in importation of some raw materials and some machinery. Some of them are delayed at the Lagos port. This kind of thing increases the cost of operations but the banks don't want to hear this. Their concern is that we gave you what you asked for, so why are you asking for more instead of repaying us. We are just asking the banks to give us a little more money, just a fraction of what they've given us before (Tell Magazine2009).

The implication is that should the project collapse the entire loss will fall on the Government of Kwara State. The farmers simply do not have any financial commitment.

Aside from the above guarantees, the government has extensively supported the project. Some government support was clearly documented in the terms of the contract cited earlier. But it has also been reported that the Kwara State Government budgeted 2.65 billion naira for irrigation in the state. Of this 1.8 billion naira went to Shonga Farms alone. It was arguably because of this that the government, in its 2010 budget, asserted that 'We have also awarded the contract for the construction of Shonga irrigation project to ensure all-year farming and remove one of the major impediments that the project has confronted' (Saraki 2009).

Irrespective of such support, lack of transparency in the agreement between the farmers with the government, which may at least in part be responsible for the rising debts of the farms, may torpedo the entire project. While government has a duty to provide infrastructural support for foreign investors, its guarantee of private loans to such enterprises is questionable.

Lessons for Local and Foreign Interests in African Agriculture

It is clear that the most important lesson from the Shonga Farms project for addressing increasing foreign interests in African agriculture is the need for transparency in both operations and agreements. At the very least, this will help reduce both the perception and reality of government corruption to a minimum. While it is important that the government should provide infrastructural support for such foreign farmers, care must be taken to ensure that local farmers are also supported.

A second lesson is the need for African governments to be more careful in dealing with the expropriation of local lands by foreign farming businesses. Given the size of these farms and the relatively extensive government support they have been receiving, it is likely that the farms will grow even bigger. More foreign farms are already being attracted to the state. The implication is that the pressure on the domestic population to give up more land has only just begun. The land takeover experience for the Shonga Farms has been documented thus:

> In line with the agreement, Saraki forcefully took the lands of the people of Tsonga District of Edu L.G.A. in the name of acquisition. The attempts by the natives to resist the illegal and unlawful takeover of their lands for transfer to foreigners met brutal suppression [from] the law enforcement agents who were savagely and ruthlessly deployed by Saraki. In the process some of the natives were killed, many maimed or injured and many sent to prison. The acquisition and transfer of the natives' lands to the Zimbabweans was against the Land Use Act 1978 which allows government to take over lands from people only for Overriding Public Interest and Forbids government from taking from one person for the purpose of transferring same to another Nigerian talk less of foreigners (Elombah Perspective 2010).

Specifically, the greatest concern of locals is the belief that these new investments may jeopardise the livelihood of the local inhabitants who, aside from being among the poorest and most vulnerable Africans, depend solely on these lands as their source of livelihood. In order to put this point in context, it is important to appreciate the fact that the land given to the thirteen Zimbabwean farmers belonged to thirty-three local farming communities in the state and represented their major source of livelihood *(Tell Magazine 2009)*. The consequences of such land expropriations, especially when not thoroughly thought through are well known in history. The ugly experiences of Central American countries with the privatisation of indigenous lands should be avoided at all costs.

As more and more local lands are being excised for the benefits of big farms, such conflicts are bound to intensify. One way of mitigating them is to involve the local community in such investments. Their land should, for instance, be able to give such communities some shareholding in the company structure. Representation of the community on the board and management of such foreign farms will no doubt greatly reduce potential conflict. It will also help enshrine the ancillary benefits of the location of big farms for such communities. These include: employment opportunities and the provision of social facilities like schools, hospitals and drinking water. If need be, government should provide generous tax breaks in order to ensure that such facilities are provided.

Another issue concerns the transfer of skills. The conventional wisdom is that this should be immaterial in a labour intensive industry like agriculture. This is however not true under all circumstances. It is for instance well known that highly populated countries like China and India are constantly under pressure to employ their excess workforce abroad. There are now allegations that China, for instance, has even gone to the extent of exporting its prison labour to Africa. For foreign engagement in African agriculture to be sustainable in the long run, there is need for clear agreements with respect to allowable foreign labour within such businesses. This is even more the case given that most of the emerging foreign agricultural businesses in Africa, especially those from populous capitalist states like India, are likely to be family businesses. The tendency will therefore be for family members to control all the key sectors of such businesses. Under such a scenario, there will be very little room for skills transfer to locals. With respect to the Shonga Farms project, for instance, a pertinent question is: why were the Zimbabwean farmers unable to transfer skills to local Zimbabweans after several years of operating in that country? Although Zimbabwe benefited from their good agricultural practices, the post-expulsion performance of the agricultural sector in Zimbabwe is evidence that very little transfer of technology and skills took place throughout the period that the white farmers dominated the agriculture industry of that country. Addressing such matters is important if Africa is to benefit from the emerging foreign investments in its agriculture.

A final issue that needs to be agreed from the outset concerns the use of the locally cultivated agricultural products given that the incentives for the Zimbabwean farmers and for farmers from countries with food deficits at home like India, China and Saudi Arabia will be different. While the Zimbabwean farmers are essentially commercially independent companies, with little relationship with any home country, the same cannot be said of the farmers from many other countries operating in Africa. With strong support from their home governments, it should be expected that reducing their home country's food deficits would be one of the objectives of such farmers. Furthermore, the ban of some agricultural product exports in countries with an agriculture product deficit like India has created a market that can be satisfied by international farmers from such agricultural production deficit countries. At the time of writing there were some eighty Indian companies trying to get land in Ethiopia. All their products will be exported to India. A government ban on non-Basmati rice exports has also driven Indian companies to grow such rice in Africa in order to sell it overseas.

It is therefore unlikely that African food security would be the objective of the foreign farmers in Africa. There are great potentials for conflict in the near future. In order to minimise such conflicts, African countries need to engage proactively with the foreign farmers from the very beginning in order to establish clear agreements.

Conclusion

The Shonga Farms project in Kwara State Nigeria presents lessons for both foreign farmers and Africans in the plan to get such foreign farmers to assist with agricultural development in Africa. For such ventures to last, they must be mutually beneficial to all stakeholders. Specifically, the host communities should be compensated for lands taken from them. Arguably the best way of doing this is by making such communities stakeholders in the business ventures concerned. Rules regarding transfer of skills and foreign labour restrictions must be spelled out from the beginning. Notwithstanding, the government must grant generous concessions to these foreign farmers in order to help them overcome the extensive bottlenecks of doing business in Africa. However, under no circumstance should this include loan guarantees. Whatever concessions and agreements are arrived at must be transparent and publicly available for scrutiny and criticism. Similar concessions should also be available to local farmers. The current situation in Shonga Farms where the real interests and obligations of the state in such projects have been subject to wild degrees of speculation must be prevented. Such secrecy and lack of transparency may endanger the future of the Shonga Farms project especially now that the tenure of the Saraki administration has ended. Iyiola Oyedepo, a former commissioner for agriculture in the state, publicly asserted that the foreign farmers came to the state without any form of capital to set up a farm business in Shonga, stressing that the government had to do everything for the farmers, including paying compensation on land acquired by private businessmen... The whole arrangement is a fraud. If a foreign investor is coming to any country, they ought to come with their capital. This would include their resources and skill. But I know that these people did not come to Kwara with any capital. Anything you find in Shonga farm today was paid for by the state government. It is like Julius Berger coming to Nigeria and asking the federal government to buy all the equipment it would need! That is why I say the arrangement is a fraud, and the truth would become clear when Bukola Saraki vacates power.

Interestingly Saraki has now left office. Should the new administration in Kwara State have cause to unravel this entire project, the state and the local communities will no doubt be far worse off than they were before the project. The acrimony is unlikely to do future foreign investments in the state any good. African countries and foreign investors in the continent's agriculture can avoid such outcomes by making all the relevant agreements in their agricultural cooperation transparent from the beginning. If this can be done, African economies that depend mainly on agriculture will no doubt immensely benefit from such ventures because 'for the poorest people, GDP growth originating in agriculture is about four times more effective in raising incomes of extremely poor people than GDP growth originating outside the sector' (Webber and Labaste (2010:1).

References

African Business Series, n.d., *Kwara State: Nigeria's Garden of Eden*, <http://www.kwarastate.gov.ng/kreport.pdf>

African Development Bank, 1995, *Future Energy Requirements for Africa's Agriculture*, Rome: Food and Agriculture Organization of the United Nations.

Akinola, A., 1986, 'Prospects and Problems of Foreign Investments in Nigerian Agriculture', *Agricultural Administration and Extension* 24:223–32.

Castel, V. and A. Kamara, 2009, *Foreign Investments in Africa's Agricultural Land: Implications for Rural Sector Development and Poverty Reduction*, African Development Bank Development Research Brief Number 2 (April).

Elombah Perspective, 2010, 'The Grand Fraud Called Zimbabwean Farms/Investment Project in Kwara State Nigeria', <http://www.elombah.com/index.php?option=com_content&view=article&id=4414:the-grand-fraud-called-zimbabwean-farmsinvestment-project-in-kwara-stat&catid=48:world-news&Itemid=69>

Food and Agricultural Organization, 2008, *Current World Fertilizer Trends and Outlook 2011/12*, Rome: Food and Agriculture Organization of the United Nations.

Food and Agricultural Organization, 2010, *Climate Change Implications for Food Security and Natural Resource Management in Africa*, Twenty Sixth Regional Conference for Africa (Luanda, Angola, 3–7 May 2010).

Goswami, R., 2010, *African Landrush*, <http://farmlandgrab.org/11985>

Huggins, C., 2010, 'The Commercial 'Land Rush' – Human Rights-based Versus Corporate Social Responsibility Models', < http://farmlandgrab.org/13227>

India-Africa Forum Summit, 2008, *Africa India Framework for Cooperation*, New Delhi: 8–9 April.

Kwara State, n.d., *About Kwara State*, < http://www.kwarastate.gov.ng/about-kwara-state.html>

Nairaland, 2009, *The Delayed Harvest in Kwara*, <http://www.nairaland.com/nigeria/topic-251408.0.html>

Otte, M. and P. Chilonda, 2002, *Cattle and Small Ruminant Production Systems in Sub-Saharan Africa: A Systematic Review*, Rome: Food and Agricultural Organization of the United Nations.

Pelum Association and Practical Action, 2005, *The Crisis in African Agriculture: A More Effective Role for EC Aid?*, accessed at <www.africanvoices.org.uk>

Reij, C. and E. Smaling, 2008, 'Analyzing Successes in Agriculture and Land Management in Sub-Saharan Africa: Is Macro-Level Gloom obscuring Micro-Level Change?', *Land Use Policy* 25: 410–20.

Saraki, A., 2003, Inaugural Speech, 29 May.

Saraki, A., 2006, Governor Bukola Saraki's Address at the 2006 World AG Expo.

Saraki, A., 2008, Address by His Excellency, Dr. Abubakar Bukola Saraki the Executive Governor of Kwara State, on the Occasion of the launching of Kwara State Association of Nigeria, United Kingdom Branch, on Saturday July 26.

Saraki, A., 2009, The 2010 Budget Speech delivered to the Kwara State house of Assembly by His Excellency Dr. Abubakar Bukola Saraki, the Executive Governor of Kwara State on Tuesday 22 December.

Saraki, A., 2010, Address delivered by H.E. Dr. Abubakar Bukola Saraki, Executive Governor of Kwara State, Nigeria KSANG 2010 Convention, Seattle, United States of America, July 4th.

Saraki, A., n.d. My Biography: Abubakar Bukola Saraki, <http://www.abubakarbukolasaraki.com/my-biography>

Silver-Greenberg, J., 2009, 'Agribusiness and Global Investors are Scooping up Farmland: Are Corporate Farmers the New Colonialists?', *Business Week*, 25 November.

Toulmin, C., 2008, 'Securing Land and Property Rights in Sub-Saharan Africa: the Role of Local Institutions', *Land Use Policy* 26:10–19.

Vashisht, D., 2010, *India's Punjabi Farmers Investigate Farming in Africa, African Agriculture: News, Views about Agriculture in Africa and Beyond*, <http://www.africanagricultureblog.com/2010/07/indias-punjabi-farmers-investigate.html>

Von Braun, J., 2008, 'Food and Financial Crises: Implications for Agriculture and the Poor', Brief prepared for the CGIAR annual general meeting Maputo, Mozambique, December, <http://www.ifpri.org/PUBS/agm08/jvb/jvbagm2008.pdf>

Webber, C. and P. Labaste, 2010, *Building Competitiveness in Africa's Agriculture: A Guide to Value Chain Concepts and Applications*, Washington, DC: World Bank.

7

Land Grab in Kenya: Risks and Opportunities

Samwel Ong'wen Okuro

Introduction

Agriculture has direct linkage to food security, while mining and tourism are indirectly linked to food security through their competing demands for land use and their potential to supply incomes for food consumption. Agriculture supports more than 70 per cent of Africa's population. The sector employs the largest number of workers and generates a significant share of GDP in most countries. The main purposes of agricultural production are to meet food security needs, supply inputs to the agricultural industry and earn much needed foreign exchange (ECA 2004). In Africa, land is regarded not simply as an economic or environmental asset, but as a social, cultural and ontological resource. Land remains an important factor in the construction of social identity, the organisation of religious life and the production and reproduction of culture. The link across generations is ultimately defined by the complement of land resources which families, lineages and communities share and control.

In Kenya, agriculture remains the backbone of the economy contributing approximately 25 per cent of the GDP and employing about 75 per cent of the labour force (Alila and Atieno 2006). Over 80 per cent of the Kenyan population live in rural areas and derive their livelihoods directly or indirectly from agriculture. Small-scale farmers, popularly referred to as smallholdings, are particularly important; they are estimated to employ 60 per cent of the labour force, produce about 70 per cent of the marketed output and most of their own food (Nyikal 2007). The development of smallholder agriculture is therefore interlinked with poverty reduction since most vulnerable groups like the pastoralists, the landless and subsistence farmers depend on agriculture as their main source of livelihoods.

However, in the past decade or so, the convergence of global crises in food, energy, finance and the environment has driven a dramatic revaluation of land ownership. Powerful transnational and national economic actors from corporations to national governments and private equity funds have searched for 'empty' land often in distant countries that can serve as sites for fuel and food production in the event of future price spikes. This is occurring globally, but there is a clear North-South dynamic that echoes the land grabs that underwrote colonialism and imperialism. In addition, there is South-South dynamic, with economically powerful non-northern countries such as Brazil and Qatar getting significantly involved. The land, water and labour of the global South are increasingly being perceived as sources of alternative energy production (primarily biofuels), food crops, mineral deposits (new and old), and reservoirs for environmental services (Saturnino et al. 2011: 209). The pace and the extent of these land deals has been rapid and widespread (GRAIN 2008). In these large scale land acquisitions, sub-Saharan Africa has become an attractive destination (Cotula et al. 2009), due to the perception that the continent contains large amounts of apparently vacant farmland and a regime of weak land rights protection.

Nowadays farmland grabs are moving fast, contracts are being signed, bulldozers are hitting the ground, land is being aggressively fenced off and local people are being evicted from their territories with devastating consequences. As expected these new land deals have increased competition over land access and use particularly between smallholder agricultural producers and the new corporates. This new and direct competition with local users for land, which previously mainly sustained local livelihoods, has led several non-governmental organisations and media to label the land deals as 'land grabs' in order to emphasise the fact that foreign investors are 'stealing' the land from the local poor people (Friis and Anette 2010:6). It is important to note that the World Bank has instead referred to these land deals as agricultural investment given their perceived benefits (World Bank 2010). Generally, land grabs refer to the purchase, concession or lease of vast tracks of land by wealthier food insecure nations and private investors from mostly poor developing countries on a long term basis in order to produce food crops and biofuels for export.

These land transactions are highly opaque and a few details have been made public. What is known, particularly about the scale of these activities, is however quite striking. The International Food Policy Research Institute estimated that 15 to 20 million hectares of farm land have been subject to negotiations or transactions over the last few years (Kugelman 2009). A UN-FAO study in 2009 looked at five sub-Saharan countries: Ethiopia, Ghana, Madagascar, Mali and Sudan and found documented evidence that 2.4 million hectares of land had been transferred in land deals since 2004. In Congo Brazzaville, President Sassou-Nguesso ceded 10 million hectares of fertile land to South African farmers to grow stable food crops for export alongside 70,000 hectares granted to an Italian oil company to plant oil palm monoculture plantations for agro-fuel production. One of the largest and the most notorious deals is one that ultimately collapsed: an arrangement that would have given the South Korean firm Daewoo a 99-year lease to grow corn and other crops on 1.3 million hectares of farmland in Madagascar, half of that country's total arable land.

Generally, the most common characterisation of this trend portrays capital rich Arab Gulf states and the prosperous countries of East Asia preying on the world's farmland. By the end of 2008, China, South Korea, the United Arab Emirates, Japan, and Saudi Arabia controlled over 7.6 million cultivable hectares overseas: more than five times the usable agricultural surface of Belgium. There is also European Union involvement in land grabs in Africa with five European countries (Italy, Norway, Germany, Denmark and the United Kingdom) leading the group. While these investments tend to flow from wealthier to poorer countries, the pattern is no means limited to North–South; a number of developing countries are also actively investing in their regions and across the globe. For example, India has soyabean and flower projects in Brazil and Kenya respectively.

Table 7.1: Examples of Media Reports on Overseas Land Investments 2006–09

Country investor	Country target	Plot size (ha)	Status	Source of information
Bahrain	Philippines	10,000	deal signed	Bahrain New Agency February, 2009
China	Philippines	1,240,000	deal signed	The Inquirer, January 2009
Jordan	Sudan	25,000	deal signed	Jordan Times, November 2008
Libya	Ukraine	250,000	deal signed	The Guardian, November 2008
Qatar	Kenya	40,000	deal signed	The Daily Nation January 2009
Saudi Arabia	Tanzania	500,000	deal signed	Reuters Africa April 2009
South Korea	Sudan	690,000	deal signed	Korea Times June, 2008
United Arab Emirates	Pakistan	324,000	under implementation	The Economist, May 2008

Source: International Food Policy Research Institute.

While many of these deals are for food cultivation, there is a growing interest in growing crops for agro-fuels, particularly to supply EU markets. Such crops include sugar cane, sweet sorghum, maize, castor oil, oil palm, jatropha and cassava. It has been estimated that of the land deals in Africa 30 per cent have been allocated to food crops, 21 per cent to cash crops, and 21 per cent to biofuels, with the rest distributed among conservation or game reserves, livestock and plantation forestry (Deininger 2011: 223). These figures may also differ as qualitative case studies undertaken in Tanzania and Mozambique tend to suggest that these two countries have enthusiastically embraced biofuel production (Cotula et al. 2009). The scale of investor ambition is huge, with a medium project size of 40,000 hectares, and a quarter of all projects involving more than 200,000 hectares. Some of the African countries involved in these deals include Ethiopia, Madagascar, Sudan, Tanzania, Mali, Mozambique, Uganda, DRC, Nigeria, Zambia, Ghana, Malawi, Senegal, Kenya, Liberia, the Republic of Congo, Angola, Cameroon, Egypt, Zimbabwe, Algeria, Libya, Morocco, Mauritania, Namibia, Niger and Zanzibar, which make up about half the countries on the continent. The land lease or land purchase agreements raise a number of troubling issues and questions concerning local food security. Around the world, there have been strong reactions from states, corporations and civil society groups. Some see land grabs as a major threat to the lives and livelihoods of the rural poor, and so oppose such commercial land deals. Others see economic opportunity for the rural poor, although they are wary of corruption and negative consequences, and so call for improving land market governance. Between these two positions are a range of intermediate views offered by other groups (Saturnino et al. 2011; Borras 2010).

Proponents of land acquisitions list possible benefits for the rural poor, including the creation of a potentially significant number of farm and off-farm jobs, development of rural infrastructure, and improvements in anti-poverty measures such as the construction of schools and health facilities. Other positive effects may include resources for new agricultural technologies and practices, as well as future global price stability and increased production of food crops that could supply local and national consumers in addition to overseas consumers. Others see these opportunities as reflecting unwarranted optimism, emphasising instead the threats that land acquisition presents to people's livelihoods and ecological sustainability (IFPRI 2009:2). The radical changes these deals are likely to bring to both modes of production and agriculture supply chains mean they may be yet another nail in the coffin of smallholder agricultural producers. Moreover, these deals may not be made on equal terms between the investor and the local communities. The bargaining power in negotiating these agreements is always on the side of the foreign firm especially when its aspirations are supported by the host state or local elites. The smallholders who are being displaced from their land cannot effectively negotiate terms favourable to them when dealing with such powerful national and international actors, nor can they enforce agreements if the foreign investor fails to provide promised jobs or local facilities (IFPRI 2009:2).

Recent debates on land grab in sub-Saharan Africa have been anchored on how to ensure a win-win situation for both investors and local communities. A dual approach has been proposed to help address the threats and tap the opportunities related to land grabs. First the threats need to be controlled through a code of conduct for both the investor and the host government. Second, opportunities or what the World Bank calls 'yield gaps' need to be facilitated by appropriate policies in the countries which are targets of these land grabs (IFPRI 2009). The World Bank has been a leader in this initiative by providing seven principles for responsible agricultural investment, insisting that new agricultural investment recognises and respects existing rights to land and natural resources, as well as generating desirable social and distributional impacts. However, these principles have been critiqued by many commentators, including civil society groups, who argue that 'the set of principles, however, are not embedded in a political analysis of how they might actually work in practice... it does not address the fundamentally important question of who wins, who loses, and why, and what are the social, political and ecological drivers and consequences of these processes?' (Saturnino et al. 2011:210). The World Bank itself could not find any convincing examples of 'wins' for poor communities or countries, only a long list of losses. With all the talk of 'win-win' outcomes ringing hollow against the reality of impacts of these deals on local communities, smallholder agricultural producers and workers, some governments, such as Argentina, Brazil and New Zealand, are responding with promises of legislation to cap or discipline foreigners' abilities to acquire domestic farmland. Others, such as Cambodia, Ethiopia and Ghana are using both the law and brute force to suppress local contestation. In the run-up to the 2012 elections in Mali, the opposition Party for National Renewal challenged President Touré to disclose all details of land leases amounting to several hundred thousands of irrigated hectares granted in the Office du Niger. In Sudan, the most 'land grabbed' country in Africa, villagers are now rising up against the government in Khartoum for having seized their lands. There are some who believe that promoting transparency in land acquisition deals can somehow lead to 'win-win' outcomes. However, even if done 'transparently' the transfer of large tracts of land, forests, coastal areas and water sources to investors is still going to deprive smallholder farmers, pastoralists, fishing and other local communities of crucial, life sustaining resources for generations to come. In many countries, there is an urgent need to strengthen systems that protect the land tenure of peasants and small-scale food producers, and many social movements have been fighting for recognition of their rights to land for many years.

Drivers of Large Scale Land Acquisitions in Africa

While it is acceptable that a thorough theoretical understanding of the motives behind the rampant land grabs and land changes in Africa are still to be established (Lambin and Geist 2006; Cecilie and Anette 2010), this chapteris guided by global and empirically established trends. It raises four key questions in agrarian political economy: who owns what, who does what, who gets what, and what do they do with the surplus wealth created?

Generally, motives behind the rampant land acquisition across Africa are diverse (Cotula et al. 2009; Shepard and Mittal 2009). Studies such as Cotula et al. (2009) and World Bank (2010) seem to identify the following interrelated factors as the main drivers of land grabs particularly in Africa: food security, biofuels, non-food agricultural commodities, private sector expected returns, emerging carbon markets, enhanced agricultural technology, availability of under-utilised farmland, and host country incentives. Historically, today's thirst for land looks like there-appearance – in a new form – of a phenomenon that occurred in Africa in the 19th century: when European colonialism gobbled up farmland in Africa under the pretext that Africa had cheap, idle and under-utilised land at the disposition of prospective European investors. The colonisers appropriated much of the most fertile land for themselves, pushing local peoples onto marginal land for their own production. However, current overseas land investments differ from their predecessors in significant ways. Their scale is much larger; they emphasise staples instead of cash crops; they are concluded on the basis of agreements instead of through the barrel of a gun; and they are spearheaded by more government led investment than in the past (Shepard and Mittal 2009). Nevertheless, beneath this rush is the historical warped notion of Africa having under-utilised land up for grabs. In explaining their interest in Africa, the manager of a major private investment fund involved with land acquisition was quoted as saying that 'Africa has most of the underutilized fertile land in the world' (Jung-a et al. 2008). The chief executive of another fund emphasised that 'land values are very, very inexpensive' (Henriques 2008). As observed by Cotula et al. (2009: 62) empirical data on land availability in Africa remains limited – as even where land is under-utilised and seems abundant, it is still likely to be claimed by somebody. In other words, concepts such as available, idle, waste land used to justify land allocation to investors need critical analysis. IFPRI (2009) warns that in most instances there is some form of land use, often by the poor for grazing animals and gathering fuel wood or medicinal plants. These uses tend to be undervalued in official assessments because their products are not marketed but they can provide valuable livelihood sources to the poor. Large scale land acquisition may further jeopardise the welfare of the poor by depriving them of the safety net function that this type of land and water use fulfils. It can therefore be concluded that land grabs are driven not by the availability of under-utilised land in sub-Saharan Africa but by the fact that in Africa these investors can easily exploit corrupt or highly indebted governments with little ability to regulate transactions or prevent buyers from targeting the poorest rural communities or expelling people with non-traditional land titles from their lands (World Bank 2010).

While it cannot be denied that the food price crises of 2007–08 had a significant impact on the world food system forcing a number of countries to rethink their food security by acquisition of farmland in developing countries, it is equally evident that increased pressures on natural resources, water scarcity, export restrictions imposed by major producers when food prices were high, and growing distrust in the functioning of regional and global markets have pushed countries which are short of land and water to find alternative means of producing food for their hungry and swelling populations (IFPRI 2009). There are a number of factors threatening food supply and security globally (Shepard and Mittal 2009). These include skyrocketing food prices in 2008 that increased import bills and inflation rates; harsh and unpredictable climatic conditions; poor soils and scarce land and water in many areas; combined with economic and demographic growth. These factors have led many nations, particularly in the Middle East and Asia to re-examine domestic food security policies. For example, while cereal agriculture in the Gulf countries is in irreversible decline, the population of the region will double from 30 million in 2000 to nearly 60 million by 2030. Food inflation has been a serious issue in several Gulf states, with higher food prices driving inflation in the wider economy. These price rises are particularly problematic in relation to the large migrant blue-collar workforce in the smaller Gulf states and concerns about social unrest. Consequently, many governments in this region are looking to stabilise food supplies by acquiring foreign lands for food production in the hopes of averting domestic social unrest and political instability over food price and supply. These states have moved quickly to extend control over food producing lands abroad. Qatar, with only 1 per cent of its land suitable for farming, has purchased 40,000 hectares in Kenya for crop production and recently acquired holdings in Vietnam and Cambodia for rice production, and in Sudan for oils, wheat and corn production. Other countries such as United Arab Emirates, China, Japan, and South Korea are also seeking to acquire land as part of a long term strategy for food security (Shepard and Mittal 2009).

The surging demand for agro-fuels and access to new sources of raw materials for manufacturing goods is also driving land purchases. The term agro-fuels describes liquid fuels derived from food and oil crops produced in large-scale plantations styled as industrial production systems. These agro-fuels are blended with petrol and diesel for use primarily as transport fuel. Bio-fuels, on the other hand, refer to the small-scale use of local biomass for fuel. The demand for agro-fuels has increased rapidly over the past several years as oil dependent countries establish ambitious targets for agro-fuel production and for incorporating biodiesel and bioethanol with traditional transport fuels. Often, these are pursued to ensure energy security, rural development and export development (Dufey et al. 2007). Presently, European companies appear to dominate land acquisition for agro-fuels in Africa. The UK company Sun Biofuels has acquired land in Ethiopia, Tanzania and Mozambique to grow jetropha while the UK based CAMS Group bought about 45,000 hectares in Tanzania to produce ethanol from sweet sorghum. The German company Flora Eco has spent US$ 77 million in land purchases in Ethiopia for bio-fuel production using contract farming. In the US, Renewable Fuel Standard aimed to increase ethanol use by 3.5 billion gallons between 2005 and 2012, and the European Union aims to increase the proportion of biofuels used in land transport to 10 per cent by 2020. With these and other impetuses, the use and production of biofuels has skyrocketed over the past several years such that the quantity of US corn used to produce ethanol increased by 53 million metric tons between 2001 and 2007.

Attracted by this huge demand and market, private and government sponsored investors, mainly from OECD member countries, are targeting vast tracks of land to produce crops for agro-fuels in developing countries which generally have comparative advantage in such production due to low labour and land costs and, in some cases, land availability. To gain acceptance, these companies emphasise the environmental and social benefits of their business: working with the local community, creating employment, and helping to develop the local economy. The totality of such claims has given birth to what has commonly been labelled 'the biofuels complex' (Saturnino et al. 2011:576), in which the recent expansion of industrial biofuels expresses several trends in global political economy. These include the global commodification of time honoured local energy supplements and the consolidation of corporate power in the energy and agribusiness sector. The biofuels revolution responds to an assumed 'energy crisis' as the cost of capital input (production, processing and transport) rises in an age of peaking oil supplies. In addition, a desire to reduce dependence on Middle Eastern oil drives governments to develop an industrial biofuels complex which delivers energy security. At the same time, biofuels represent a new profitability frontier for agribusiness and energy sectors beset with declining productivity and/or rising costs (Magdoff 2008; McMichael 2009; Houtart 2010; McMichael 2010). Biofuels are also presented as a route to reducing or transforming energy use patterns in ways that can ameliorate environmental concerns without affecting economic growth (Saturnino et al. 2011:576). It is however important to point out that existing studies have shown that biofuels production has the potential to undermine food production (Weis 2010) and accelerate deforestation trends (Gouverneur 2009).

While securing food supply is seen as the dominant driver of large scale land acquisition in Africa, the role of private investors is also critical. The hunger of investors who view farmland as investment poised to produce significant returns is also fuelling the land grab. Many wealthy investors have recently turned their attention to agricultural acquisitions. These groups include Morgan Stanley, Goldman Sachs, Black Riock Inc, Qudra Abu Dhabi based Investment Company, a Swedish Investment Group, and a British Investment Group among others. These investors anticipate benefiting from soft commodity markets through investment in land, farming and associated activities. The principal actor facilitating these land deals is the International Financial Corporation (IFC), the private sector arm of the World Bank Group, which finances private investment in the developing world by advising governments and businesses and encouraging a 'business enabling environment' in developing countries. The IFC is thus the leading promoter of land policy reforms in developing countries to remove red tape that could inhibit foreign direct investment. In addition, the IFC has been working with developing countries to change land laws to increase the permissible quantity of land under foreign ownership and develop simple and transparent procedures for investors to acquire and secure property rights at a reasonable costs. The IFC and some donor governments have also convinced developing countries to view foreign investment as capable of bringing new technologies, developing productive potential, facilitating infrastructure developments, and creating employment and supply of food to local markets (Cotula et al. 2009). In other words, that foreign investment in land can be a win-win situation for both the investor and receiving host country.

The Case of Kenya

It is important to point out from the onset that land grabs are relatively recent phenomena. Details about the status of the land deals, size of land purchased or leased, and amounts invested are often murky and difficult to establish. Similarly, there are still relatively few scientific studies and reports about the magnitude and consequences of the deals in Africa. The deals have, however, gained significant attention in international media and NGOs around the world, which remain the main source of information on the land deals so far (Smaller and Mann 2009). The few serious studies which have been undertaken seem to conclude that unequal power relations in the land acquisition deals have the potential of putting the livelihoods of the poor at risk. Land grabbing forecloses vast stretches of lands and ecosystems for current and future use by peasants, indigenous peoples, fishing communities and nomads, thus seriously jeopardising their rights to food and livelihood security. It captures whatever water resources exist on, below and around these lands, resulting in the de facto privatisation of water.

It has also emerged that the violation of international human rights law is an intrinsic part of land grabbing through forced evictions, the silencing (and worse) of critics, the introduction of non-sustainable models of land use and agriculture that destroy natural environments and deplete natural resources, the blatant denial of information, and the prevention of meaningful local participation in political decisions that affect people's lives. Moreover, giving land away to investors will result in a type of farming that will have much less powerful poverty-reducing impacts than if access to land and water were improved for the local farming communities. It directs agriculture towards crops for export markets, increasing the vulnerability to price shocks of the target countries. Even where titling schemes seek to protect land users from eviction, land grabbing accelerates the development of a market for land rights with potentially destructive effects on livelihoods. This chapter further considers the cases on Dominion Farms Limited, the Qatar Tana River Delta, and the Karuturi Global deals to assess and comment on these observations.

While land grab is a recent phenomenon, in Kenya it can be traced to the period of British colonialism. It resurfaced recently in 2004 when Dominion Farms Limited, a subsidiary of Dominion Group of Companies based in the US, was leased about 2,300 hectares within the fertile River Yala Swamp at the ludicrously cheap rate of €12,000 a year to produce rice, vegetables and fish. In addition, it said it would rehabilitate at least one school and one health facility in each of the Siaya and Bondo districts. The land in question was trust land under the custody of Bondo and Siaya county councils. However, the community benefited from the resource base of this area through a combination of economic activities such as extensive small-scale farming, livestock keeping, and hunting of wild animals, collection of firewood, papyrus reeds, herbal plants, and sisal (Food First Information and Action Network 2011). The Yala swamp thus supported several communities that utilise the wetland's natural resources to provide for their families and secure their livelihoods. The issue came to media attention when the company went against the memorandum of understanding signed between the firm, the local council and the Ministry of Lands, stipulating that the company would confine itself to the 2,300 hectares, by expanding its activities and reportedly using more than 65 per cent of the swamp's total area to conduct agricultural activities.

On 10 May 2011, the Food First Information and Action Network held a symposium in which several impacts of the project on community livelihoods were identified. According to community representatives, the deal, which granted the company a 25-year lease, has seen community land submerged by water due to the hydro-electric generation plant constructed by the company on the River Yala. This has resulted in people's homes and farms being flooded, and in the loss livestock. The representatives alleged that over 500 families are facing forced eviction by the company, which sought to expand its activities. The case of Erastas Dildo, a 33 year-old from Yala River Swamp, is an example of how these large scale land acquisitions operate. Dildo is a small scale farmer who owns three hectares of land. It is fertile land, where the corn turns bright green and grows two metres tall, where the cattle are as fat as hippos and the tomato plants bend under the weight of their tomatoes. There are three small brick houses on the property. Erastas harvests his corn twice a year, and vegetables and tomatoes grow all year-round. One hectare produces €3,600 worth of corn a year, a lot of money by Kenyan standards. Things changed when Erastas was contacted by Dominion Farms. Dominion, which planned to grow rice, vegetables and corn on the land, wanted to include Erastas Dildo's three hectares in its venture. The Dominion representatives offered to pay him about 10 cents per square metre. Erastas turned them down, and now they are making life difficult for the farmer.

Their most effective weapon is a dam they have built. When Erastas tried to harvest his corn last year, it was under water. The Dominion were manipulating water levels to get rid of Erastas. When that did not work, Dominion sent in bulldozers, thugs and sometimes even the police (Business Week 2009).

Gondi Olima, a worker with Friends of Yala Swamp, observed that under its contract, Dominion agreed to renovate at least one school and one medical facility in each of the two local districts. They drove out 400 families instead. According to Olima, 'at first the Dominion venture created new jobs, as day labourers were hired to clear the site with machetes, but then the company brought in more and more equipment...now they have so many machines that workers are no longer needed' (Business Week 2009). Land grabs thus have the potential to dispossess small scale farmers on a large scale because more than 60 per cent of the population in Kenya are small farmers. Large-scale land acquisition could be disastrous for the population. Those who lose their fields lose everything.

In the Siaya District of Kenya, families say Dominion has not offered as many jobs as it claimed in the six years since it arrived. Villagers accuse it of polluting water and sickening farm animals (Business Week 2009). Charles Onyango Apiyo, aged thirty-nine, raises cattle in Siaya. A year ago, he says, ten of his cows wandered onto Dominion property. The entire herd of 150 was confiscated by company employees and taken to a police station. The cattle were held for almost two weeks, during which time twenty died. More perished from dehydration on the trek back to his land. However, Dominion Farms denied the farmers' accusations and points out that it had already built eight classrooms, donated gateposts and awarded educational scholarships to sixteen children, as well as providing beds and electricity for a hospital ward. Dominion President Calvin Burgess boasts that his company provides employment for hundreds of local residents and has reduced instances of malaria. In addition, Dominion plans to sell rice to African governments and export farm-raised fish to Europe (Business Week 2009).

A similar scenario emerged in 2008 when the president announced that the Qatar government would be given 40,000 hectares in the Tana River Delta in return for building a modern US$2.4 billion port in Lamu. The delta is one of Kenya's last wildernesses. One of the most important bird habitats in Africa is the flood plain of the river Tana, which flows 1,014 kilometres from Mount Kenya to the Indian Ocean. The Tana River Basin encompasses 126,028 km2 in the eastern part of Kenya, an area currently suffering from extreme drought. It supports a population of approximately 15 million people, with 10 million living within the basin. In the lower catchment, irrigated agriculture is practised on the river's riparian land. Flood recession farming is practised on the rivers flood plains. The Tana Delta is a key ecological resource. It is a source of fish for the local communities, a lifeline for the coastal agricultural community and a source of pasture for the pastoralists during the dry seasons. It is also an important habitat for some endangered species of birds, monkeys and fish.

On signing the land deal, the Kenya government argued that the second port was to complement Mombasa, which serves as a gateway for goods bound for Uganda and Rwanda and is struggling to cope with the large volumes of cargo. By building docks in Lamu, Kenya hopes to open a new trade corridor that will give landlocked Ethiopia and the autonomous region of South Sudan access to the Indian Ocean. Qatar was to use the land to grow vegetables and fruits. In addition to Qatar, the government also gave Kenya owned Mumias Sugar Company and another foreign company about 66,000 hectares for biofuels. Here again, the subsistence agricultural communities were forcefully removed from the Tana Delta to pave way for the production of vegetables, fruits, sugarcane and Jetropher. The Tana Delta Qatar project is not only pushing people off plots they have farmed for generations, stealing their water resources and raising ethnic tensions that many fear will escalate into war, but also destroying a unique wetland habitat that is home to hundreds of rare and spectacular birds.

The extent of the destruction of region's biodiversity was captured by Francis Kagema of Nature Kenya as follows: 'No proper research has been done into what wildlife is here, and now the habitat is disappearing. There is no evidence of what we are losing... You don't need to be a scientist to see the situation here is critical and the land grab is terrible. This is supposed to be the wet season. The elephants have already gone, the hippos are going, birds are less and less.' Similar observations were made by Gamba Manyatta arguing that 'This is not a good place. Children have died, we have typhoid and malaria now. We were healthy before and our children went to school. This river is the drainage for pesticides from all the big farms. The proper river has been diverted to irrigate them and now we just get their poison. When we were evicted they showed us the maps, and we saw many more villages who don't yet know they are to be evicted too. Where will they all go?' (Guardian 2011).

These testimonies suggest that the land grab projects are likely to devastate the social fabric and livelihoods of communities in the Delta, and destroy unique wetland and floodplain ecosystems.

In May and August/September 2009 FIAN International investigated four cases of land grabbing in Kenya and Mozambique in detail and on the spot. The Kenyan investigation focused on the Yala Swamp and Tana River Delta. In all the cases, the FIAN report noted that '[l]and grabbing denies land for local communities, destroys livelihoods, reduces the political space for peasant oriented agricultural policies and distorts markets towards increasingly concentrated agribusiness interests and global trade, rather than promoting sustainable peasant agriculture for local and national markets and for future generations'. According to Tom Odenda, the co-ordinator of the Kenya Land Alliance, 'the evidence shows that there is no greater engine for driving growth and reducing poverty and hunger than investing in agriculture but it must ensure that people can access the food that is produced. What we are seeing is that the food is mainly for export. The state has become the agent of land lease and that is why the new constitution emphasises that the land belongs to Kenyans ...we have no problem if the food was being produced for Kenya. Isn't it the height of recklessness in leadership for the government to give out land to Qatar when Kenya is food insecure and we are literally being fed? Where is the logic?' (News from Africa 2011).

Behind the scenes, the Indian government has been busy prioritising agriculture as a key area of engagement with Africa. Indeed, India is using all sorts of strategies to encourage Indian companies to buy mega farms in Africa to meet food shortages in India. Consequently, Indian firms have invested around US$3 billion in Ethiopia, Kenya, Mozambique, Senegal and Madagascar to produce a wide variety of food crops (rice, sugar cane, maize and lentils)for their home market and also crops used to produce biofuel. The Indian government is actively encouraging investments in land acquisition programmes by providing cheap lines of credit to the governments of Ethiopia, Senegal, Kenya, Madagascar and Mozambique. Some of India's leading companies in land grab include Varun, Ruchi and Karuturi.

Presently, the biggest Indian company with significant investment in Kenya is a Bangalore-based company, Karuturi Global, which bought farm land in Kenya in 2007 to grow sugar cane, oil palm, rice and vegetables. Karuturi Global is currently among the leading producer of floriculture products in Kenya. The company is doing well in Kenya and Ethiopia because the two countries have duty free export status into the EU while freight costs are lower by over 25 per cent due to lower taxation. The labour costs are similar to in India. Today, the company produces 555 metre stems per year, more than 95 per cent of which are grown in Kenya and Ethiopia and are exported globally. It also plans to increase production of sorghum, sugar cane and palm oil – African expansion is now right at the centre of Karuturi's long-term growth, which will see the company become a billion dollar multinational agricultural business by the middle of the next decade.

To integrate itself into Naivasha, the company started investments in 'social infrastructure'. At any one time the firm employs between 4,000 and 5,000 workers, depending on seasonal requirements. Karuturi funds schooling for the children of its staff, through nursery, primary and secondary levels, and has expanded an existing health centre into a fully-equipped hospital. Karuturi Sports, a Kenyan Premier League football team, plays on a watered pitch attached to the company's headquarters.

Underneath this seemingly win-win situation, the presence of Karuturi Global in Naivasha has led to serious environmental concerns around Lake Naivasha. These include loss of water, unsustainable increases in population, and the over-use of pesticides and fertilisers. These have been compounded by poor labour practices: stories abound of flower farm workers sufferings from chemical exposure and enduring long hours of low wages in the farm fields and processing facilities. Recently, hundreds of flower workers at a Naivasha flower farm protested against low wages and poor working conditions, as labour unrest continued in the horticulture sector. The 800 workers from Vegpro farm accused the management of being insensitive to their plight. Workers at two other flower farms, Karuturi and Aquilla, have also protested at what they termed poor terms of employment. According to one of the workers, they are earning about US$1.2 a day, which is substantially below what is stipulated by the labour regulations.

Conclusion

While the magnitude and effects of land grabs in Kenya have not been adequately studied, anecdotal evidence seems to suggest that a win-win situation may not be attainable in the near future. In many of the instances in Kenya, as is the case in the rest of the world, smallholder farmers have been forcefully evicted from their holdings with inadequate or no compensation at all. There have also been weak environmental and biodiversity impact surveys of the affected areas leading to worsening environmental and biodiversity loss. The rush for farmland in Kenya for biofuel production has significantly led to a decrease in subsistence agricultural production and new forms of poverty. Optimistic promises that such investment would also reinvigorate depressed rural economies, by virtue of employment creation and improved livelihoods, have proven to be vastly overstated, if not unfounded in many cases. A number of the incentives offered by governments to attract foreign land investments reinforce the disadvantage of not only the smallholder producers but also the labour force, mainly women. While new land investment has provided employment opportunities for women, often these jobs are temporary, low paid and insecure. Women also suffer sexual exploitation and bear extra responsibilities. The Kenya case study demonstrates that the new phase of land grabs is not significantly different from the historic process associated with colonialism and neo-colonialism. The language of both the government and the developers to acquire land in the Tana Delta, arguing that such lands are 'unused' or 'empty dry land', is a telling example of the new form of colonialism and neo-colonialism.

References

Alila, P. and R. Atieno, 2006, 'Agricultural Policies in Kenya: Issues and Processes', Paper presented during *Futures Agriculture Consortium Workshop*, Nairobi University, 20–22 March.

Cotula, L., S. Vermeulen, R. Leonard and J. Keeley, 2009, *Land Grab or Development Opportunity: Agricultural Investment and International Land Deals in Africa*, London: IFAD.

Deininger, K, 2011, 'Challenges Posed by the New Wave of Farm Investment', *Journal of Peasant Studies*38(2): 217–47.

Dufey, A., S. Vermeulen and W. Vorley, 2007,*Biofuels: Strategic Choices for Commodity Dependent Developing Countries*, Amsterdam: Common Fund for Commodities.

ECA, 2004, *Land Tenure Systems and their impacts on Food Security and Sustainable Development in Africa*, Addis Ababa: Economic Commission for Africa.

Friis, C. and R. Anette, 2010, *Land Grab in Africa: Emerging Land Systems in Teleconnected World*, GLP Report No. 1 GLP-IPO Copenhagen.

Gouverneur, E., 2009, 'The Palm Oil Land Grab', *Le Monde diplomatique*, 5 December.

GRAIN, 2008, *The 2008 Land Grab for Food and Financial Security*, Barcelona: GRAIN.

Houtart, F., 2010, *Agrofuels: Big Profits, Ruined Lives and Ecological Destruction*, London and Amsterdam: Pluto and Transnational Institute.

Jung-a, S., C. Olivier and T. Burgis, 2008, 'Madagascar Farm Lease: Daewoo to Pay Nothing for Vast Land Acquisition', *Financial Times*, 20 November.

Magdoff, F., 2008, 'The Political Economy and Ecology of Biofuels', New York: Monthly Review Press.

McMichael, P., 2009, 'Agro-Fuels Project at Large', *Critical Sociology* 35(6): 825–39.

McMichael, P., 2010, 'Agrofuels in the Food Regime', *The Journal of Peasant Studies* 37(4):609–30.

Nyikal, R., 2007, 'Financing Smallholder Agricultural Production in Kenya: An Analysis of Effective Demand for Credit. African Crop Science', AAAE Conference Proceedings, pp. 193–7.

Saturnino, M., R. Borass Jr., I. Hall, I. Scoones, B. White, W. Wolford, 2011,'Towards a Better Understanding of Global Land Grabbing: An Editorial Introduction', *Journal of Peasant Studies*38(2): 209–16.

Saturnino, M., R. Borass Jr., P. McMichael, I. Scoones, 2010, 'The Politics of Biofuels, Land and Agrarian Change', *Journal of Peasant Studies* 37(4): 575–92.

Shepard, D. and Anuradha Mittal, 2009, *The Great Land Grab: Rush for World's Farmland Threatens Food Security for Poor*, FAO: The Oakland Institute.

Weis, T., 2010, 'The Accelerating Biophysical Contradictions of Industrial Capitalist Agriculture', *Journal of Agrarian Change* 10(3):315–41.

World Bank, 2011, *Rising Global Interest in Farmland: Can it Yield Sustainable and Equitable Benefits?*, Washington, DC: World Bank.

8

Pastoralism, Social Protection and Vision 2030 in Kenya: Possibilities and Prospects

Introduction

Pastoralists inhabit many parts of northern Kenya, many of which are arid and semi-arid. Pastoralists suffer from vulnerabilities related to scarcity because of the arid and semi-arid conditions. The region suffers from shortages of water and pasture, which often lead to conflict. This chapter argue that Kenya needs to deploy social protection strategies for pastoralist groups in Kenya in order to protect them from various social, economic, political and environmental hazards and calamities. There is need for structures and institutions that should be deployed in order to protect Kenyans who inhabit these regions from destitution and vulnerability.

The chapter is based on research which investigated the availability of social protection structures and institutions among pastoralists in northern Kenya. The paper makes a case for social protection in Kenya. Northern Kenya needs social protection, which consists of policies and programmes designed to reduce poverty and vulnerability by promoting efficient labour markets, diminishing people's exposure to risks, and enhancing their capacity to protect themselves against hazards and interruption or loss of income. The paper critiques Vision 2030 and suggests mechanisms by which pastoralists can be incorporated in Kenya's development more meaningfully. It is argued that Vision 2030 has not addressed the plight of pastoralists in political, economic and social realms in ways that would integrate them advantageously in national, regional and global market places. How do pastoralists engage new global realities? The paper shows that with ICT and the introduction of cell phones in rural areas, pastoralists are part of the global market place. They follow auctions on livestock on the stock exchange and stock market as well as produce carcasses for export and domestic production. The paper shows that pastoralists are increasingly becoming aware of the importance of selling and offloading herds at an advantage, before drought sets in. Pastoralists in Kenya seem ready to deal with the challenges of the twenty-first century.

It is suggested that social protection will moderate the impact of shocks among pastoralist groups in the region. Social protection will sharply improve incomes by allowing better access to the market. Modern roads and an international airport will help the livestock sector, which is the mainstay of economic activities in the region. Social protection and economic support through micro enterprises can also enhance the productive capabilities of pastoralist men and women in northern Kenya, reducing poverty and inequality and stimulating pro-poor growth.

The Millennium Development Goals and Kenya's Vision 2030

The Government of Kenya is committed to the Millennium Development Goals (MDGs) and has focused on lowering extreme poverty rates and attending to the escalating HIV/AIDS pandemic in the country. Northern Kenya suffers from extreme levels of poverty and has poverty incidence levels of 90 per cent in some counties, far higher than the national average of 60 per cent. Since 2003, the government of Kenya has introduced universal primary schooling as part of its commitment to providing education for all by 2015. Against this background, Kenya Vision 2030 was conceived and launched as a national framework to address the MDGs and Kenya's own peculiar development needs.

Vision 2030 promises to open up northern Kenya, but one wonders if this plan will be different from previous plans which promised a lot of for the region, such as provision of water, but were never implemented. Perhaps one of the greatest highlights is the projected development of Isiolo town into a resort city that will serve a huge catchment area that includes Aberdares, Samburu and Meru national parks. Isiolo played host to the popular American reality TV show 'Survivor' when it was shot in Samburu. Isiolo has also hosted many films and will therefore be the resort city of choice for many. Vision 2030 seeks to attract local and international investors to make this a reality, to optimise tourism potential and the city's capacity to cater for a large number of visitors. There is a need to ensure that Vision 2030 is promoted in tandem with social protection capacity in northern Kenya in order to take care of the interests of local herders in the region.

In 2007 the government of Kenya created the Ministry of State for Development of Northern Kenya and other Arid Lands. Creation of this ministry stimulated new interest in the region after many years of neglect and marginalisation. Before then, the region was regarded as a development backwater and pariah region. There is a realisation that policy interventions can improve the well-being of the region with, among other things, infrastructure development, such as the modern tarmac road from Isiolo to Marsabit which opened up the region from early 2011. The government of Kenya also proposed to build a fifth international airport in Kenya at Isiolo town (after Nairobi, Mombasa, Eldoret and Kisumu), the first such facility in northern Kenya, and likely to open up the area even further.

In 2011, the then Minister of Planning and Vision 2030 in Kenya admitted that it was not going to be possible for Kenya to achieve all the Millennium Development Goals as well as Vision 2030. This was not surprising because in Kenya, plans are often simply made to satisfy policy and donor correctness. This has been the practice since independence in the 1960s when in one of the Water Master Plans, the government of Kenya indicated that by the year 2000, every Kenyan home would have pipe borne clean and potable water. In 1995, just five years away from 2000, and on realising that it was not going to achieve this goal, the plan was revised to read that by 2000 every home would be at least 10 kilometres from pipe borne clean and potable water. It was therefore, not surprising to many Kenyans when the Minister for Planning called for the revision of some of the goals in Vision 2030. Although when Vision 2030 was unveiled in 2009 many stakeholders received the news with a great deal of excitement, the pastoralists were not as excited. This is because many of the plans in Kenya have always tended to favour farmers and not herders or pastoralists (Amutabi 2009a; 2009b).

When Vision 2030 was unveiled in 2009, many stakeholders received the news with a great deal of excitement, except the pastoralists in Kenya. The pastoralists were left out for many reasons. First, the focus in Vision 2030 seemed to be on agriculture, industry and infrastructure development in major cities, which are all located outside the pastoralist regions. Second, the creation of the Ministry of Northern Kenya meant that pastoralists were no longer regarded as part and parcel of the rest of Kenya. Third, the lack of a clear government policy on livestock and development, as compared to agriculture, has undermined the pastoralist economy and exposed herders to exploitative middlemen from southern Kenya who often buy cattle during periods when pastoralists are most vulnerable. Fourth, the perennial drought, famine, livestock diseases and insecurity problems in northern Kenya have not been addressed in Vision 2030 in ways that are clear to the area's residents. Fifth, many NGOs have been pushing for irrigation schemes, many of which have been undermined by lack of government support and the threat of wildlife (Amutabi 2006). The lack of clear policies on social protection for pastoralists has implications for development in Kenya. Many pastoralists do not have access to clean water, good roads, schools and health services compared to their counterparts in the south. Policies on disaster preparedness and disaster management, and early warning and drought monitoring are lacking.

Problems Afflicting Northern Kenya

Northern Kenya and pastoralist rangelands remain backwaters of Kenya's development focus (Amutabi 2009a). Scarcity of water, insecurity and livestock-related problems are the three major evils that afflict northern Kenya (Amutabi

2009b). The government of Kenya should end the ambivalence and policy silences around pastoralists and northern Kenya and create structures of inclusion through social protection. Social protection will enhance the capacity of poor and vulnerable persons in northern Kenya to manage economic and social risks such as scarcity of water, pasture and other general problems such as unemployment, exclusion, sickness, disability and old age. There are simple programmes such as harvesting of rain water, providing irrigation canals from major rivers like the Tana River, and sinking of boreholes in strategic places than could be introduced without a lot of capital. Such projects can only succeed if identified by and implemented in collaboration with all the stakeholders, especially local people.

Government agencies and NGOs in Kenya have had little success in northern Kenya largely as a result of pursuing top down policies instead of bottom up options (Amutabi 2006). Government agencies have tended to use development models from the north, for which there are no models for pastoralists. They lack proper development models rooted in the local culture and ethos of nomadic pastoralists of northern Kenya. This perception of development focuses attention on importing development paradigms and ideas from the North, and results in the absence of a maintenance culture, which is a necessary condition of sustainable development. Development of the rangelands can only succeed through bottom up approaches under social protection. This will be different from top down approaches which have tended to undermine the pastoralist ethos and survival mechanisms, seeing them as primordial.

Herders have occupied the same savannahs with wildlife in East Africa for over 2,000 years. Present research suggests that shared grazing between wild and domestic herds may be mutually helpful. Locking out and evicting pastoralists from national reserves and game parks through restictive fencing does not solve the problem of rangeland use. It creates greater problems by forcing pastoralists into greater antagonism with farmers and other pastoral populations. Some NGOs in Kenya have moved in to limit environmental degradation in the rangelands, while creating structures and institutions of empowerment for pastoralists (Amutabi 2006). These include Action Aid, the Kenya Energy and Environment Organizations (KENGO), Kenya Pastoralist Survival Forum, The Pastoralists Forum, the Environment Liaison Center International (ELCI), and the Society for the Protection of the Environment in Kenya (SPEK). The problem has been that some of these NGOs focus on preserving the environment with very little attention given to the social protection of pastoralists.

During drought and after cattle raids, many pastoralists often lose large herds. Many become destitute while others die due to lack of sources of revenue and food. They clearly need social protection that targets supporting groups that have been excluded from formal and informal economic and social structures such as the labour market, especially women, youth and the disabled. Through a combination of interrelated activities, social protection aims at improving living and working conditions for those dependent on the informal economy and other vulnerable groups who face challenges in finding formal employment. The intention of social protection is to provide mechanisms for people to survive against the ravages of nature, marginalisation and poverty, and reduce susceptibility among vulnerable groups such as pastoralists. Although there are attempts to develop infrastructural facilities as well as income generating capacities in northern Kenya, there is a need for people to be involved in some of the decisions in lieu of the top down approach that presently dominates government thinking and some parts of the NGO world.

There has been a lot of wastage in the use of resources in northern Kenya. There are twenty-seven national parks in the region, which generate a lot of revenue for central and local governments. Unfortunately, much of the revenue is lost in corrupt deals and wasteful practices. Since social protection encourages efficient utilisation and tapping of the environment and use of resources in a sustainable manner, many county governments in northern Kenya need training on how to apply social protection in their respective communities. Since social protection aims at promoting access to basic needs and enhancing potential and capacity of marginal groups, the intention of any intervention mechanism would be to focus on specific target groups. Social protection seeks to equip people with skills and knowledge, to allow them to protect themselves from vulnerability and disruptions, such as preventable diseases in cattle and humans, environmental degradation, catastrophes such as drought and flooding, as well as loss of livelihoods. Northern Kenya would be an ideal candidate for this type of knowledge (Amutabi 2009a).

Making a Case for Social Protection for Pastoralists in Northern Kenya

The Kenya Land Conservation Trust has pointed to the lack of commitment by the government in the interests of northern Kenya, given the lack of direction on the same, in Vision 2030. The Kenya Land Conservation Trust commented that 'Although Vision 2030 targets key areas and opportunities, some of which may complement the pastoral livelihoods of those in north-eastern Kenya, nothing specific was identified to support communities in this region [to] develop opportunities outside of the major towns or National Parks'. Clearly, northern Kenya needs social protection programmes in order to enable residents to survive catastrophic episodes they are forced to endure yearly due to factors that are clearly not of their making. Access to basic needs such as water and food is a human right which social protection should guarantee. Social protection consists of policies, formal and informal interventions as well as specifically designed structures to cater for vulnerabilities and lessen human suffering. Besides the harsh climate and their almost inhabitable physical terrain, pastoralists have often been excluded from much of the development in Kenya largely as a result of being on the fringes of the national economy and activities (Amutabi 2009a).

The government of Kenya tends to pay more attention to farming than toherding of animals, an approach that favours some sections of the country more than others. In agricultural policies, the focus is often on crops and exotic breeds, and not on the borana and zebu cattle which the pastoralists raise (Amutabi 2009a). The colonial government pursued similar isolationist and discriminative projects in northern Kenya. Zwanenberg has observed that,

> The colonial view had consistently been that pastoral, and particular nomadic activities, were primitive, backward and to be discouraged. This view underlay the permanency of the stock control regulations, and especially the quarantine [screening] regulations, which precluded any official encouragement of stock trade (Zwanenberg 1973:224).

Policies that incorporate social protection vis-à-vis cattle are likely to alleviate the suffering of people in the region. The issue to highlight is that the life of pastoralists is intimately and intricately intertwined with that of their livestock. Any policy intervention should therefore have livestock in its framing. Livestock provides much of the livelihoods and sustenance of pastoralists (Ndege 1992). Therefore policies that incorporate livestock keeping in social protection are likely to alleviate the suffering of people in the region.

Northern Kenya needs social protection policies because it is evident that development policies in northern Kenya have not been working since the 1950s. Government policies and development approaches, models and programmes are inappropriate and potentially disastrous to pastoralists in northern Kenya, especially because they create dependency (Hogg 1982; 1986). Hogg has argued that it was the nature of the pastoralist society that allowed the development of dependent structures. This is different from the argument in this paper. The pape recommend social protection, arguing that it will not engender dependency because social protection allows for the creation of structures and institutions of empowerment. The problem lies with development approaches that have been used in the past that did not take cognisance of local voices and needs. Local dynamics and mechanisms should be incorporated into any preparation of development approaches and models for northern Kenya.

The United Nations Research Institute for Development sees social protection as involving prevention; the management and overcoming of situations which often adversely affect the quality of people's lives (UNRID 2008). Therefore, social protection consists of policies and programmes designed to reduce poverty and vulnerability by promoting well-organised labour markets, minimising people's exposure to risks, and enhancing their capability to manage economic and social risks, such as joblessness, segregation, disease, disability, insecurity and old age. In northern Kenya, social protection mechanisms and strategies must by and large involve livestock because this is the economic backbone of the region. Any plans for social protection must revolve around the improvement of the livestock sector through provision of water and pasture.

There are six main areas in social protection that can be applied to northern Kenya. First is what is called social insurance programmes which are supposed to cushion people from risks associated with societal problems such as sickness, unemployment, destitution, being orphaned, injury, and old age. Northern Kenya has many individuals who need social insurance from the government because many of them have become victims of certain circumstances, largely because of government neglect and poor policies. Improvement of livestock quality and making sure that there is adequate water and pasture in the rangelands will improve the state of residents in northern Kenya. There has been much talk about providing water from the Tana and other big rivers to supply northern Kenya, but this has remained largely on paper. With the devolved system of government, many parts of northern Kenya are likely to experience rapid development if they receive adequate water supplies.

There are many young and old people who have often been exploited in the rangelands of northern Kenya. Child labour is rampant for example, where young boys and girls are employed as herd boys and girls and trained in handling dangerous weapons such as AK-47 and M16 for protection of herds (Simala and Amutabi 2005). Frequently girls are married off early in exchange for dowries, usually involving hundreds of livestock (Amutabi 2009b). Many adults have lost their livestock to raiders due to poor security arrangements and lack of proper insurance against theft of livestock. If farmers have insurance for their crops, it only makes sense for herders to be given insurance for their livestock as well; otherwise this would amount to segregation and discrimination. The region has many economically internally displaced people (IDPs) and economic refugees occasioned by bad government policies that have not given pastoralists social, economic and political security.

Second, there are social assistance programmes which are predicated on the provision of some kind of welfare service to the most vulnerable groups, many of which may not have adequate access to basic life sustaining components such as water, food, shelter, clothing, security and education due to policy neglect or marginalisation. Third, social protection takes care of environmental refugees as a result of drought, floods, earthquakes and other natural catastrophes. Such problems are common among pastoralists in northern Kenya largely as a result of a fragile ecosystem and harsh environment that receives very little annual rainfall.

Fourth, social protection focuses on micro-finance and micro-enterprises, popularised in Bangladesh, where the government needed to create an enabling environment in which people's vulnerabilities are minimised through credit schemes which do not require colossal collateral or complicated and sophisticated lending mechanisms. The aim is to address vulnerability at the community level, including through the provision of soft loans against major securities, especially to women, many of whom do not have property largely as a result of societal prohibitions and inheritance laws and regulations. Some NGOs have tried to introduce micro-finance schemes and enterprises in northern Kenya in order to minimise vulnerability. But despite many years of operations in the region, northern Kenya residents remain vulnerable (Amutabi 2006). Fifth, social protection focuses on the market, especially around access and protection of consumers and suppliers. In northern Kenya, livestock marketing is brokered and controlled by agents from the south who often swindle pastoralists of their livestock through marketplace tricks and manipulation.

Why Northern Kenya Needs Social Protection

Northern Kenya needs social protection because pastoralists have been left out of many of the government development programmes in Kenya for many reasons. One of the reasons is that the focus in Vision 2030 is on agriculture, industry and infrastructure development in the major cities, which are all located outside the pastoralist regions. A critical examination of the current and previous budgets reveals that many development projects tend to be located in the south among farmers. Some scholars have suggested that herders have consistently received little or no attention from the government since the colonial days, but this should not be as an excuse because fifty years after independence all parts of Kenya should have equitable development.

Previous development plans in Kenya and Vision 2030 have not addressed the plight of pastoralists in political, economic and social realms, in ways that would integrate them advantageously in national, regional and global market places. The isolation of northern Kenya from the rest of the country has left the area to stagnate in general development (Dahl 1979). It is for this reason that many scholars think that the constitution promulgated in 2010 will assist the development of pastoralists and northern Kenya through devolution. In the devolved structure, county governments will have the final say on how funds are spent. Pastoralist counties in Kenya include Isiolo, Marsabit, Garissa, Mandera, Wajir, Baringo, Keiyo-Marakwet, Kajiado, Laikipia, Narok, Samburu, Turkana and West Pokot, and are likely to have more resources allocated to them in order to catch up with the rest of Kenya.

Although Kenya offers wide-ranging tourism products such as great diversity of flora and fauna in national forests and national parks, as well as coastal marine tourism and eco-tourism, very little passes to the common people in terms of direct earnings. Vision 2030 highlights many challenges and opportunities to take advantage of the development prospects in the tourism sector. It addresses some issues that are relevant to the possible development in northern Kenya, especially infrastructure development. Besides focus on tourist attractions, Vision 2030 seeks to increase and expand product choices for Kenya while improving the quality of destinations in northern Kenya such as Garissa, Isiolo, Marsabit, Maralal, Archers'

Post and Lodwar among others. Vision 2030 also mentions improvements in the general infrastructure and security of northern Kenya. Perhaps the most fascinating feature of Vision 2030 is the recognition of stakeholder participation, which calls for improved coordination and collaboration among private and public sector actors in the region.

Social protection is not only a concern for the government, but other stakeholders in development such as NGOs. Many scholars have pointed out that the problems of development in northern Kenya are predicated on institutional weaknesses and failure (Amutabi 2006; Fratkin 1998; Fratkin and Smith 1994; Hogg 1992); and Fratkin and Roth 1990). They argue that new changes are also occurring due to the influence of capitalism and globalisation. Commenting on the work of NGOs in northern Kenya, Elliot Fratkin has pointed out that new changes brought about by capitalism are hurting pastoralists in the region:

> Pastoralists have increasingly shifted economy from subsistence production (produ-
> cing mainly milk for the household consumption) to commercial production (beef
> and dairy products for sale both to domestic and export markets). This increased
> commoditization of livestock economy has led to large transformations of pastoral
> society, including increased polarization of pastoralists into 'haves' (owning private
> ranches) and 'have-nots,' with poor pastoralists working for wealthier kinsmen or
> migrating to towns in search of low paying jobs such as watchmen, or for women as
> maids or prostitutes (Fratkin 1998:22).

Kenya needs social protection due to the effects of globalisation. Due to lack of proper protection policies and breakdown of informal structures and institutions many pastoralists are ending up in urban areas performing manual tasks, and working as guards and prostitutes. These problems are occasioned by breakdown of informal and formal social and cultural structures and institutions.

The creation of the Ministry for the Development of Northern Kenya and other Arid Lands has been regarded by others as a step back because it means that pastoralists were no longer regarded as part and parcel of the rest of Kenya. But this is negative thinking. Great efforts that seek to elevate areas that have previously been left behind must be applauded. The ministry has embarked on many development projects which need to be supported by county governments as encapsulated in the new 2010 constitution. The ministry needs to incorporate social protection into its programmes in northern Kenya in order to target all the pastoralists together with their herds. Pastoralists have suffered from drought and famine, as well as warfare and cattle diseases such as smallpox, rinderpest and foot and mouth diseases in the past. They need carefully prepared development interventions in health care, education and food security, which are likely to vastly enhance their quality of life.

Lack of clear government policies on livestock improvement compared to crop farming and agriculture in general has undermined the pastoralist economy and exposed herders to exploitative middlemen from southern Kenya who often buy cattle during periods when pastoralists are most vulnerable (Amutabi 1999). Poor timing of offloading herds during drought and the right time to buy new stock for recovery after droughts have affected marketing of livestock by herders. Herders often sell when they are most vulnerable and are therefore often exploited by middlemen who buy their livestock at ridiculously cheap rates. There is need for social protection by the government, to buy the animals at reasonably competitive prices similar to the the scheme the government has with cereal producers in Kenya. The Kenya National and Cereals Board often buys excess maize from farmers and places it instorage. This increases benefits for farmers because it saves them from exploitation by middlemen and commercial millers.

Through social protection pastoralists would be assisted by the government in selling and offloading herds at an advantage before drought sets in and the pastoralists in Kenya would be able to deal with the challenges of the twenty-first century. Kenya needs social protection, more so in parts of northern Kenya which have been marginalised for a long time. This is because besides lack of potable water, northern Kenya suffers from persistent drought. Drought periods (1982–87; 1991–92; 1994; 2000; 2008–09; 2010–11) have plagued the northern region more than anywhere else in Kenya and have led to destitution both among semi-agriculturalists and pastoralists. Pastoralists' animals have died for lack of pasture and adequate supply of water. The droughts had the double impact of reducing agricultural projections and food security and led to serious outbreaks of famine in many parts of the country. Kenya was for a long time self-sufficient in food production, especially up to the 1980s, but is not any more as a result of frequent droughts. During the drought periods, agro-based manufacturing fell, and water shortages resulted in decreased production in the generation of electricity (as over 90 percent of electricity in Kenya is hydro-generated) and therefore in the industrial sector.

Due to recurrent famine in northern Kenya, some scholars have suggested that the region be given more attention by the state. Despite the incidence of perennial drought, famine, livestock diseases and insecurity problems have not been addressed in Vision 2030. While pastoralism usually implies nomadism, moving one's herds (with all or part of the human population) to available pasture and water, some pastoralists combine dry land farming with livestock keeping, a model of livelihood known as agro-pastoralism or semi-sedentary pastoralism. In eking out a living in these tough conditions, pastoralists have had to endure a number of problems. The lack of clear policies on social protection for pastoralists has implications for development in Kenya. Many pastoralists do not have access to clean water, good roads, schools and health services compared to their counterparts in the south. There is need for inclusion of more social protection structures and institutions among pastoralists in northern Kenya.

Land is an important resource for all Kenyan communities. In communal lands such as among pastoralists in northern Kenya, drought has often resulted in livestock and crop failure and hunger for many pastoralists. Subsequent to the drought have been poor and unreliable rainfall patterns since the 1990s, which has led to lower yields in agro-pastoralist activities along river valleys. Because of inheritance laws and regulations, the farm-holding size per household has decreased significantly due to continued subdivisions owing to inheritance practices. Over-cultivation has affected the quality of soils. Many of the soils which were low in fertility have deteriorated due to excessive cropping in recent years (Amutabi 1999). Rangeland productivity has been decreasing due to overgrazing, and high rural-urban migration by male household members has resulted in a shortage of farm labour.

Like other policy areas, social protection policies involve choices and priorities, for example between mere social safety nets and promotion of sustainable livelihoods, between short-and long-term alleviation and elimination of poverty, between universal and targeted programmes, conditional and unconditional schemes, food and cash transfers, etc. Criteria must be set for selecting which households, and who within them, should receive benefits. If schemes are conditional, then on what: participation in education, health, nutrition and, or work programmes? Is such participation by the poor and needy in fact constrained by demand or supply factors? Is it possible to improve institutional and management capacity?

Vision 2030 has not addressed the lack of capital and markets for livestock keepers in northern Kenya. There is a need for mechanisms and ways in which pastoralists can be incorporated in Kenya's development more meaningfully. Since the colonial period, Kenya has pursued policies based on the containment, pacification and sedentarisation of pastoralists. These policies have created hostility between the government and pastoralists, mainly in northern Kenya. Sir Charles Elliot, one of the colonial commissioners (governors) of the East African Protectorate (later Kenya), had no reservations about displacing pastoralists from their traditional lands: 'I cannot admit that wandering [ethnic] groups have a right to keep other superior races out of large tracts of land merely because they have acquired the habit of struggling over more land than they can utilize' (Kenya National Archives 1933-34:67). This kind of attitude dominated thinking in government even after Kenya became independent. There is a condescending attitude that seems to govern thinking about herders.

In the colonial period, the Crown Lands Ordinance of 1902 gave the governor power to lease or sell land to settlers in Kenya. This saw many white settlers arrive in Kenya from South Africa and Britain (Maxon 1992). Colonial policy was to confine the pastoralists in 'native' reserves, while the authorities appropriated much of their free-range space for other purposes. Even after the Devonshire White paper of 1923 declared that the interests of natives were supreme when they conflicted with those of whites and Asians, things did not change for the pastoralists (Maxon 1992:

67). This attitude has not changed significantly many years after independence. In 2010 Kenya unveiled a new constitution after an acrimonious referendum, but the chapters, articles and sections on land still gave provisions for trust land in northern Kenya. This means that land ownership arrangements will still be different in the region compared with other parts of Kenya. The same argument used to undermine the pastoralist communal land owning culture is also used to denigrate land utilisation practices in the region.

Development stakeholders in Kenya use double standards in their discussion of land use patterns in northern Kenya compared to southern Kenya, and how they treat them. Formal and informal institutions are willing to grant loans and development opportunities to farmers in the south, but unwilling to do the same for herders. This has been going on for many years. Zwanenberg has noted that,

> Pastoral peoples of Kenya ... did indeed live very close to the margins of existence all the time. They were exposed to recurrent food shortages and famines, and suffered greatly from diseases and malnutrition. They had to cope with an unreliable climate and frequent drought, and their technology, although well adapted to environmental conditions, was limited (Zwanenberg 1973:223).

Clearly land use policies have been discriminatory. Unequal development between northern and southern regions existed and is evident in the poor infrastructure, lack of policing and civil authority structures and institutions, lawlessness and high levels of insecurity and the dominance of an underground economy and other illegal activities in the north, compared to the rest of Kenya. There have even been suggestions to indicate that there was some collusion between southerners and colonial officials in exploiting northern Kenya. Why are the pastoralists the most marginalised people in Kenya despite the fact that livestock keeping has often made very high returns on domestic and international markets? Why have pastoralists not benefitted from good prices for their livestock like those in other parts of Kenya? It is possible that social protection would alleviate the suffering of pastoralists if intervention policies were created in order to harness all the potential in northern Kenya, and especially to improve the quality of herds in the region.

The colonial government's policy towards pastoralist communities was based on a perspective which saw pastoralists as practising an uneconomic and irrational herding system based on accumulation for its own sake (Fratkin 1998). Attempts have been made to undermine pastoralism as a practice, with the clear objective of gradually eradicating it as a mode of livelihood and lifestyle. Many NGOs have done this through funding irrigation projects such as Perkerra and Kiina on the Ewaso Nyiro River in collaboration with the government of Kenya both in the pre-independence period and still today. Introduction of cultivation and use of land through irrigation has exacerbated the plight of the pastoralist in arid and semi-arid areas. The effect of pastoralists' dependency on aid and the vulnerable livestock sector, and the tendency for them to be 'empowered' as far as food supply is concerned, has been to deprive pastoralists of valuable pasture. Permanent water sources have been affected through diversion of water into irrigation canals. Many seasonal rivers such as Ewaso Nyiro and Turkwell that have increasingly been used in irrigation schemes are rendered dry most of the year. This has led to the deaths of many livestock leading to more pressure on the few water sources in the region. The result has been more conflicts over water and pasture in the region.

The indigenous land tenure system, where they practiced a 'communal' land tenure system in which sharing was less fractious and land was plenty, served pastoralists well for generations. Tenure in this context was thus a social and cultural institution: a relationship between individuals and groups or ethnic groups consisting of a series of rights and duties with respect to the use of land (Akong'a and Kareithi 1996; Birgegard 1993). In northern Kenya, sharing of resources has been rendered problematic by the continued existence of the colonial Trust Land Act, because of communal ownership of land and access to grazing fields.

Northern Kenya has some of the largest national parks in Kenya, such as the Samburu and Marsabit national parks, which earn Kenya significant revenue from tourist earnings as well as from harvesting some of the animals for export to foreign zoos through culling (Amutabi 2009c). Butherders have benefited very little from these activities. The government often sees the herdersas a threat to wildlife and efforts have been intensified to fence them out using electric fences. Clearly this is unwarranted because the struggle between animal conservationists and Kenyan herders need not be hostile. In some areas, Kenya has had policies where residents around national parks and reserves receive a portion of the tourist revenues through local country councils, especially among the Maasai. This is done by use of game scouts and guards. Many herders in Kenya do follow the logic that wild animals, mainly ungulates like gazelles, wildebeest, zebras, and elephants are part of their environment and graze their animals freely alongside this wildlife. So long as these wild animals do not directly threaten their households or livestock, herders are enthusiastically preoccupied with their protection. There is therefore no good reason why eco-tourism and conservation that incorporates local herders as important stakeholders in conservation, as is done among the Maasai, cannot be extended to fellow pastoralists in northern Kenya.

A lot of the land loss in northern Kenya is due to political and economic factors as the government has been increasing its demand for foreign revenue gained by renting out land for commercial farming to Arab states for wheat, corn and rice, as well as for raising beef cattle,ostriches and turkeys. This has resulted in reduced and fragmented grazing areas and increased the impact of droughts and scarcity on pastoralists in northern Kenya. Fratkin has asserted, 'The process of commoditization divides up formally communal shared grazing resources, and polarizes pastoral society into private ranchers and poor pastoralists'. Fencing has forced pastoralists to graze their livestock on an ever-shrinking range of inferior quality land (Raikes 1981). It might explain why droughts in 1999–2000, 2002–03 and 2010 led to more deaths of livestock and loss of human life in Turkana district compared to other districts in northern Kenya (Amutabi 2009a).

The other noticeable tendency in the approach of the government and some NGO operations in northern Kenya is an emphasis on modernisation-type projects such as privatisation of land among pastoralists, which has been going on in northern Kenya since the 1990s. The greatest hindrance to pastoralism in northern Kenya is the enclosure, privatisation and fencing of grazing lands which exclude former owners. Recognition of traditional land tenure is fundamental for the continuation of pastoralism in Kenya. Many herders in northern Kenya realise that this recognition will not come without great effort and pastoralists are progressively organising to defend their rights.

Modernisation and new technologies such as vaccination of livestock against many diseases as well as the introduction of artificial insemination have helped improve the quality of life of pastoralist herds. There are however some pursuits of modernisation that are inimical to pastoralist interests, such as fencing. Some policy makers in Kenya have also pushed for eco-tourism and the creation of group ranches. These modernisation projects, whose concern is with economic material improvement, do not much benefit the very poor, but the relatively wealthier elements of Kenya, particularly the African upper class who occupy senior positions in government. These projects also benefit senior politicians who have been allocating themselves pastoralists' land in northern Kenya through proxies. Many of the group ranches are managed by political cartels whose eco-tourism activities are dominated by the educated and elites in society. By incorporating Kenya's upper class from southern Kenya in the acquisition of huge chunks of land in northern Kenya, and by privatising it through issuance of land title deeds, the government and the international community are collaborating in exploiting pastoralists. The land question in northern Kenya is a 'human rights violation' because it is a form of exploitation.

Most common types of social protection include social assistance, where resources, either cash or in-kind, are transferred to vulnerable individuals or households with no other means of adequate support, such as to single mothers, the homeless, or the physically or mentally disabled. Pastoralists are socially coherent and dependent groups. When a family remains alone, it becomes vulnerable to raids and other calamities. The separation of northern Kenya from the rest of the country was part of the divide-and-rule policy and produced a form of economic apartheid. Since the white settlers were mainly in the south, they instituted quarantines protecting their livestock from diseases that they believed to inhere in the pastoralist herds in the north. Thus from 1912 up until today Isiolo town has been a screening centre for onward livestock. Large blocks of quarantine facilities built during the colonial period are still in use. In this quarantine regime, animals had to be screened for 'native diseases' before they could travel south to where large markets such as Nairobi were located. The good news is that this is changing due to Vision 2030, which seeks to make Isiolo a major resort town for Kenya and replace its image as a quarantine, screening and holding town.

Quarantine laws were discriminatory and segregated against Africans. The laws and regulations sought to protect the herds of white settler ranchers from competing against pastoralists' livestock. The intention was to shelter settlers from open market competition. Government regulation denied pastoralists outlets for excess livestock leading to unhealthy congestion in their areas. Clearly, the laws were meant to protect white producers in Kenya and the colonial government did not care about what happened to the pastoralists. Quoting a Government livestock expert report, Raikes wrote in 1981,

> For many years the pastoral native reserves have been in perpetual quarantine. This has been caused partly by the presence of disease, but largely by economic considerations. The expenditure at any time of comparatively small sums on veterinary services for these areas would have enabled them rapidly to be liberated from quarantine with "*disastrous effect upon the price of stock and stock products within the colony*" (Raikes1981:118).

Quarantine still takes place in Kenya. There are warnings issued by veterinary officials from time to time against cattle diseases, such as foot and mouth, affecting mainly northern Kenya. Government officials are often too sensitive to transient and cross-border ethnic groups such as the Boran and Sakuye in northern Kenya, who often move back and forth across the international border. In the colonial period, screening focused mainly on Contagious Bovine Pleura Pneumonia (CBPP), a cattle disease, which was very prevalent in northern Kenya. George Ndege has pointed out that during the interwar years colonial policies regarding cattle movement and quarantine particularly hurt the pastoralists (Ndege 1992). Why has Kenya's independent government retained these quarantine laws? Research has revealed that CBPP, which made quarantine necessary and was the sole justification for it, has been eradicated since the 1970s, but the quarantine still remains in place. This has enraged many pastoralist leaders and the NGO community in Kenya. But the quarantine served other purposes in colonial Kenya. It has emerged that screening of livestock allowed the colonial government to gauge pastoralist economic production, and enabled it to keep track of pastoralists income for taxation.

Conclusion

Kenya's Vision 2030 is not sufficiently exhaustive and needs to do more for herders and pastoralists. Pastoralists in Kenya need social protection. Many of their problems emanate from informal and formal institutional failure. Social protection, which consists of policies and programmes designed to reduce poverty and vulnerability by promoting efficient labour markets, diminishing people's exposure to risks, and enhancing their capacity to protect themselves against hazards and interruption or loss of income would be a fitting intervention. This chapter has shown that like other Kenyans, pastoralists are changing through their long history of contact with other societies. They also collaborate with other groups in economic, political and cultural realms.

Although Vision 2030 seeks to improve the state of people in the whole of Kenya, policies governing rangelands in northern Kenya must be friendly to herders. Pastoralists have shared the same space with wild animals, for many years in a symbiotic relationship. It is therefore wrong for wildlife conservation groups, mainly from Europe and the US, to advocate draconian measures that encourage the government of Kenya to lock out or evict or strictly restrict human activities within park precincts. For this reason the development of Isiolo into a resort city will enhance the status of northern Kenya. One hopes that Vision 2030 will not be hijacked by careerists in Kenya's civil service who have always undermined the role of stakeholders. It must be recognised that pastoralists would like to have input into what affects them. Eco-tourism was a good idea but it has been hijacked by elites and middlemen who have invested in hotels and tourist resorts at the expense of the ordinary people. Fault has also been found with the group ranches, which have been presented as an alternative to communal land ownership, for being manipulated by elites who have rented some of them to outsiders and pocketed the proceeds.

References

Amutabi, Maurice N., 1999, 'The Role of Politicians in Livestock Marketing Policy in Kenya'. Paper presented at a conference on the theme, 'Rethinking Livestock Marketing in Kenya' organised by Egerton University's Tegemeo Institute of Agricultural Policy and Development and Action Aid Kenya, held in Isiolo, Kenya.

Amutabi, Maurice N., 2005a, 'Captured and Steeped in Colonial Dynamics and Legacy: The Case of Isiolo Town in Kenya', in Steven Salm and Toyin Falola, eds, *African Urban Spaces in Historical Perspectives*, New York: University of Rochester Press.

Amutabi, Maurice N., 2005b, 'Transient, Mobile "Nations" and the Dilemma of Nationhood in the Horn of Africa: Interrogating Nomadic Pastoralists, Insecurity and the Uncertainty of Belonging', in Felicia Arudo Yieke, ed., *East Africa: In Search of National and Regional Renewal*, Dakar: CODESRIA.

Amutabi, Maurice N., 2006, *The NGO Factor in Africa: The Case of Arrested Development in Kenya*, New York: Routledge.

Amutabi, Maurice N., 2009a. 'The Livestock Sector in Kenya', in Maurice N. Amutabi, ed., *Studies in the Economic History of Kenya: Land, Water, Railways, Education, and*

Entrepreneurship, New York: Edwin Mellen Press.

Amutabi, Maurice N., 2009b, 'Colonial Legacy and Underdevelopment in Northern Kenya', in Maurice N. Amutabi, ed., *Studies in the Economic History of Kenya: Land, Water, Railways, Education, and Entrepreneurship*, New York: Edwin Mellen Press.

Amutabi, Maurice N., 2009c, 'Water and Development in Kenya: Problems and Potential', in Maurice N. Amutabi, ed., *Studies in the Economic History of Kenya: Land, Water, Railways, Education, and Entrepreneurship*, New York: Edwin Mellen Press.

Amutabi, Maurice N. and I.K. Simala, 2005, 'Small Arms, Cattle Raiding and Borderlands: The Ilemi Triangle', in Willem van Schendel and Itty Abraham Itty, eds, *Illicit Flows and Criminal Things: States, Borders, and the Other Side of Globalization*, Bloomington: Indiana University Press.

Birgegard, L.E., 1993, *Natural Resource Tenure: A Review of Issues, Experiences with Emphasis on Sub-Saharan Africa, Rural Development Studies*. Uppsala: Swedish University of Agriculture Science/International Rural Development Centre.

Dahl, G. S., 1975, *Suffering Grass: Subsistence and Society of Waso Borana*, Stockholm: Stockholm University Press.

Fratkin, Elliot, 1994, 'Pastoral Land Tenure in Kenya: Maasai, Samburu, Boran, and Rendille Experiences, 1950–1990', *Nomadic Peoples* 34/35:55–68.

Fratkin, Elliot, 1997, 'Pastoralism: Governance and Development Issues', *Annual Review of Anthropology* 26: 235–61.

Fratkin, Elliot, 1998, *Ariaal Pastoralists of Kenya: Surviving Drought and Development in Africa's Arid Lands*, Boston, MA: Allyn and Bacon.

Galaty, J.G., 1994, 'Rangeland Tenure and Pastoralism in Africa', in E. Fratkin, K. Galvin, and E.A. Roth, eds, *African Pastoralist Systems*, Boulder, CO: Lynne Rienner Publishers.

Hogg, R., 1982, 'Destitution and Development: the Turkana of Northwest Kenya', *Disasters* 6(3): 164–8.

Hogg, R., 1986, 'The New Pastoralism: Poverty and Dependency in Northern Kenya', *Africa* 65(3):319–33.

Hogg, R., 1992, 'NGOs, Pastoralists and Myth of Community: Three Case Studies of Pastoral Development', *Nomadic Peoples* 30: 122–46.

Kenya Land Conservation Trust, 2011, *Tourism, Vision 2030 and Pro-Pastoralist Livelihoods in North-Eastern Kenya: Ecotourism in Northern Kenya Policy Brief – Enhanced Livelihoods in the Mandera Triangle (ELMT)*, Nairobi: Kenya Land Conservation Trust.

Kenya National Archives, 1933–34, 'Kenya Land Commission of 1933', Part II, chapter 1, p. 185, paragraphs 635 and 642.

Raikes, P. L., 1981, *Livestock Policy and Development in East Africa*, Uppsala: Scandinavian Institute of African Studies.

Simala, I.K. and Maurice N. Amutabi, 2005, 'Small Arms, Cattle Raiding and Borderlands: the Ilemi Triangle', in Willem van Schendel and Itty Abraham Itty, eds, *Illicit Flows and Criminal Things: States, Borders, and the Other Side of Globalization*, Bloomington: Indiana University Press.

Zwanenberg, R.M.A.Van,1972, 'The Economic Response of Kenya Africans to European Settlement, 1903-1939', in Bethuel A. Ogot, ed., *Politics and Nationalism in Colonial Kenya*, Nairobi: East African Publishing House.

9

Cross-border Migrations, Regional Integration and Conviviality in the Gulf of Guinea: Reality and Prospects

Emmanuel Yenshu Vubo and Humphrey Ngala Ndi

Introduction

The Gulf of Guinea region has always been a sphere of migrations, the production of identities and trans-ethnic as well as inter-ethnic relations. Although many countries in West and Central Africa lay claim to the Gulf of Guinea (GG) for strategic, military or security reasons (Angola, Benin, Burkina Faso, Cameroon, Cape Verde, the Central African Republic, Chad, Congo, Côte d'Ivoire, the Democratic Republic of Congo, Equatorial Guinea, Gabon, Gambia, Ghana, Guinea, Guinea Bissau, Liberia, Mali, Niger, Nigeria, São Tomé and Príncipe, Senegal, Sierra Leone and Togo), only Guinea, Guinea Bissau, Sierra Leone, Liberia, Ghana, Togo, Benin, Nigeria, Cameroon, Equatorial Guinea (EQ), Republic of Congo, Angola and Gabon are Gulf of Guinea states in the strict sense of the term. The GG states are endowed with an infinite wealth of natural and human resources. Gold, oil, diamond and bauxite abound and the first three African exporters of crude oil (Angola, Nigeria and Equatorial Guinea) are found therein. A large part of the African evergreen and mangrove forest is found in the GG. Nigeria, the most populous country in Africa is also located there. Other economically important states in this region are Côte d'Ivoire, Gabon, Ghana and Cameroon.

These states have combined to endow the region with a colourful *métissage* of people. The mixing of people on the Atlantic coast of wWest-central Africa pre-dates the colonial era. Such movements were in all directions: north to south or east to west involving Bantu speaking peoples. Some of the factors that account for inter-ethnic contacts over the *longue durée* in the modern period are the slave trade and commercial activities promoted by European traders and prospective colonial powers. The partitioning of Africa, while creating, carving and crystallising boundaries between colonial spheres, thus restricting movements across the new frontiers, triggered new internal movements under a labour imperative. This explains the movement towards colonial plantations and public work projects (roads, railway construction sites). Developments following the First World War were also responsible for the reshuffling of peoples. The retreat of German forces to Fernando Pó and the partitioning of the former German Cameroon between Britain and France were responsible for a new series of migrations and the erection of new spaces and frontiers likely to control population movements. The resulting contacts between peoples in this period gave rise to new forms of identity awareness, what Bourdieu has called the 'social categories of perception' that were in reality 'principles of a vision and division' of the world. Besides the colonial dichotomy between subject and citizen, new categories were introduced to take care of an awareness of the difference between insiders and outsiders such as the division between natives and strangers. Independence inherited both this legacy and also ushered in new forms of movements both within and across the post-colonial state boundaries: regular movements across the linguistic divide in Cameroon, the continuing presence and movement of Nigerians (especially the Igbo) within and across the commercial cities of Cameroon, and the movement of anglophone Cameroonians to Nigeria.

The development of sub-regional economic schemes was the basis of new waves of migration in the Central African sub-region. Although the dominant destinations are countries rich in oil but with a human resource deficit such as Gabon and Equatorial Guinea in the post-1980 period, or Nigeria in the 1970s, other countries have also hosted migrants from across the region. For example, migration towards Cameroon has been a function of its status as an economic and cultural power or its stability in a region marked by civil wars. Moreover the continuing patterns of ancient population movements, where former colonial boundaries at times split the same peoples into different national spaces, has been a very strong factor in what can be considered as cross-border migrations. These migratory movements have given rise to new forms of distinctions between insiders and outsiders, especially of nationals and non-nationals, grafted to older distinctions derived from the colonial era and resulting in several crises (expulsion of non-nationals, xenophobic attacks, violent attacks, and diverse forms of confrontations). Although belonging to the same economic community, the status of migrants in the CEMAC region has often been problematic within some countries (Cameroonians in Gabon and Equatorial Guinea, Equatorial Guineans in Cameroon, Central African Republic nationals in Cameroon) even resulting in diplomatic incidents or prolonged border closures. This situation is paradoxical not only because these countries all belong to CEMAC but also because they display characteristically very homogenous political, social and cultural characteristics that are supposed to cushion rather than exacerbate tensions resulting from cross-border movements and contacts between their peoples. On the contrary, Cameroonian migrants in Nigeria seem to live at greater ease with Nigerians in spite of the fact that Nigeria belongs to an entirely different economic social and fiscal dispensation (ECOWAS). Conversely, Nigerians have enjoyed relatively peaceful existence within Cameroon although there are incidents that tend to project their status as non-nationals (harassment by corrupt government officials, threats of expulsion and mass repatriation). Nigeria itself has also been the host of nationals from countries in the Gulf of Guinea as well as the larger west African region but it appears to be more a starting point for migrations to smaller countries (Equatorial Guinea, Gabon, São Tomé and Príncipe).

This paper attempts to investigate the crises of identity which have often occurred with the contact of different peoples moving across recognised borders within the states of the Gulf of Guinea in the contemporary context. The question is: can African countries lay claims to transnational projects and still insist on practices that exclude non-nationals in their own countries? How can this apparently be overcome in practical terms? The chapter sets out to achieve the following objectives:

- identify, characterise and classify the various cross-border movements in the Gulf of Guinea;
- examine the nature and outcomes of contacts in areas of destination of migrants;
- identify and examine the causes of crises arising from cross-border migrations especially as related to the identity question in the countries of destination. In this regard, a small survey was made of the experience of non-nationals from the Gulf of Guinea living in Cameroon;
- examine the prospects for alternative models of regional integration in the Gulf of Guinea.

Pattern and Character of Movements

The economic potentials of this region have meant the dynamics of migration date back many centuries in time, to the caravan traders from north Africa who came in search of spices and other commodities; the attraction of the strong Soninke Ghana empire that collapsed in the fifteenth century; the slave trading kingdoms; and to the Muslim wars of conquest and colonial invasion orchestrated frequent movements across the territory (Metogo 2006). Whereas in the past, people moved to escape conquest by muslim jihadists, slave raiders, or to resist colonisation, movements in the post-colonial era are almost entirely dominated by economic motives. Movements due to economic incentives are strong and have dynamic patterns determined by changes in the economic fortunes of various countries in the region. For example, from the 1990s, Equatorial Guinea emerged from decades of misery to become the new *El Dorado* of the GG through 'black gold' (oil), taking over from Gabon and Nigeria which had been prominent migrant destinations in the preceding two decades. Presently, Angola is fast becoming a prized destination for migrants following the end of twenty-five years civil war in 2002. For a long time, Chadian refugees sought protection in north Cameroon and many have settled there permanently.

Internal Movements

North-South Movements

These are movements from the dry Sahelian belt to the humid forest zones of the GG. The Sahelian belt of West Africa extends from Senegal to Cameroon. Examples of such movements abound and include: informal migrants from Burkina Faso and Mali who seasonally move to work on the cocoa farms of Ghana and Côte d'Ivoire, and Malian migrants working in the groundnut producing regions of Senegal. Besides the people heading for agricultural destinations are also a host of informal migrants whose primary destinations are the towns and cities along the coast of the GG. In these towns, they faithfully accept and execute the menial jobs which the nationals often disdain. These include petty trading, garbage collection, gardening and ambulatory shoe mending.

Movements to Oil Producing Countries (Resource Frontiers)

Another type of movement in the GG involves job-seeking migrants, originating in countries with low economic growth rates ravaged by high levels of unemployment, to countries with high growth rates providing greater avenues for employment and prospects of a better life. The countries sustaining high growth rates in this region are basically those producing oil with the exception of Nigeria. Nevertheless, the Nigerian oil boom of the 1970s was a veritable magnet for the entire region drawing migrants from almost all countries but notably Ghana, Benin, Togo and Cameroon. Today the current wave of migration is towards Gabon and Equatorial Guinea. Between 1997 and 2002, for example, real Gross Domestic Product (GDP) growth for Equatorial Guinea stood at over 50.1 per cent per annum. The growth rate for Gabon has not been very outstanding but the small population implies high GDP growth rates per capita (Table 9.1). Police estimates today show that migrants constitute over a third of the population of Equatorial Guinea (300,000). Most of these imigrants are illegal and notably originate in Cameroon, Nigeria, Senegal and Mali. In Gabon, a large segment of the population is also made up of people who have escaped the difficult climate of the West African Sahel. The sahelian countries mostly fall into the low income category and generate huge numbers of migrants. The countries labelled fragile have potential for growth in real GDP but have been weakened by internal conflict and civil wars which have besieged their economies from taking off.

Other oil producing countries like the Republic of Congo and Angola have not witnessed waves of immigration that are particularly striking because of domestic political instability. They are still recovering from such strife and may soon have to face their own waves of immigrants. As Table 9.1 below shows, many countries in the GG are in the low income bracket.

Table 9.1: Growth in real gross domestic product (GDP) for selected countries of the GG

Country	1997–2002	2003	2004	2005	2006	2007	2008	2009
Oil exporting countries								
Angola	4.9	3.3	11.2	20.6	18.6	21.1	16.0	12.8
Cameroon	4.5	4.0	3.7	2.3	3.2	3.5	3.8	4.6
Congo	2.7	0.8	3.5	7.8	6.2	-1.6	9.1	12.1
Equatorial Guinea	50.1	14.0	38.0	9.7	1.3	21.4	7.4	4.6
Gabon	0.0	2.4	1.1	3.0	1.2	5.6	3.9	7.0
Nigeria	6.8	10.3	10.6	5.4	6.2	5.9	6.2	8.1
Low income countries								
Benin	5.1	3.9	3.1	2.9	3.8	4.6	5.1	5.7
Burkina Faso	5.7	7.3	4.6	7.1	5.5	3.6	4.5	5.6
Ghana	4.3	5.2	5.6	5.9	6.4	6.3	6.5	5.8
Mali	5.0	7.2	2.4	6.1	5.3	3.1	4.8	5.2
Niger	4.1	7.7	-0.8	7.4	5.2	3.2	4.4	4.5
Fragile countries								
Sierra Leone	3.8	9.5	7.4	7.3	7.4	6.8	5.5	5.9
Togo	0.0	5.2	2.4	1.3	4.1	2.1	2.5	3.5
Guinea	4.2	1.2	2.3	3.0	2.4	1.8	4.5	4.7
Guinea Bissau	-2.1	-0.6	2.2	3.2	1.8	2.5	3.2	3.1
Liberia	-	-31.3	2.6	5.3	7.8	9.5	8.6	14.3
Côte d'Ivoire	1.0	-1.7	1.6	1.9	0.7	1.6	2.9	4.7

Source: International Monetary Fund (2008:55).

Though migration appeals to many, because of the economic benefits of remittances, life has not always been comfortable for these migrants. They are often accused of being responsible for crime, political and economic problems. Nigeria for example, in 1983, had to expel illegal migrants whose presence had become pugnacious to the nationals. Similar expulsions have occurred from Gabon and Equatorial Guinea.

Refugee Movements

Africa has the highest number of refugees in the world. A refugee is defined by UNHCR as any person who cannot return to his or her own country because of a well founded fear of persecution for reasons of race, religion, nationality, political association or social grouping. Refugeeism develops because of two main factors: internal conflict or civil war, and famine. Refugee movements due to internal conflict in the GG include the following: Chadian refugees to Cameroon; Liberian refugees to Ghana; and Sierra Leonean refugees to Côte d'Ivoire. In addition to refugees, there are thousands of internally displaced persons in the region. These types of movements are recurrent in Nigeria due to ethic and religious conflicts, and in Côte d'Ivoire due to political instability.

Deportations

Movements under the stress of deportation have become common originating mainly from the economically more attractive economies in the GG. As indicated earlier, migrants are resented in most of these countries and are easily associated with criminal conduct, civil and political disobedience. Providing a representation of how locals view migrants in Equatorial Guinea, Engonga, a local sociologist, has explained that the influx of immigrants into Equatorial Guinea has increased locals' wariness because the imigrants out-compete the locals for jobs and have an immense spirit of entrepreneurship to which locals are not accustomed. It is reported that migrants have virtually taken over the oil villages around the capital, Malabo. In Gabon, migrants are looked upon in the same way even though the more objective nationals affirm that imigrant workers are more loyal, obedient, inventive and courageous than nationals. For example, in Gabon, Cameroonians, Senegalese and others accept living and working in places that the Gabonese disdain.

Movements for Education

Movements for education are equally important in the GG. Nigeria exerts a major pull on students within the ECOWAS zone of the GG. In the CEMAC zone, Cameroon attracts students from virtually all the other members of the economic and monetary community. There is a large colony of students from Equatorial Guinea in the University of Buea, Cameroon for example. Similarly there is an impressive number of students from Chad and the Central African Republic studying in the predominantly francophone universities of Cameroon.

External Movements

There is a small but strategically important number of European, Asian and American migrants in the GG. A majority of them are involved in oil exploration along the coastal sedimentary lowlands of the region, notably in the Niger delta, off the coast of Kribi and in Rio del Rey. Many are also involved in prospecting for minerals, exploiting forests, and in engineering and construction.

Chinese migrants have become very significant in the countries of the Gulf of Guinea. They are involved in commerce, engineering and oil prospecting. Figure 9.1 below shows a generalised directional pattern of the migratory movements in the Gulf of Guinea.

Figure 9.1: Pattern of Labour Migration in the Gulf of Guinea

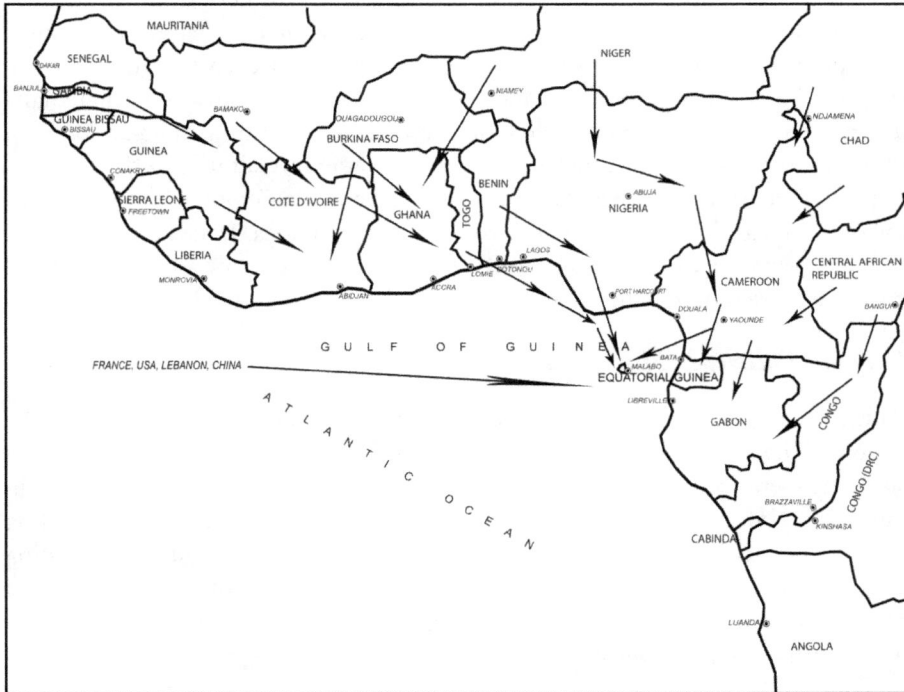

Nature and Outcome of Contacts in Areas of Destination

A variety of trends can be ascertained when it comes to the nature and outcome of contacts in areas of destination. The attitudes of the nationals fluctuate depending on a number of factors.

Occupation of Migrants

There is a difference in attitude towards migrants between occupations and professions where competition is high and those in which there is little or no competition. Migrants in menial jobs or in liberal professions (teaching, accounting and banking) are less the focus of resentment or hostility from nationals than are skilled blue-collar workers such as construction workers. This has also been a function of the fluctuations in economic trends between boom, stagnation and recession; or between poles of prosperity and poverty.

Political Implications of Alien Presence

This links internal politics of identity to migrant presence, where there is fear of the 'alien' who can pass for a 'national'. This is the situation of border peoples such as the Burkinabes in Côte d'Ivoire (who may pass for Dioula) and Nigerians in Cameroon (for reason of history and who are unfortunately placed where some anglophones are openly clamouring for secession). In fact, cross-border peoples in general play on an undeclared and unofficial dual nationality and can actually live peacefully across borders. They may also tend to claim a singular status in times of border disputes such as the armed movements claiming to fight for the independence of Bakassi separately from Nigeria and Cameroon at the time when the two countries were striking deals over the disputed area. In fact the area at the interface between CEMAC and ECOWAS in the Gulf became a haven of armed groups of mixed nationalities.

Varying Political Climates and the Nature of Diplomatic Relations

Political climate has often dictated the way migrants are treated within the regions. The lax management of borders during the colonial period under a labour imperative led to mass free movement of work-seeking migrants within the two regions irrespective of colonial rule; labour needs were the over-riding factor. Plantations and public work of all sorts (railway, road and building construction projects in urban centres) were principal poles of attraction. In this period, distinctions between nationals and non-nationals either did not exist or were minimal since citizenship did not exist.

It is the political management of statehood through emphasising boundaries that created the category of nationals when the new status of statehood was equated with nationhood, or elites sought to define or create nationhood at independence:

> The new governments, anxious to identify their own national territories as sove-
> reign and independent states exacted immigration laws and regulations governing
> conditions of entry, residence and employment of non-nationals, the aim being to
> reduce the flow of immigrants as a whole and limit entry to authorised immigrants
> who were admitted on their special skills (Adepoju 2005b:3).

In this dispensation, migrants from the colonial era – the lingering presence of Nigerians in Cameroon and vice versa; many West Africans in Côte d'Ivoire – became an embarrassing and complex legacy to manage in many countries.

Internal conflicts further led to new cross-border movements or reinforced the continuing presence of those 'non-nationals'. For instance, the civil war in Nigeria, which mostly affected the east from which most migrants in Cameroon originated stabilised their presence in Cameroon, despite stereotyping (e.g. the use of the term 'Biafranis' to refer to Ibos).

When the press reported a massive repatriation of Nigerians from Cameroon in 2005 immediately became the source of a diplomatic incident, with the Nigerian government worried about the plight of nationals seemingly driven out of a neighbouring country. Cameroon, apparently caught off guard by the events, denied being behind the incident and indicated that if Nigerian nationals left then it was voluntary. Top-level meetings between Cameroonian and Nigerian officials ensued. As was to be expected all else was diplomacy as usual as the press reported their pledges to good neighbourliness, protection of each other's nationals and eventual search for solutions. One point remained clear: a large number of Nigerians had opted to leave and take residence in their home country. Secondly, if one goes by press reports, conditions of residence had become more difficult for the majority and especially the less wealthy. The third fact is that the event, not being forced or organised repatriation, was not linked to the complicated border conflict that had strained diplomatic relations between the two countries. This is all the more plausible because, despite official diplomatic differences over the settlement of the boundary dispute characterised by the ruling of the International Court of Justice in The Hague and bilateral discussions, the residency question of nationals on either side had never been the issue. Even when raised by Nigerian authorities, under pressure from interest groups, in relation to the residents of the disputed Bakassi area, Cameroon did not hesitate to accept that Nigerians could continue to live in that territory in the same way as other Nigerian nationals lived in Cameroon. Prior to the massive return of Nigerians there had been an estimated two million Nigerians in Cameroon. These figures are polemical and differ according to the political issues with which they are connected. When it comes to portraying the people as the source of some trouble, they are represented as being in excessive numbers. When it does not befit such a cause the numbers are less gigantic. By and large Nigerians live peacefully within Cameroonian territory and indeed enjoy near-nationality status. The only clear difference is that they have to obtain residence permits. It is not clear how many of them have naturalised. The incident referred to above is the first ever reported case of Nigerians returning to their homeland since the detachment of Southern Cameroons from Nigeria in 1961 following the plebiscite on independence on 11 February of that year. It should be noted that the reverse is also true.

Following independence and reunification of Southern Cameroons with the French speaking Republic of Cameroon, many English-speaking Cameroonians either moved to Nigeria in search of jobs, especially with the oil boom, or for university education where the dominant French university of Yaoundé was an important obstacle to higher education for many anglophone youngsters. Cameroonians were not the only foreigners who were attracted by the opportunities offered by the oil boom and the derived economic and social development. When these prospects faded non-nationals in Nigeria were requested to leave, and many did, or were constrained to, with the crunch of deteriorating economic conditions. The category of Cameroonians who continued to live in Nigeria were university students, either self-sponsored or on Cameroon government scholarships. Movement to Nigeria on academic grounds became more restricted with the creation of a university in Buea along the lines of an English-speaking tradition. These developments have kept the number of Cameroon nationals living in Nigeria at a very low level proportionately, in relation to the number of Nigerian nationals living in Cameroon. The question that arises is: how was this possible? The question is appears to be banal since everybody can point to the period of British colonial rule in Southern Cameroons. What is forgotten in this case however is that the presence of Nigerians in Cameroon extends beyond the former territory of southern Cameroons, and that the ethnic origins are more diverse than the predominantly Ibo population of the colonial days. The other dimension of the question that cannot be answered in very clear terms is why Nigerian nationals did not immediately return after independence but rather continued to expand their presence in Cameroon to the point of integration. One needs to explore how they have been able to integrate whereas southern Cameroonians were not able to integrate in Nigeria but rather preferred to associate with French speaking Cameroonians and eventually have been integrating into the Cameroonian social fabric, as distinct from the polity, which is still problematic. This is all the more striking as literature on southern Cameroons colonial history has continued to highlight the Ibo episode as the ultimate reason for the political choice to dissociate from Nigeria in preference for southern Cameroons.

We posit that the presence of Nigerians in Cameroon was possible because of the absence of a real threat that Nigeria could pose to the new state of Cameroon. Secondly, accommodation between nationals and non-nationals has been more or less harmonious and did not pose any problem of any significant proportion at the level of the citizens. Thirdly the argument holds that the return of Nigerian nationals is symptomatic of the degeneration of economic conditions and the austerity of the packet of measures put in place under successive Structural Adjustment Programmes (SAP). The crisis in Côte d'Ivoire is also testimony of how integration or partial integration of non-nationals can lead to the most obnoxious political developments in the current contexts where the contours of the polities are just being shaped. Occasional problems of conviviality between Cameroonians and nationals of Gabon and Equatorial Guinea fall into this category.

Experiences of Non-Nationals of GG Countries in Cameroon

Identity of Non-Nationals

Respondents to the survey were drawn from four of Cameroon's neighbours: Nigeria, Equatorial Guinea, Chad, Central African Republic (CAR) and Congo. From the 101 persons interviewed, 50 were from Nigeria (which has the largest number of foreigners living within Cameroon), 37 from Equatorial Guinea, 8 from Chad, and 3 each from CAR and Congo Brazzaville. This sample was selected through a combination of quota, purposive and snow ball sampling' methods. The first two groups were targeted according to the proportion of their residents in Cameroon given that these are the most important communities of foreigners within the national territory, Nigeria out-distancing Equatorial Guinea in this regard. These were countries with the most active trans-frontier population movements in the southern part of Cameroon with the highest concentrations being in the cosmopolitan regions of the littoral and south west where the study took place. The mean age of the respondents was 34.5 (standard deviation: 12.9) with range 56 (lowest age 19, highest 77). This points to the wide range of persons that we interviewed representative of different age groups. Two-thirds of the sample was male (66.3 %) while the rest was female. The disproportion in favour of men within the sample results from the fact that there are more male immigrants than female ones and from their availability in public places where the interviews were conducted. While sixty-four respondents declared their religious affiliation as Christian and five said they were Muslims, as many as thirty-two did not respond to the question. Around two-fifths (39.6 %) of the sample were married as opposed to 56.4 per cent who were unmarried, and 4 per cent who were widowed. Eight of the married respondents had got married to Cameroonians.

Most respondents (71.3 % had moved into the country for the first time only within the past ten years (2001–10) although movements date as far back as the 1970s. Figures about other movements into the country confirm the idea of regular movements into Cameroon and into different urban centres. The motives of these movements are given in decreasing order as: studying (38.6 per cent from Equatorial Guinea in the main, although not exclusively), business (26.7 %; Nigerian traders in the majority), employment (16.8 %), marriage (9.9 %), visits (5 %), acquisition of nationality (1 %), and evangelism and unspecified others (1 %). These motives tie in closely with the occupations of the respondents.

The statistics point to the wide gamut of activities these immigrants are involved in. It is interesting to note that there are even unemployed persons looking for jobs in the sample. In terms of actual employment only 50.5 per cent of the sample declared they were employed as against 47.5 per cent and two non-responses. Nigerians are the most employed being self-employment as traders (majority), mechanics, hair dressers, farmers, christian missionaries, teachers and dressmakers. Dates of first employment correlate closely with date of first entry into the country.

The respondents from Nigeria possess certificates at all levels just as they are involved in a wide variety of occupations or professions. The respondents from Equatorial Guinea are mainly secondary school leavers as they pursue their studies in Cameroon. We should note those with little education from the three other countries (Chad, CAR, Congo) as well as the well-educated from Nigeria and Equatorial Guinea. There are also uneducated people from four of the five countries under study.

Nearly half of the sample population (45.5 %) do not visit their home countries regularly while 18.8 per cent do so less than once a year, 23.8 per cent once a year, and 4 per cent twice a year. Only two persons said they visited their home countries four or more times a year. Respondents from Nigeria (26) are among those least likely to return to their home countries although some of them say they do so less than once a year (16). It is significant to note that only 22 persons from Equatorial Guinea visited once a year and that some do not return at all. The Chadian, Central Africans Republic nationals and Congolese do not return at all.

Employment Situation

Only half of the sample (50.5 %) was employed. This employment follows the type of occupations indicated above. The unemployment figures are augmented by the students from Equatorial Guinea. If these are discounted then only 14 per cent of the respondents are really unemployed. It is important to note that 12 per cent of the respondents are applicants from four of the five countries, which points to the fact that Cameroon also attracts people looking for jobs. Nigerians are the most employed and mostly as traders although they are to be found in a variety of other occupations. A third of this sample (34.7 %) is self-employed. Most respondents have been employed between one and ten years (34 out of 55), while 6 persons were employed between 11 and 20 years, 4 between 21 and 30 years, and 2 between 31 and 40 years. It is interesting to note that some of the respondents have worked for as many as 40 years. The employment situation correlates with date of first movement into the country.

Relations with Nationals

We set out to measure relations between the non-nationals and the nationals in neighbourhoods, work places, worship sites and associations as well as between children and among the public. We also wanted to understand their experiences in cross-country marriages and friendships with Cameroonians as well as likely domains of conflict. Relations within the neighbourhoods were rated by the majority (96 %) as friendly, cordial or welcoming as against only 4 per cent who assessed them as unfriendly. Almost in the same way, 90.1 per cent of the sample thought that relations at work were good as against only one person who declared that they were negative. Only two thirds (67.3 %) of the sample opted to give an opinion about relations at religious worship sites, this being positive. The rest did not give any opinion. The trend of positive relations was confirmed with 94.1 per cent reporting good relations in public with only 4 per cent thinking that they were discriminatory or hostile. Relations within associations were considered to be good by 39.6 per cent with another 10.9 per cent speaking positively about the freedom of association accorded to foreigners. Relations between children are considered to be good by the 35.6 per cent who opted to address that issue (representing those who came into contact with this group, similarly for those judging relations at sites of worship).

Only 14 respondents indicated that there were marriages between members of their families and people of the host country. These relations were generally rated positively: six persons reported happily married couples while 8 persons reported love and respect between in-laws. Almost half of the sample (45.5 % as against 52.5 %) reported friendships between their families and people of the host country. These relations were positively rated: they were said to be marked by love and respect (33) or by partnership in development (13). Only one person reported a conflict, and this was in business, related to exploitation in a business deal.

The values highlighted in coping within the host country are hard work (14.9 %), loyalty to job site (2 %), cordial relations with neighbours (41.1 %), respect for the law and citizens (36.6 %), good management of financial resources (2 %) and support for spouses (2 %). A third of the respondents (33.7 %) have a positive view of Cameroonians in the domain of interpersonal relations and ethos. However, 14.9 per cent identify certain vices (drunkenness, flirting, maltreatment of tenants by landlords, vindictiveness) in their host country. The other lessons were more personal to the respondents.

Relations with Officials

Only 7 of the 23 respondents who came into contact with council officials thought that the relations with its officials were good as against 9 who thought that they were the object of victimisation when they were known to be illegal immigrants. Six others reported embarrassment. This trend is reported with taxation officials where only 6 respondents say the relations are friendly whereas 15 reported exploitation or embarrassment. On the other hand, it is significant to note that immigration officials are judged to be good and duty-conscious by almost a third, 31, as against the 22 who hold a contrary view. Views are divided about utility provision officials and national police officials. Relations with school officials are rated as friendly by 14 respondents while 4 thought that the former exploited foreigners. Car park officials are assessed by two-fifth of the sample as good while another fifth hold a contrary view.

Perception of Relations between Home and Host Countries

Relations between the home countries of respondents and Cameroon are unanimously rated on a positive note as very good (71.3 %) and good (28.7 %). The treatment of foreigners by nationals is described as very good (59.4 %), good (37.6 %), bad (2 %) and very bad (1 %). We can deduce therefore a very positive relationship that ties in with the assessment of the relations reported above.

Problems, Solutions and Lessons Learnt

Problems encountered by the incomers are the same as those observed by the nationals. These are essentially social problems that have little to do with their status as immigrants. This points to the normality of their situations, to the extent that they can be described as feeling at home. The proposed solutions are also commonplace and consistent with the problems identified. The lessons learnt by half of the sample (51.6 %) are personal or moral ones with no direct bearing on relations with nationals. Almost two-fifths (38.3 %) speak well of Cameroonians when they refer to their own lessons. The latter are referred to as kind, understanding, peaceful, undiscriminating, hardworking, well-educated and blessed with bilingualism. This contrasts with only 18.9 per cent who attribute negative characteristics to their hosts: vindictiveness (11.8 %), exploitative as tenants (1 %), drunks and flirts (1 %), or not 'business conscious' (5 %).

Perspectives for the Future

The majority of the respondents (82.2 %) saw the future in largely positive terms as very bright (5 %), bright (75.2 %), or normal, as against only nine persons who think it is not promising and eight who are uncertain. Close to three-fifths of the respondents plan to stay in Cameroon.

One might be tempted to conclude that Cameroon and Cameroonians have good attitudes towards non-nationals within the Gulf of Guinea to the extent that it could be a model. This contrasts with other countries (Gabon, Equatorial Guinea) where non-nationals are occasionally harassed. This is due to Cameroon's central position as a junction point between countries in Central, West and North Africa. We may wonder at this level of tolerance towards non-nationals in a country where non-natives in some metropolitan areas are labelled and treated as 'strangers' according to an autochthony ideology that has unfortunately found its way into the constitution (Yenshu Vubo 1998; 2003; 2005; 2011). This apparent hospitality is also at variance with the rather irregular delays in the naturalisation process observed of late as well as a law prohibiting dual nationality for Cameroonians dating back to the post-independence days characterised by repression. The study also reflects a period in which non-nationals are not being harassed as in earlier times.

Explaining the Situation

Two factors account for the nature of relationships that develop between nationals and non-national within the Gulf of Guinea, namely badly defined national boundaries that automatically determine nationality and problematic regional integration schemes.

Badly Defined, Blurred and Problematic Frontiers

National boundaries that were arbitrarily demarcated by colonial powers were totally oblivious to the realities of trans-ethnic or expansive universal ethnic spaces. This had the effect of balkanising and containing groups that stand astride the modern states in the region, controlling with them the movement of people. This had been compounded by the post-colonial state's resort to dogmatic principles of the blurred concept of statehood such as the OAU's principle of maintaining boundaries inherited from colonialism, backtracking from or questioning colonial policy of condoning labour movement across boundaries under a labour imperative, and the definition of citizenship in essentialist terms as related to 'roots' or ethnic ancestry, this being close to an ethnic vision of the 'nation state'. The paradox is that this new form of ethnicity was often grafted to ethnic preoccupations (unresolved differences) that the new countries were grappling with, pulled as they were between national cohesion and competition between elites that turned back to their groups of origin for some form of legitimacy. Such trends in political attitudes tended to place itinerant peoples without a sense of 'homeland' and people whose homelands were either not in any single country or stood astride two countries in a rather awkward, marginal, problematic or advantageous positions. In the case of the Hausa and Fulbe they have taken up residence in almost every country of west and west central Africa and can take advantage of their trans-territoriality and status as a people of all countries but they may either fit into local politics defined in term of locality or autochthony or be excluded or marginalised.

For instance, the Fulbe in Cameroon succeeded in achieving a comfortable position in the Ahidjo era as a dominant ethnic category both in the north and the whole country. But this position was revised and challenged by both the Biya successor regime and local peoples (both in the north and elsewhere) who cast them as aliens. The Mbororos faction of this group is particularly the focus of conflict for people who consider themselves to be indigenous peoples or 'first arrivals'.

Consequently, the Mbororos have tried to reverse this situation by defining themselves as indigenous minorities, a category borrowed from transnational jargon but entirely miscontrued by political elites at state and local levels. Even when accepted within the political game, these peoples can only marginally fit in because the locals are or should be given priority as the real actors.

In some cases, border peoples can enjoy the privilege of near dual citizenship without the defining legal qualifications. In this case, they can only be at best active participants in one state or maintain and be obscurely defined within the two. Such an ambiguous status can also be observed with border peoples who move to areas across the border and feel at home to the extent that their consciousness equates a sense of homeland with being within the state or totally ignores the existence of the state. This has been observed over the years with the Efik and their neighbours who have inhabited the Cameroonian peninsular of Bakassi to the extent that this was used as an argument by Nigeria to assert its sovereignty over the area. Even when the dispute over the area was resolved in favour of Cameroon, the status of these 'Nigerians' was one of the lingering contentious issues.

The same is true of movement of border peoples (Dioula, Senoufo) between Burkina Faso and Côte d'Ivoire, whose ancient kingdoms and territorial limits extended astride the current borders of the two countries. Movements of peoples of Burkinabé origin and settlement within the north of Côte d'Ivoire or in the reverse direction in both the colonial or post-colonial eras were at times in a spirit of total ignorance of the partitions into different states. These free cross-border movements, overlooked and even encouraged by the Houphouët-Boigny regime, have actually been a source of suspicion from politicians whose definition of citizenship in ethnic terms tends to attribute the northerners (Dioula, Senoufou) to the Burkinabés.

This triggered the ill-defined concept of *ivoirité* that became a strong political tool: there were no documents to define the concept although it was used extensively to imply 'aliens' in the broad sense. But more specifically (and paradoxically) nationals were suspected of or assimilated by ethnic identity with citizens of Burkina Faso. Moreover this was inscribed exclusively within the politics of exclusion and did not extend to actions such as mass expulsion. Politicians from the south (Bedié who invented the term, even to some extent Gbagbo) increasingly tended to restrict the real identity of Ivoirians to those with origins from the south albeit imprecisely. This development accounts for a long period of political confrontation where the dominant question was who was an Ivoirian and by extension who could become the country's president. Successive presidents from the south tended to be comfortable with the view that *ivoirité* might not accommodate all northerners, some of whom were suspected of being foreigners, showing or sharing ethnic characteristics with Burkinabés, although this fell short of openly excluding northerners. The increasing resort to this veiled argument led to an attempt to topple the Gbagbo government by an essentially northern group and to the protracted civil war. The stress on the identification of citizenship as a prelude to elections and the eligibility of Ouattara (a northerner) for the presidency, a matter that touched on his 'questioned' citizenship or nationality, validates the point.

Closely related to the definition of the status of cross border peoples is the management of these borders. In fact, no policies exist other than the fixation of territorial limits and sovereignty on either side of territorial divides. This leaves the ordinary people with no choice other than to ignore the arbitrary colonial creations and violate the boundaries, deeply connected as they have been over time with peoples across the new structures.

Problematic Regional Integration Schemes

One way beyond this impasse seemed to have been the regional integration schemes starting with the Economic Community of West African States (ECCAS), which was a veritable precursor in the design of policies to manage mass cross-border migration (Adepoju 2005a:4–7; 2005b:5–13) and then more recently the Economic Community of Central African States (ECCAS). Although ECOWAS has achieved relatively greater success than ECCAS in term of achieving a 'borderless' policy where citizens can move freely across state boundaries or where restrictions are reduced to the minimum, both schemes have faced circular crises connected with relations between national and non-nationals where the same factors are at play.

A common labour policy, which would cover all categories of workers, migrants and nationals, has not been adopted. Economic prosperity in some countries has attracted workers from countries with less opportunities but consequent recession has also led to the expulsion of non-nationals by the states as well as xenophobic attitudes towards them from nationals (either fuelled or appropriated by governments). This was the case with Nigeria's expulsion of citizens from certain ECOWAS countries at a time when this regional organisation was designing policies to cope with cross-border migrations (Adepoju 2005b:6). In fact, the organisation has had a chequered history in the implementation of its own measures towards a border-free zone. Some countries have been complacent about non-nationals in periods of peace, economic prosperity and political stability but resorted to hostility towards non-nationals in periods of recession, with the justification that aliens aggravate a 'host country's economic conditions (ibid.) while disregarding their contributions to the countries themselves including in areas of labour, skills in the professions, training in the educational sector and business amongst others. The illusion, as with some ideologies of identity politics, is to explain social crises – in this case working economic conditions (unemployment, fall in real wages) – by resorting to the vilification of the 'other', presented as the scapegoat. In some cases this scapegoat can be political as in the case of certain ethnic groups suspected of collusion with the nationals to tilt the balance of the vote. This is the effect of ethnically defined conceptions of the nation state in terms of space and citizenship.

In either case, both elites and local peoples are active, the first as flag bearers (in the name of serving as protectors of peoples or the national interest) and the second as principal victims. Either way, the observed effect is the diversion of attention from the real causes of the problems to some imaginary aliens who should be held responsible, as well as the development of a short-lived nationalist feeling which serves no other purpose than to rally nationals around the leadership (whatever their performance might be) and thus serve as a political tool. To suggest that there may be manipulation would far-fetched. What is at work is a twofold process where disenchanted locals may attack non-nationals who are perceived as the source of misfortune for nationals, as well as being criminals, as against the good nationals or even the good category – by dint of either some sort of purity *(ivoirité or congolité)* – while the leadership is resorting to the expulsion of non-nationals, blamed for some unfortunate incidents with nationals, or as alleged irregular migrants. This is the case of Cameroonians who have been regularly attacked and whose homes have been vandalised in Equatorial Guinea by nationals both as a result of personal conflicts with nationals, and because the Cameroonians are seen to be taking advantage of the oil boom much more than the nationals. Such incidents are followed by expulsion by the government of Equatorial Guinea whose action seems to complement that of the governed. In this case, Equatorial Guinean students, living and studying in Buea, Cameroon were also brutalised in retaliation by youngsters who believed they were acting in a 'patriotic' spirit.

Absence of a Citizenship Policy within Regional Schemes

It is not clear whether clear-cut policies exist in the common management of citizens within single regional schemes as the focus is on facilitating movement of people while the issues of residence and the protection of non-nationals are overlooked. People may move but the binary distinction between nationals and non-nationals is a serious operational obstacle to the enjoyment of integrated spaces.

Contrasting Pulls between two Political Drives that Generate Contradictory Demands and Expectations on Individual State Spaces

This is the contradiction between 'nationalist drives' and regional integration schemes. Protecting 'national' space has become an instinctive mode of governance for leaders to which regional schemes emerge only in contradiction. As Nyamnjoh (2007) has remarked about globalisation, one illusion of regional schemes is that people are invited to feel at home everywhere within the scheme but are reminded that the bounds of the state have not yet disappeared. The fate of the migrant is the extreme dimension of the dilemma of the person in the South torn between the unfulfilled dreams of both a nation state in the making and the increasing promises of a universal existence that transcends the bounds of the nation state. In the words of Serge Latouche:

> What is suggested to people of the Third World is an absurd national identity and the false belief of belonging to a global community. The former is both theoretically and practically absurd: theoretically because the concept of nation losses meaning within a global community and practically since nations created by the West have not fully matured from within. The latter is an illusion because the person (ironically transformed into an abstraction) is emptied of any substance by the fact that differences in access to available wealth have been maintained, created and exacerbated. The "westernized" person of the Third World is a destitute, neither fully a citizen of the world since suffrage is tied to tax-based voting rights…nor a national of any viable state since nationhood policy derived from the colonial experience is nothing else but mimicry.[1]

This has been aggravated by the fact that 'the popular rhetoric around globalisation is all about free flows of factors of production (including labour) and consumer goods, regardless of attempts by states to control or confine them' (Nyamnjoh 2007:76). Vidal Villa (1996) argued that one of the main obstacles standing in the way of globalisation is the nationalism of nation states. As a result, the growing tendency towards internationalism or transnational fashions, as found in regional continental or sub-continental regional blocks, meets with difficulties of application because of recourse to prevailing and perennial state-building logics of the inter-state system and the near ethnic appeal of nationalisation. Serge Latouche ([1989]2005) has captured the logic of state building in the following words:

> This nation-state order will in time and at the same time be an international statist order: the nation-state is subject to international law ; it is sovereign because it has no legitimate authority below and above it while societies that have not yet adopted it as a model lack a legal existence and, as such, have to be discovered, conquered and civilized; the totality of sovereign powers that rule the planet constitute a society of nations or a contractual association of member states.[2]

This explains the tendency to continue to inscribe economies within the confines of the nation-state, which is the principal obstacle related to labour mobility. Global level arrangements of a political nature (common passports, common currency) have thus often been oblivious to local level issues (residency within the region) that should constitute some of the building blocks of viable integration.

In the final analysis, the elites some states within regional integration schemes tend to adopt the same posture as ethnic groups within states as they perceive regional integration as nothing more than a patchwork of entities with no strong ties between them. In fact, the reality is not far from this as the CEMAC region has been identified as the least integrated of such projects in Africa.

Factors Related to Level of Economic Growth and Political History of the Regions

The relative underdevelopment of the region characterised by substantial differences in prosperity between countries provokes the movement of people to periodic poles of attraction providing jobs across borders. Identity issues related to nationality become central in the competition for scarce jobs, firstly between persons with the same level of skill, and then between persons of different skills levels. In the final analysis, the natural expectation is that nationals have a priority over non-nationals. Non-nationals who end up clinching jobs are often the object of resentment and even hatred. When recession sets in, elites would tend to primarily target non-nationals as failures are even attributed to the non-nationals, particularly when austerity measures have been put in place. Such discriminatory attitudes, perceptions and practices derive from an implied and assumed regular function of states to provide jobs for nationals either as a matter of responsibility that goes with sovereignty or as social policy palliatives to ward off unrest and contestation from discontented groups. In either case, the state presents itself as not yet ready for the reality of regional integration that appears as an alien structure either imposed externally or as a fashion in which no one believes, the reality – of power, economy, international responsibility – being with the state.

This situation renders these sub-regional schemes largely as incomplete or dwarfed projects, this being a function of political history. It is evident that although ECCAS has extended its influence to the lusophone and Hispanic countries (São Tomé and Príncipe and Equatorial Guinea), which are demographically insignificant anyway, its elementary origins and primary territorial limits coincide with the former French colonial sphere of the Afrique Equatoriale Française (AEF) where the political motive can be imputed to the lingering neo-colonial influence of France. This argument is buttressed by France's continual involvement in the activities of this organisation ever since the birth of UDEAC (Union Douanière et Economique de l'Afrique Centrale) through the subsequent transformations in status and configuration to ECCAS in its present form, added to the former colonial power's paternalistic posture in the control of key issues especially monetary policy (through the franc) and political leadership. Such a situation abstracts issues of control from member states and transfers them to the former colonial power, the presence of the two non-francophone states making no difference. The regional integration scheme thus appears to be an affair of heads of states who have reluctantly entered into a contractual relationship over which they have no real control. It can be said to hang above states that are themselves also hanging above their own societies or constitute 'un Etat sans nation' (a state without a constituent nation) in the way Alain Touraine (2000: 83) pondered about the European Union. In this regard, such a scheme is doubly removed from society and social concerns such as labour and relations between citizens of all countries. Moreover, the involvement of the former colonial power in settling matters of hegemony (Cameroon vs. Gabon) alienates countries and strengthens nationalist feelings rather than the cooperation necessary for collective policies. There have been reports about animosity towards Cameroonians in Gabon, this not being unrelated to the competition for ascendancy in the region. Such competition is fuelled by France's preference for Gabon. The abstraction of the scheme from the societies of the states concerned explains the low level of integration within the region: in fact, it is the lowest in the African region.

The problems of a political nature in the ECOWAS region are slightly different although there are common dimensions with what can be observed in the ECCAS region. Instead of one dominant colonial history, the sub-region came under the control of three colonial powers, Britain, France and Portugal. As such, some states belong to different unions with ideologies and programmes that may entirely cohere, or else conflict with, those of the regional union. ECOWAS' 'bold attempt to stimulate the kind of homogeneous society which once existed in the sub-region' (Adepoju 2005) has achieved little success at an institutional level with the society left out of its programme. The concern is with easing free movement of people and maintaining the reality of boundaries inherited from the colonial period.

Prospects for Alternative Models of Regional Integration in the GG

A problematic status for migrant non-nationals has emerged and with it a crisis of conviviality within some countries in specific periods at both official and societal levels. We have explained this situation in relation to the rather dogmatic and idealised definition of the nation state as absolutely coinciding with colonial territorial boundaries within which bounds citizenship and nationality are framed with respect to ethnic origins and to the exclusion of others. Such a restricted and narrow definition is facing difficulties of an operational and ideological nature. Operationally, it is oblivious to the colonial antecedents that moved peoples across territorial boundaries under a labour imperative, the trans-territorial character of some border peoples, and the emerging reality of internationalism/ transnationalism, triggered by the end of economic nationalism and the globalisation that goes with it. In ideological terms, the current form of the nation that Benedict Anderson (1983:15) defined as an 'imagined community – and both imagined as limited and sovereign' and, which is the key contextual idea on which modernity was premised (Llobera 1996; Touraine 2005), is coming under serious challenge (Latouche [1989] 2005:110). In fact, a major and decisive crisis of the order of the nation state that is likely to lead to the transformation of the world system is constituted around nations ('la fin de la société des nations' Latouche [1989] 2005:136), and is characterised by a trans-nationalisation of economies, a 'de-territorialisation' of societies, and globalisation of culture (Warnier [1999] 2007; Appadurai 1996), rendering the stress on the nation state anachronistic.

This trend is compounded by challenges from forces from below which are weakening the idea of the nation in favour of ethnic communities[3] in the name of cultural rights (Touraine 2005:267). 'In sum, the nation-state is much less than before a general frame for collective existence',[4] concludes Alain Touraine (2005:65). Edgar Morin, for his part, feels that the nation state has simply lost its mobilising utopia: 'The historic vitality of the nation-state is worn out today'.[5]

Paradoxically, African elites had adopted a totally different option – that of the old form of the nation-state – at a time when these developments set in, precisely at the end of the 1960s (Wallerstein 1991:72–3; Wieviorka 2004:283):

> Taking Fanon as prophet, they adopted the ethnic vision of the nation as opposed to the elective one. They preferred cultural identity – a modern form of Volkgeist – the "every plebiscite" or the idea of a secular association. If liberation movements without exception gave birth to repressive regime, it is because, like political romanticism, they tooled interpersonal relations on the mystical model of fusion rather the legal option of contract. They also imagined liberty as collectively wielded rather than an individual entitlement.[6]

This explains the fashions nation-building sought to achieve: the dream of uniting heterogeneous people through a certain mystique of fusion, the international dimension being a resort to protecting boundaries and restricting citizenship to ethnic nationals (to the exclusion of earlier migrants) as well as cross-border migrations, with the attendant difficulties we have demonstrated.

These limitations argue in favour of a rethinking of the current practices and the search for solutions consistent with the spirit of the times. Above everything else, this must start with the leaders abandoning the anachronistic vision of the nation-state, the rethinking of citizenship within regional integration schemes, the possibility of common labour policies and a redefinition of residency conditions (requirements, responsibilities, entitlements and rights). These go beyond the classical inter-state management of movements of persons and expectations of neutrality, alluding to issues of participation in local political life (eligibility for certain offices and the right to vote at certain levels) as in other spheres (economy and culture). This rethinking process can gain inspiration either from experiences from other regions that have experienced relatively more success (the European Union) or from local experiences of tolerance and accommodation of migrants taken over from the colonial era (Nigeria and Cameroon; Côte d'Ivoire during the Houphouët-Boigny era), the hosting of refugees from neighbouring countries and reciprocity in border-free attitudes. Beyond these piecemeal national policies, there needs to be critical assessment of the regional integration projects themselves. There is a definite need to move beyond the current style of regionalism. Edgar Morin has argued in favour of confederate forms as a way out:

> The world has to be told that the ideal is no more the independence of nations but the confederation of nations that will ensure autonomy in independence.[7]

This is all the more urgent in an area where countries share a common destiny within the same geographical space with identical demographic, historical, cultural and economic realities. This may not be the forum for the proposals for a Gulf of Guinea Union or Entente with a confederate status but it is an idea worth exploring out of the current configuration of the regional schemes.

Notes

1. 'Ce qui est proposé aux populations du tiers monde … consiste en une identité nationale absurde et une appartenance fallacieuse à une communauté universelle. La première est absurde théoriquement et pratiquement. Théoriquement, car la nation n'a pas de sens dans une communauté universelle, pratiquement, car les nations créées par l'Occident ne correspondent pas à aucune maturation locale. La seconde est fallacieuse car le statut de l'homme, ironiquement réduit à une abstraction, est vidé de tout contenu par la seule différentiation maintenue, créée et exacerbée, celle de la quantité des richesses disponibles. Ni citoyens du monde à part entière, car le suffrage est censitaire…ni national d'un Etat authentique, car la politique « nationalitaire », nés artificiellement de la colonisation, n'a d'autre racine à affirmer qu'un mimétisme généralisé, « l'occidentalisé » du tiers monde est un clochard' (Latouche [1989] 2005: 113). (Translation from French to English by Yenshu Vubo).
2. 'Cet ordre national-étatique sera dans le temps, et du même moment, un ordre international-étatique. L'État-nation est le sujet du droit international, il est souverain. Nulle puissance légitime au-dessus, nulle dessous. Les sociétés qui n'ont pas adopté la forme nationale-étatique n'ont pas d'existence juridique, elles sont à découvrir, à conquérir et à civiliser. L'ensemble des souverains qui dominent la planète forme une société des nations, ou une association contractuelle des États membres.' (Translation from French to English by Yenshu Vubo).
3. 'affaiblissement des communautés nationales et le renforcement des communautés ethniques'. (Translation from French to English by Yenshu Vubo).
4. 'Au total, l'État national est beaucoup moins qu'avant un cadre général d'identification collective'. (Translation from French to English by Yenshu Vubo).
5. 'La fécondité historique de l'État-nation est aujourd'hui épuisé'. (Translation from French to English by Yenshu Vubo).
6. 'Avec Fanon pour prophète, ils choisi la théorie ethnique de la nation au dépense de la théorie élective, ils ont préféré l'identité culturelle – traduction moderne du

Volkgeist – au « plébiscite de tous les jours » ou à l'idée d'« association séculaire ». Si, avec une régularité sans faille, ces mouvements de libération ont sécrété des régimes d'oppression, c'est parce qu'à l'exemple du romantisme politique, ils ont fondé les relations interhumaines sur le modèle mystique de fusion, plutôt que celui juridique – du contrat, et qu'ils ont pensé la liberté comme un attribut collectif, jamais comme une propriété individuelle' (Finkielkraut 1989: 99). (Translation from French to English by Yenshu Vubo).

7.	'L'idéal à annoncer au monde n'est plus l'indépendance des nations, c'est la confédération des nations, qui leur assure l'autonomie dans l'interdépendance'. (Translation from French to English by Yenshu Vubo).

References

Adepoju, A., 2005a, 'Creating a Borderless West Africa: Constraints and Prospects for Intra-Regional Migration'. Draft article of the Migration without Borders Service, UNESCO.

Adepoju, A., 2005b, 'Migration in West Africa', Global Commission on International Migration (GCIM)'. Paper prepared for the Policy Analysis and Research Programme.

Adepoju, A., n.d., *Fostering free movement of Persons in West Africa: Achievements, Pitfalls and Prospects for Intra-Region Migration.*

Anderson, B., 1983, *Imagined Communities*, London: New Left Books.

Appadurai, A.,1996, *Modernity at Large: Cultural Dimensions of Modernity*, London and Minneapolis: University of Minnesota Press.

Finkielkraut, Alain, 1987, *La défaite de la pensée*, Paris: Gallimard.

Latouche, S., [1989] 2005, *L'Occidentalisation du monde: Essai sur la signification, la portée et les limites de l'uniformisation planétaire*, Paris: La Découverte.

Llobera, Josep, 1964, *The God of Modernity: The Development of Nationalism in Western Europe*, Oxford: Berg.

International Monetary Fund, 2008, *World Economic and Financial Surveys: Regional Economic Outlook: Sub-Saharan Africa*, Washington, DC: IMF.

Mañe, D.O., 2005, *Emergence of the Gulf of Guinea in the Global Economy: Prospects and Challenges*, IMF Working Paper, Washington, DC: IMF.

Metogo, G., 2006, *Security and Stability in the Gulf of Guinea*, Pennsylvania: USAWC Strategy Research Project, U.S. Army War College, Carlisle Barracks.

Morin, E., [1965] 1999, *Introduction à une politique de l'homme*, Paris: Seuil.

Nyamnjoh, F. B., 'From Bounded to Flexible Citizenship: Lessons from Africa', *Citizenship Studies* 11(1): 73–82.

Touraine, Alain, [1996] 1997, 'Vrais et faux problèmes', in Michel Wievorka, ed., *Une société fragmentée? Le multiculturalisme en débat*, Paris: La Découverte.

Touraine, Alain, 2005. *Un nouveau paradigme: pour comprendre le monde aujourd'hui*, Paris: Fayard.

Vidal Villa, José Maria, 1996,'Ten Theses on Globalization', in UNESCO Chair on Sustainable Development, ed., *Social Development: Challenges and Strategies*, Rio de Janerio: UFRJ/EICOS.

Wallerstein, I., 1991, *Geopolitics and Geoculture: Essays on the Changing World System*, Cambridge and Paris: Cambridge University Press and Maison des Sciences de l'Homme.

Warnier, J. P., [1999] 2005, *La Mondialisation de la culture*, Paris: La Découverte.

Wieviorka, Michel, 2001, *La Différence*, Paris: Balland.

Wieviorka, Michel, 2004, 'The Making of Differences', *International Sociology* 19(3): 281–97.

Yenshu Vubo, E., 'The Discourse and Polities of Indigenous/Minority People's Rights in some Metropolitan Areas of Cameroon', *Journal of Applied Social Sciences* 1(1): 25–41.

Yenshu Vubo, E, 2003, 'Levels of Historical Awareness: the Development of Identity and Ethnicity in Cameroon', *Cahiers d'Etudes africaines* 43(3): 591–628.

Yenshu Vubo, E, 2005, 'The Management of Ethnic Diversity in Cameroon: The Coastal Areas', in E.S.D. Fomin and J. W. Forje, eds, *Central Africa: Crises and Reform*, Dakar: CODESRIA.

Yenshu Vubo, E, 2011, *Inventer un espace public africain en Afrique: Le défi de la diversité ethnique*,Paris: Harmattan.